DISCARD

Contemporary Soviet Society

Contemporary Soviet Society

a statistical handbook

Compiled, with translation, by

Michael Ryan

Lecturer in Politics and Russian Studies
University College of Swansea

Edward Elgar

Published by
Edward Elgar Publishing Limited
Gower House
Croft Road
Aldershot
Hants GU11 3HR
England

Edward Elgar Publishing Company
Old Post Road
Brookfield
Vermont 05036
USA

British Library Cataloguing in Publication Data
is available.

ISBN 1 85278 349 4

Printed in Great Britain by
Billing & Sons Ltd, Worcester

Contents

Acknowledgements

I am happy to express my gratitude to a number of people whose helpfulness has materially assisted me in the task of compiling this book. The existence in print of the first results of the 1989 Soviet population census was drawn to my attention by Stephen White, and Michael Berry told of me about the availability of the (then) new journal **Statisticheski Press-Byulleten.** Jackie Johnson, Librarian of Birmingham University's Centre for Russian and East European Studies, expended time and effort in supplying me with photocopied materials; I am particularly grateful for her assistance. Mervyn Matthews lent me one source, whilst John Cule and Richard Taylor gave me books which they obtained during their visits to the Soviet Union, thus expediting my access to important data. Once again, David and Taya Martin willingly answered queries about points of Russian usage. Of course, I alone am responsible for any errors of translation.

I also wish to thank Edward Elgar for his patience over the delay in completing this book, and to Julie Leppard for her sympathetic advice about preparing the camera-ready copy for it. As ever, I am indebted most deeply to Ann Ryan, my wife, whose tolerance and encouragement in this connection has extended far beyond the temporary loan of her word processor.

Michael Ryan
University College of Swansea

Foreword

Before the advent of glasnost, as is widely known, the Soviet authorities were notoriously selective in publishing information about many highly significant aspects of Soviet society. There can be no doubt that they collected a substantial volume of data on social trends and social conditions, but they normally deprived the general public of facts which reflected badly on the government and Communist Party of the Soviet Union. For example, over a number of years in the recent past it was impossible to ascertain the current figure for the infant mortality rate, a very basic social indicator routinely available in most countries.

After Mikhail Gorbachev gained supreme power in 1985, some time elapsed before evidence of a totally new approach started to emerge. In 1988 a major contribution to our knowledge about Soviet population trends was made by the publication of the demographic handbook **Naselenie SSSR 1987**. Also in that year, apparently, the USSR Ministry of Health ceased to classify any of its morbidity and mortality data as secret. The statistical yearbook for the economy, **Narodnoe khozyaistvo SSSR**, included detailed information about environmental pollution for the first time and in the following year it broke new ground again by including a section on crime.

However, not all the figures which are reproduced in this book reflect an openness on the part of the State Committee on Statistics, the agency responsible for the preparation of the above-mentioned sources and for the monthly journal **Statisticheski Press-Byulleten.** As will be seen, certain tables derive from the widely-read weekly newspaper **Argumenty i Fakty,** which at times has incurred the leadership's displeasure in its pursuit of the principle of glasnost. It is that source which provided me with striking data on the incidence of leprosy and plague.

All the same, at the time of writing it is still not possible to document in detail certain areas of interest for which details are easily accessible in Britain and many other countries. The distribution of income and wealth constitutes one such area for which relatively little useful tabulated data can be obtained.

By contrast, it is now possible to learn much about the views expressed by ordinary people on a wide range of contemporary issues (including the performance of Gorbachev himself). In 1988 the authorities' concern to improve the chances of perestroika was apparently the main reason for the establishment of a large research centre charged with conducting nation-wide surveys of public opinion. Findings from some of these surveys are reproduced in the final section of this handbook.

It is a basic but highly important observation that, for a whole range of social indicators, the figures which refer to the entire USSR in fact conceal substantial variations as between different areas within its vast land mass. Consequently I have always sought to include breakdowns at least to the level of the fifteen Union Republics and, within them, by urban and rural areas respectively. At the time of writing another - and most compelling reason - for giving readers as much information as possible about spatial variations is provided by evidence that the possible disintegration of the Union can no longer be written off as journalistic exaggeration.

Implicit in the notion of a social indicator is the idea of comparability and, in conformity to it, I have sought to reproduce data which are expressed in relation to a population base as well as in the form of absolute numbers. Another note which can be recorded here is that the sections of this book which deal with education and illness are mainly concerned not with the provision of services as such but with their outcomes - levels of educational attainment and incidence of specific diseases.

Except for **Naselenie SSSR 1987**, all the sources used in compiling this handbook were published either in 1989 or the early months of 1990. As well as yielding the most up-to-date information available, these sources also contained tables which cover longish periods of time; I have included some of them on the ground that they offer valuable insights into changing patterns in Soviet life. In that connection it seemed especially important to enable readers to compare data from the population censuses which were carried out in 1979 and 1989, in so far as findings which relate to the latter year were available when work on this handbook came to a halt.

For ease of reference I chose to depart from the format of Soviet statistical handbooks by creating an index and a contents page which lists broadly-drawn subject headings. When dubiety arose over the most appropriate location of a table, I took into account the overall structure of the individual subject divisions.

As for editorial alterations, I have adopted different conventions in different contexts. Where modifications were made to the continuous prose passages, it seemed appropriate to record the fact (unless the editing was so light that mention of it would be pedantic). In the case of time series, however, I thought it unnecessary to draw attention to the occasional omission of data for a particular year or years and I have not recorded the substitution, in three tables, of percentage increases where the original gives 1989 data as a percentage of 1979 data.

In the case of certain tables I have adopted a layout which differs from the one to be found in the source. Sometimes this has involved separating out some of the columns for presentation in a second, subsequent table. The small amount of replication which occurs is mainly between tables and continuous prose translations and may be thought useful as a cross-check for accuracy.

Although this is not the place to discuss the collection and processing of Soviet social statistics, it is implicit in some of what has been said above that far greater official importance now attaches not only to the public dissemination of the end-product but also to the accuracy of what appears in print. Interesting evidence of concern on the part of the central authorities to improve recording practices at local level is given in a passage which refers to very substantial under-reporting of infant deaths in various areas of the Union (see p. 246).

******

When transliterating Russian Cyrillic symbols into the Latin alphabet, I have chosen - like others - to depart from purist conventions in minor respects, particularly by simplifying adjectival-type endings and by omitting the hard and soft signs. To adopt such simplifications, it can be argued, has the advantage of rendering transliterated words somewhat less puzzling or outlandish in appearance to those readers who are not familiar with the superbly expressive mother tongue of a great nation.

The major divisions within what is known as the administrative-territorial structure of the Union of Soviet Socialist Republics (USSR) are the fifteen Soviet Socialist Republics (SSRs). Also termed Union Republics, these areas were delimited basically by reference to the historical homelands of the larger ethnic groupings within the USSR.

The picture becomes somewhat complex below the level of Union Republics. Subordinate to them are Autonomous Soviet Socialist Republics (ASSRs), which are smaller nationality-based divisions, and two main categories of region, the krai (plural: kraya) and the oblast (plural: oblasti).

Generally speaking, a krai will contain one or more of the smallest divisions which recognise the existence of ethnic minorities; those units are termed autonomous oblasti and autonomous okruga. Most of them are located within the Russian Soviet Federative Socialist Republic, which helps to explain the presence of the adjective 'federative' in its title. It should be added that economic planning regions have been delimited within the the Russian SFSR and the Ukrainian SSR. [Ed.]

******

Population of USSR at post-war censuses

	Millions
1959 (January 15)	208.8
1970 (January 15)	241.7
1979 (January 17)	262.4
1989 (January 12)	286.7

Over the ten years following the census of 1979 the population of the USSR increased by 24.3 million persons, or by 9.3%.

Source: **Pravda** 1989, 29 aprelya, s. 2.

Areas and population of Union Republics, 1959 and 1970

	Area in sq. km. (thousands)	Population (thousands) 1959	1970
USSR	**22 403.0***	**208 827**	**241 720**
Russian SFSR	17 075.4	117 534	130 079
Ukrainian SSR	603.7	41 869	47 126
Belorussian SSR	207.6	8 056	9 002
Uzbek SSR	447.4	8 119	11 799
Kazakh SSR	2 717.3	9 295	13 009
Georgian SSR	69.7	4 044	4 686
Azerbaidzhan SSR	86.6	3 698	5 117
Lithuanian SSR	65.2	2 711	3 128
Moldavian SSR	33.7	2 885	3 569
Latvian SSR	64.5	2 093	2 364
Kirgiz SSR	198.5	2 066	2 934
Tadzhik SSR	143.1	1 981	2 900
Armenian SSR	29.8	1 763	2 492
Turkmen SSR	488.1	1 516	2 159
Estonian SSR	45.1	1 197	1 356

* Includes 90 000 sq. km. in respect of the White Sea and 37 300 sq. km. in respect of the Sea of Azov. These figures are not allocated to the areas of individual Republics.

Source: **Nar. khoz. SSSR 1988**, s. 19.

Population of Union Republics, 1979 and 1989

	Thousands 1979	1989	% increase
USSR	**262 436**	**286 717**	**9**
Russian SFSR	137 551	147 386	7
Ukrainian SSR	49 755	51 704	4
Belorussian SSR	9 560	10 200	7
Uzbek SSR	15 391	19 906	29
Kazakh SSR	14 684	16 538	13
Georgian SSR	5 015	5 449	9
Azerbaidzhan SSR	6 028	7 029	17
Lithuanian SSR	3 398	3 690	9
Moldavian SSR	3 947	4 341	10
Latvian SSR	2 521	2 681	6
Kirgiz SSR	3 529	4 291	22
Tadzhik SSR	3 801	5 112	34
Armenian SSR	3 031	3 283	8
Turkmen SSR	2 759	3 534	28
Estonian SSR	1 466	1 573	7

Source: **Pravda** 1989, 29 aprelya, s. 2.

Population of economic regions and major territorial-administrative divisions, 12 January 1989

Abbreviations: obl. = oblast AO = Autonomous oblast
AOk = Autonomous okrug

| | Thousands | | | % increase |
	Total	Urban	Rural	1979-1989
USSR	**286 717**	**188 791**	**97 926**	**9**
Russian SFSR	**147 386**	**108 419**	**38 967**	**7**
Northern region	**6 125**	**4 689**	**1 436**	**9**
Karelian ASSR	792	646	146	8
Komi ASSR	1 263	954	309	13
Archangel obl.	1 570	1 152	418	7
incl. Nenets AOk	55	34	21	17
Vologda obl.	1 354	881	473	3
Murmansk obl.	1 146	1 056	90	19
North-west region	**8 279**	**7 172**	**1 107**	**8**
Leningrad*	5 020	5 020	–	9
Leningrad obl.	1 659	1 093	566	9
Novgorod obl.	753	524	229	4
Pskov obl.	847	535	312	-0.4
Central region	**30 379**	**25 077**	**5 302**	**5**
Bryansk obl.	1 475	992	483	-2
Vladimir obl.	1 654	1 310	344	5
Ivanovo obl.	1 317	1 075	242	-0.3
Kalinin obl.	1 670	1 194	476	1
Kaluga obl.	1 067	735	332	6
Kostroma obl.	809	555	254	1
Moscow*	8 967	8 966	1	10
Moscow obl.	6 686	5 307	1 379	7
Orel obl.	891	555	336	-0.1
Ryazan obl.	1 346	885	461	-1
Smolensk obl.	1 158	788	370	3
Tula obl.	1 868	1 514	354	-2
Yaroslavl obl.	1 471	1 201	270	3
Volgo-Vyatka region	**8 457**	**5 830**	**2 627**	**1**
Mari ASSR	750	459	291	7
Mordvin ASSR	964	545	419	-3
Chuvash ASSR	1 336	773	563	3
Gorki obl.	3 713	2 869	844	0.5
Kirov obl.	1 694	1 184	510	2
Central Black-earth region	**7 741**	**4 667**	**3 074**	**-1**
Belgorod obl.	1 381	871	510	6
Voronezh obl.	2 470	1 507	963	-0.3

	Thousands Total	Urban	Rural	% increase 1979-1989
Kursk obl.	1 339	775	564	-4
Lipetsk obl.	1 231	771	460	0.5
Tambov obl.	1 320	743	577	-5
Volga region	**16 411**	**12 022**	**4 389**	**6**
Kalmyk ASSR	322	147	175	10
Tatar ASSR	3 640	2 658	982	6
Astrakhan obl.	998	680	318	9
Volgograd obl.	2 593	1 969	624	5
Kuibyshev obl.	3 266	2 638	628	6
Penza obl.	1 502	930	572	0
Saratov obl.	2 690	2 000	690	5
Ulyanovsk obl.	1 400	1 000	400	10
North Caucasus region	**16 737**	**9 588**	**7 149**	**8**
Dagestan ASSR	1 792	783	1 009	10
Kabardino-Balkar ASSR	760	465	295	13
North Osetin ASSR	634	436	198	6
Chechen-Ingush ASSR	1 277	530	747	11
Krasnodar kraï	5 115	2 776	2 339	6
incl. Adyge AO	432	225	207	7
Stavropol krai	2 855	1 531	1 324	12
incl. Karachai-Cherkes AO	418	204	214	13
Rostov obl.	4 304	3 067	1 237	5
Ural region	**20 287**	**15 165**	**5 122**	**4**
Bashkir ASSR	3 952	2 522	1 430	3
Udmurt ASSR	1 609	1 122	487	8
Kurgan obl.	1 105	605	500	2
Orenburg obl.	2 174	1 414	760	4
Perm obl.	3 100	2 396	704	3
incl. Komi-Permyak AOk	159	47	112	-8
Sverdlovsk obl.	4 721	4 113	608	6
Chelyabinsk obl.	3 626	2 993	633	5
West Siberia region	**15 003**	**10 916**	**4 087**	**16**
Altai krai	2 822	1 582	1 240	6
incl. Gorno-Altai AO	192	52	140	12
Kemerovo obl.	3 175	2 774	401	7
Novosibirsk obl.	2 782	2 078	704	6
Omsk obl.	2 140	1 452	688	10
Tomsk obl.	1 001	690	311	16
Tyumen obl.	3 083	2 340	743	63
incl. Khanty-Mansi AOk	1 269	1 150	119	123
and Yamalo-Nenets AOk	487	379	108	209

	Thousands Total	Urban	Rural	% increase 1979-1989
East Siberia region	9 155	6 583	2 572	12
Buryat ASSR	1 042	641	410	16
Tuva ASSR	309	145	164	16
Krasnoyarsk krai	3 595	2 619	976	12
incl. Khakass AO	569	413	156	14
and Taimyr (Dolgano-				
Nenets) AOk	55	37	18	25
and Evenki AOk	24	7	17	55
Irkutsk obl.	2 831	2 279	552	11
incl. Ust-Ordinski				
Buryat AOk	136	25	111	3
Chita obl.	1 378	899	479	12
incl. Aginski-				
Buryat AOk	77	25	52	11
Far East region	7 941	6 021	1 920	16
Yakut ASSR	1 081	721	360	29
Primorski krai	2 260	1 751	509	14
Khabarovsk krai	1 824	1 430	394	16
incl. Jewish AO	216	143	73	13
Amur obl.	1 058	716	342	13
Kamchatka obl.	466	379	87	23
incl. Koryak AOk	39	15	24	15
Magadan obl.	543	440	103	17
incl. Chukot AOk	158	115	43	19
Sakhalin obl.	709	584	125	8
Kaliningrad obl.	871	689	182	8
Ukrainian SSR	51 704	34 591	17 113	4
Donetsk-Dnieper region	21 778	17 226	4 552	3
Voroshilovgrad obl.	2 864	2 474	390	3
Dnepropetrovsk obl.	3 883	3 233	650	7
Donetsk obl.	5 328	4 810	518	3
Zaporozhe obl.	2 081	1 577	504	7
Kirovgrad obl.	1 240	743	497	-1
Poltava obl.	1 753	991	762	1
Sumy obl.	1 433	886	547	-2
Kharkov obl.	3 196	2 512	684	5
South-west region	22 257	12 272	9 985	3
Vinnitsa obl.	1 932	857	1 075	-6
Volynsk obl.	1 062	519	543	5
Zhitomir obl.	1 545	818	727	-3
Transcarpathia obl.	1 252	515	737	8
Ivano-Frankovsk obl.	1 424	598	826	7
Kiev*	2 602	2 602	–	21
Kiev obl.	1 940	1 042	898	1

	Thousands Total	Urban	Rural	% increase 1979–1989
Lvov obl.	2 748	1 630	1 118	6
Rovno obl.	1 170	530	640	4
Ternopol obl.	1 169	477	692	1
Khmelnitski obl.	1 527	723	804	−2
Cherkassy obl.	1 532	810	722	−1
Chernigov obl.	1 416	756	660	−6
Chernovtsy obl.	938	395	543	5
Southern region	**7 669**	**5 093**	**2 576**	**8**
Crimea obl.	2 456	1 714	742	13
Nikolaev obl.	1 331	875	456	7
Odessa obl.	2 642	1 745	897	4
Kherson obl.	1 240	759	481	7
Belorussian SSR	**10 200**	**6 676**	**3 524**	**7**
Brest obl.	1 458	824	634	7
Vitebsk obl.	1 413	911	502	2
Gomel obl.	1 674	1 070	604	5
Grodno obl.	1 171	670	501	3
Minsk*	1 612	1 612	0	26
Minsk obl.	1 587	744	843	2
Mogilev obl.	1 285	845	440	3
Uzbek SSR	**19 906**	**8 106**	**11 800**	**29**
Karakalpak ASSR	1 214	584	630	35
Andizhan obl.	1 728	559	1 169	28
Bukhara obl.	1 141	397	744	29
Kashkadarya obl.	1 594	415	1 179	42
Namangan obl.	1 475	550	925	34
Samarkand obl.	2 778	926	1 825	29
Surkhandarya obl.	1 255	245	1 010	40
Syr-Darya obl.	1 316	407	909	37
Tashkent*	2 079	2 079	–	16
Tashkent obl.	2 157	958	1 199	20
Fergana obl.	2 153	703	1 450	27
Khorezm obl.	1 016	283	733	36
Kazakh SSR	**16 538**	**9 465**	**7 073**	**13**
Aktyubinsk obl.	738	399	339	17
Alma-Ata*	1 132	1 132	–	24
Alma-Ata obl.	978	216	762	15
East Kazakhstan obl.	934	607	327	7
Gurev obl.	755	548	207	21
Dzhambul obl.	1 050	498	552	13
Dzhezkazgan obl.	496	388	108	10

	Thousands Total	Urban	Rural	% increase 1979-1989
Karaganda obl.	1 352	1 147	205	7
Kzyl-Orda obl.	651	422	229	15
Kokchetav obl.	664	260	404	8
Kustanai obl.	1 221	616	605	13
Pavlodar obl.	944	605	339	17
North Kazakhstan obl.	600	287	313	5
Semipalatinsk obl.	838	429	409	8
Taldy-Kurgan obl.	721	325	396	9
Ural obl.	631	269	362	9
Tselinograd obl.	1 002	572	430	8
Chimkent obl.	1 831	745	1 086	17
Georgian SSR	**5 449**	**3 033**	**2 416**	**9**
Abkhazian ASSR	537	256	281	6
Adzhar ASSR	393	181	212	11
South Osetin AO	99	50	49	2
Tbilisi*	1 264	1 264	0	18
Districts subordinated to the Republic	3 156	1 282	1 874	6
Azerbaidzhan SSR	**7 029**	**3 785**	**3 244**	**17**
Nakhichevan ASSR	295	89	206	24
Nagorno-Karabakh AO	188	97	91	17
Baku*	1 757	1 757	–	13
Districts subordinated to the Republic	4 789	1 842	2 947	17
Lithuanian SSR	**3 690**	**2 509**	**1 181**	**9**
Vilnius	582	582	–	21
Moldavian SSR	**4 341**	**2 037**	**2 304**	**10**
Kishinev*	720	711	9	36
Latvian SSR	**2 681**	**1 907**	**774**	**6**
Riga	915	915	–	10
Kirgiz SSR	**4 291**	**1 641**	**2 650**	**22**
Frunze*	626	623	3	15
Issyk-Kul obl.	665	183	482	16
Osh obl.	2 010	576	1 434	29
Districts subordinated to the Republic	990	259	731	16

Table continues

	Thousands Total	Urban	Rural	% increase 1979-1989
Tadzhik SSR	5 112	1 667	3 445	34
Gorno-Badakhshan AO	161	20	141	27
Dushanbe*	604	596	8	21
Leninabad obl.	1 559	527	1 032	30
Khatlon obl.	1 703	363	1 340	39
Districts subordinated to the Republic	1 085	161	924	43
Armenian SSR	3 283	2 225	1 058	8
Erevan*	1 215	1 207	8	18
Turkmen SSR	3 534	1 603	1 931	28
Ashkhabad*	402	401	1	27
Mari obl.	815	222	593	29
Tashauz obl.	699	220	479	32
Chardzhou obl.	735	322	413	27
Districts subordinated to the Republic	883	438	445	26
Estonian SSR	1 573	1 127	446	7
Tallinn*	503	503	-	14

* The figure includes outlying settlements which are subordinated to the city.

Source: **Pravda** 1989, 29 aprelya, s. 2.

9

Rural and urban population of economic regions and major territorial-administrative divisions as percentages, 1989 and 1979

Abbreviations: obl. = oblast   AO = Autonomous oblast
AOk = Autonomous okrug

	1989 Urban	Rural	1979 Urban	Rural
USSR	**66**	**34**	62	38
Russian SFSR	**74**	**26**	69	31
Northern region	**77**	**23**	72	28
Karelian ASSR	82	18	78	22
Komi ASSR	76	24	71	29
Archangel obl.	73	27	72	28
incl. Nenets AOk	63	37	59	41
Vologda obl.	65	35	59	41
Murmansk obl.	92	8	89	11
North-west region	**87**	**13**	85	15
Leningrad*	100	–	100	–
Leningrad obl.	66	34	64	36
Novgorod obl.	70	30	65	35
Pskov obl.	63	37	55	45
Central region	**83**	**17**	78	22
Bryansk obl.	67	33	59	41
Vladimir obl.	79	21	75	25
Ivanovo obl.	82	18	80	20
Kalinin obl.	71	29	67	33
Kaluga obl.	69	31	62	38
Kostroma obl.	69	31	64	36
Moscow*	100	0	100	0
Moscow obl.	79	21	75	25
Orel obl.	62	38	55	45
Ryazan obl.	66	34	58	42
Smolensk obl.	68	32	60	40
Tula obl.	81	19	78	22
Yaroslavl obl.	82	18	78	22
Volgo-Vyatka region	**69**	**31**	62	38
Mari ASSR	61	39	53	47
Mordvin ASSR	57	43	47	53
Chuvash ASSR	58	42	46	54
Gorki obl.	77	23	73	27
Kirov obl.	70	30	64	36
Central Black-earth region	**60**	**40**	52	48
Belgorod obl.	63	37	53	47
Voronezh obl.	61	39	54	46

Table continues

	1989 Urban	Rural	1979 Urban	Rural
Kursk obl.	58	42	48	52
Lipetsk obl.	63	37	56	44
Tambov obl.	56	44	49	51
Volga region	**73**	**27**	**68**	**32**
Kalmyk ASSR	46	54	41	59
Tatar ASSR	73	27	63	37
Astrakhan obl.	68	32	67	33
Volgograd obl.	76	24	71	29
Kuibyshev obl.	81	19	78	22
Penza obl.	62	38	55	45
Saratov obl.	74	26	71	29
Ulyanovsk obl.	71	29	63	37
North Caucasus region	**57**	**43**	**55**	**45**
Dagestan ASSR	44	56	39	61
Kabardino-Balkar ASSR	61	39	58	42
North Osetin ASSR	69	31	68	32
Chechen-Ingush ASSR	41	59	43	57
Krasnodar krai	54	46	52	48
incl. Adyge AO	52	48	48	52
Stavropol krai	54	46	50	50
incl. Karachai-Cherkes AO	49	51	43	57
Rostov obl.	71	29	69	31
Ural region	**75**	**25**	**71**	**29**
Bashkir ASSR	64	36	57	43
Udmurt ASSR	70	30	65	35
Kurgan obl.	55	45	51	49
Orenburg obl.	65	35	60	40
Perm obl.	77	23	74	26
incl. Komi-Permyak AOk	30	70	24	76
Sverdlovsk obl.	87	13	85	15
Chelyabinsk obl.	83	17	81	19
West Siberia region	**73**	**27**	**68**	**32**
Altai krai	56	44	52	48
incl. Gorno-Altai AO	27	73	28	72
Kemerovo obl.	87	13	86	14
Novosibirsk obl.	75	25	71	29
Omsk obl.	68	32	63	37
Tomsk obl.	69	31	65	35
Tyumen obl.	76	24	61	39
incl. Khanty-Mansi AOk	91	9	78	22
and Yamalo-Nenets AOk	78	22	51	49

11

	1989 Urban	Rural	1979 Urban	Rural
East Siberia region	72	28	69	31
Buryat ASSR	62	38	57	43
Tuva ASSR	47	53	43	57
Krasnoyarsk krai	73	27	69	31
incl. Khakass AO	73	27	68	32
and Taimyr (Dolgano-Nenets) AOk	67	33	65	35
and Evenki AOk	31	69	35	65
Irkutsk obl.	81	19	78	22
incl. Ust-Ordinski Buryat AOk	19	81	18	82
Chita obl.	65	35	63	37
incl. Aginski-Buryat AOk	33	67	26	74
Far East region	76	24	75	25
Yakut ASSR	67	33	61	39
Primorski krai	77	23	76	24
Khabarovsk krai	78	22	79	21
incl. Jewish AO	66	34	68	32
Amur obl.	68	32	65	35
Kamchatka obl.	81	19	83	17
incl. Koryak AOk	39	61	39	61
Magadan obl.	81	19	78	22
incl. Chukot AOk	73	27	70	30
Sakhalin obl.	82	18	82	18
Kaliningrad obl.	79	21	77	23
Ukrainian SSR	67	33	61	39
Donetsk-Dnieper region	79	21	75	25
Voroshilovgrad obl.	86	14	85	15
Dnepropetrovsk obl.	83	17	80	20
Donetsk obl.	90	10	89	11
Zaporozhe obl.	76	24	71	29
Kirovgrad obl.	60	40	52	48
Poltava obl.	57	43	50	50
Sumy obl.	62	38	53	47
Kharkov obl.	79	21	75	25
South-west region	55	45	47	53
Vinnitsa obl.	44	56	35	65
Volynsk obl.	49	51	40	60
Zhitomir obl.	53	47	44	56
Transcarpathia obl.	41	59	38	62
Ivano-Frankovsk obl.	42	58	36	64
Kiev*	100	–	100	–
Kiev obl.	54	46	45	55

Table continues

	1989 Urban	Rural	1979 Urban	Rural
Lvov obl.	59	41	53	47
Rovno obl.	45	55	36	64
Ternopol obl.	41	59	31	69
Khmelnitski obl.	47	53	36	64
Cherkassy obl.	53	47	44	56
Chernigov obl.	53	47	44	56
Chernovtsy obl.	42	58	38	62
Southern region	**66**	**34**	**63**	**37**
Crimea obl.	70	30	67	33
Nikolaev obl.	66	34	60	40
Odessa obl.	66	34	62	38
Kherson obl.	61	39	58	42
Belorussian SSR	**65**	**35**	**55**	**45**
Brest obl.	57	43	45	55
Vitebsk obl.	64	36	56	44
Gomel obl.	64	36	52	48
Grodno obl.	57	43	44	56
Minsk*	100	0	100	0
Minsk obl.	47	53	36	64
Mogilev obl.	66	34	57	43
Uzbek SSR	**41**	**59**	**41**	**59**
Karakalpak ASSR	48	52	42	58
Andizhan obl.	32	68	29	71
Bukhara obl.	35	65	33	67
Kashkadarya obl.	26	74	25	75
Namangan obl.	37	63	34	66
Samarkand obl.	33	67	42	58
Surkhandarya obl.	19	81	19	81
Syr-Darya obl.	31	69	29	71
Tashkent*	100	–	100	–
Tashkent obl.	44	56	43	57
Fergana obl.	33	67	33	67
Khorezm obl.	28	72	20	80
Kazakh SSR	**57**	**43**	**54**	**46**
Aktyubinsk obl.	54	46	47	53
Alma-Ata*	100	–	100	–
Alma-Ata obl.	22	78	19	81
East Kazakhstan obl.	65	35	61	39
Gurev obl.	73	27	71	29
Dzhambul obl.	47	53	45	55
Dzhezkazgan obl.	78	22	77	23

Table continues

	1989 Urban	Rural	1979 Urban	Rural
Karaganda obl.	85	15	85	15
Kzyl-Orda obl.	65	35	63	37
Kokchetav obl.	39	61	34	66
Kustanai obl.	50	50	46	54
Pavlodar obl.	64	36	57	43
North Kazakhstan obl.	48	52	44	56
Semipalatinsk obl.	51	49	48	52
Taldy-Kurgan obl.	45	55	39	61
Ural obl.	43	57	38	62
Tselinograd obl.	57	43	53	47
Chimkent obl.	41	59	40	60
Georgian SSR	**56**	**44**	**52**	**48**
Abkhazian ASSR	48	52	47	53
Adzhar ASSR	46	54	45	55
South Osetin AO	51	49	42	58
Tbilisi*	100	0	100	0
Districts subordinated to the Republic	41	59	37	63
Azerbaidzhan SSR	**54**	**46**	**53**	**47**
Nakhichevan ASSR	30	70	26	74
Nagorno-Karabakh AO	52	48	44	56
Baku*	100	–	100	–
Districts subordinated to the Republic	38	62	37	63
Lithuanian SSR	**68**	**32**	**61**	**39**
Vilnius	100	–	100	–
Moldavian SSR	**47**	**53**	**39**	**61**
Kishinev*	99	1	99	1
Latvian SSR	**71**	**29**	**68**	**32**
Riga	100	–	100	–
Kirgiz SSR	**38**	**62**	**39**	**61**
Frunze*	99	1	98	2
Issyk-Kul obl.	28	72	25	75
Osh obl.	29	71	30	70
Districts subordinated to the Republic	26	74	25	75

Table continues

	1989 Urban	Rural	1979 Urban	Rural
Tadzhik SSR	**33**	**67**	**35**	**65**
Gorno-Badakhshan AO	13	87	14	86
Dushanbe*	99	1	99	1
Leninabad obl.	34	66	36	64
Khatlon obl.	21	79	23	77
Districts subordinated to the Republic	15	85	14	86
Armenian SSR	**68**	**32**	**66**	**34**
Erevan*	99	1	99	1
Turkmen SSR	**45**	**55**	**48**	**52**
Ashkhabad*	99.6	0.4	99.9	0.1
Mari obl.	27	73	32	68
Tashauz obl.	32	68	30	70
Chardzhou obl.	44	56	46	54
Districts subordinated to the Republic	50	50	54	46
Estonian SSR	**72**	**28**	**70**	**30**
Tallinn*	100	–	100	–

* The figure includes outlying settlements which are subordinated to the city.

Source: **Pravda** 1989, 29 aprelya, s. 2.

Intercensal population change: by Union Republic, 1979–1989 (thousands)

	Total increase	Natural increase	Migration
USSR	**24 281**	**24 450**	**−169**
Russian SFSR	9 835	8 068	1 767
Ukrainian SSR	1 949	1 796	153
Belorussian SSR	640	648	−8
Kazakh SSR	1 854	2 638	−784
Moldavian SSR	394	450	−56
Republics of Central Asia	**7 363**	**8 213**	**−850**
Uzbek SSR	4 515	5 022	−507
Kirgiz SSR	762	919	−157
Tadzhik SSR	1 311	1 413	−102
Turkmen SSR	775	859	−84
Transcaucasian Republics	**1 687**	**2 326**	**−639**
Georgian SSR	434	486	−52
Azerbaidzhan SSR	1 001	1 267	−266
Armenian SSR	252	573	−321
Baltic Republics	**559**	**311**	**248**
Lithuanian SSR	292	192	100
Latvian SSR	160	67	93
Estonian SSR	107	52	55
Central Asian, Kazakh, Azerbaidzhan SSRs	**10 218**	**12 118**	**1 900**
Other SSRs	**14 063**	**12 332**	**1 731**

Between the censuses of 1979 and 1989 the population of the
USSR increased by an average of 0.9% per annum. Minor
deviations from the average occurred in 1978-1981 and 1986-
1987. In the first period the growth rate fell to 0.8% as a
consequence of an increase in deaths, and in the second it
rose to 1% as a result of a small rise in the birth rate
and a decline in mortality.

Although the populations of all Union Republics grew during
the intercensal period, the rates of increase differ
substantially. On account of high birth rates, the growth
was greatest in the area of Central Asia - with an average
of 3% per annum. Broadly speaking, that level has been
maintained since the first post-war census of 1959. Over
the thirty year period since then the population of the
relevant Union Republics has more than doubled, increasing
by 2.5 times in Uzbekistan, 2.1 times in Kirgizia, 2.6
times in Tadzhikistan and by 2.3 times in Turkmenistan.
More than 11% of the total population of the USSR now live
in these Republics, compared to 6.6% in 1959.

A high population growth rate has also occurred in
Azerbaidzhan. However, from 1961, the birth rate there has
fallen, and the annual average increase declined from 3% in
1959-1969 to 1.7% in 1979-1989. A comparable situation is
evident in Kazakhstan, where the growth rate declined to
1.3% per annum. A contributory factor was out-migration; it
amounted to almost one third of the Republic's natural
increase. In the 1980s the lowest population growth rates
were in the Ukraine, Latvia, Estonia, Belorussia and the
Russian SFSR (at 4%-7% over the decade).

A significant differentiation is also evident in the pace
of population growth within the Russian SFSR. It ranges
from 1%-1.6% in the Volga-Vyatka, Ural, Central and Volga
economic regions to 12%-16% in East and West Siberia, and
in the Far East.

A decline in population occurred in eleven territories of
the Russian SFSR and in seven oblasti of the Ukraine. It
was most marked (at 4%-8%) in Kursk, Tambov, Vinnitsa, and
Chernigov oblasti, and in Komi-Permyak autonomous okrug.
The main explanory factor in these cases was out-migration.
Furthermore, in Ryazan, Tula, Tambov, Pskov, Sumy and
Chernigov oblasti the number of deaths exceeded the number
of births. In Pskov oblast that explanation almost
completely accounts for the population decrease.

In the majority of territories of the Russian SFSR where
the numbers of people have fallen, the rate of decrease has
slowed down. This can be seen from the table which follows
on the next page.

Population decrease in areas of Russian SFSR, 1970-1988 (percentages)
Abbreviation: obl. = oblast

	1970-1978	1979-1988
Tambov obl.	8.1	5.0
Kursk obl.	5.1	4.3
Mordov ASSR	3.8	2.7
Bryansk obl.	4.7	2.1
Tula obl.	2.4	2.0
Ryazan obl.	3.5	1.2
Pskov obl.	2.9	0.4
Voronezh obl.	1.9	0.3
Ivanovo obl.	1.4	0.3
Orlov obl.	4.1	0.1
Penza obl.	2.1	0.05

In three oblasts of the Ukrainian SSR, the percentage
decrease was higher during the years 1979-1988 than during
1970-1978. In Zhitomir oblast it was 1.8% and 3.2%; in
Chernigov oblast 3.7% and 5.7%; in Vinnitsa oblast 4.0% and
5.6%.   Source: **Stat. Press-Byull.** 1989, 9, s. 94-6.

Permanently resident population of Union Republics, at 1989 census (thousands)

	Total	Urban	Rural
USSR	285 743	187 746	97 997
Russian SFSR	147 022	107 959	39 063
Ukrainian SSR	51 452	34 297	17 155
Belorussian SSR	10 152	6 642	3 510
Uzbek SSR	19 810	8 041	11 769
Kazakh SSR	16 464	9 402	7 062
Georgian SSR	5 401	2 992	2 409
Azerbaidzhan SSR	7 021	3 806	3 215
Lithuanian SSR	3 675	2 487	1 188
Moldavian SSR	4 335	2 020	2 315
Latvian SSR	2 667	1 889	778
Kirgiz SSR	4 258	1 625	2 633
Tadzhik SSR	5 093	1 655	3 438
Armenian SSR	3 305	2 222	1 083
Turkmen SSR	3 523	1 591	1 932
Estonian SSR	1 565	1 118	447

Source: **Vestnik Statistiki** 1990, 3, s. 79.

Urban and rural population, 1959-1989

| | Millions | | % of total | |
	Urban	Rural	Urban	Rural
1959	100.0	108.8	48	52
1970	136.0	105.7	56	44
1979	163.6	98.8	62	38
1989	188.8	97.9	66	34

Source: **Pravda** 1989, 29 aprelya, s. 2.

****

Between the censuses of 1979 and 1989 the urban population rose by 25.2 million persons (which is an increase of 15%). Of that total, 14.5 million persons (58%) are accounted for by natural increase - the excess of births over deaths. A further 8.9 million persons (35%) are accounted for by in-migration from rural areas. The transformation of rural settlements into urban settlements accounts for 1.8 million persons.

In the Union taken as a whole the proportion of the population who live in urban areas was 66% in 1989, compared to 62% in 1979. The most highly urbanised Republics are the Russian SFSR (74%), Estonia (72%) and Latvia (71%). At the same time, in the Central Asian and Moldavian SSRs less than half of the population (33%-47%) live in towns. Moreover, as a consequence of the high birth rates in rural areas the proportion of urban population decreased over the period 1979-1989; it fell from 48% to 45% in Turkmenistan, from 39% to 38% in Kirgizia and from 35% to 33% in Tadzhikistan.

The rural population decreased by 0.9 million persons (by 0.9%) between the censuses of 1979 and 1989. In the Union taken as whole the proportion of the population living in rural areas fell from 38% to 34%. The rural population decreased in the overwhelming majority of oblasti in the Russian SFSR, including virtually the entire Non-Black Earth zone, in almost every oblast of the Ukrainian SSR and throughout the territory of Belorussia. The rural population decreased by 20% or more in the Mordvin and Tatar ASSRs and in Bryansk, Kursk, Sumy, Chernigov, Gomel and Grodno oblasti.

19

Nevetheless, due to a range of measures aimed at retaining cadres in the countryside, out-migration was significantly less than during the previous intercensal period. That is attested by the following data.

**Annual average for rural population change,
1970-1988** (thousands)

	Total	Natural increase	Migration	Settlements transformed
1970-1978	-763.4	985.2	-1 491.7	-256.9
1979-1988	-92.4	993.0	-909.8	-175.6

As in the past, out-migration continues to be the major cause of the decrease in the rural population. However, the intensity of out-migration is noticeably less; during the last decade it was at an average of 9.3 per 1 000 persons, compared to 14.6 per 1 000 during the period 1970-1978.

In the rural areas of several territories the high proportion of elderly people, together with out-migration, is linked to an excess of deaths over births. This phenomenon has occurred in the rural areas of all oblasti of the Central Black-Earth and Central regions, and in Gorki oblast of the Volgo-Vyatka region of the Russian SFSR, and in the Vitebsk, Grodno, Minsk, and Mogilev oblasti of the Belorussian SSR.

During the last decade the rural population has increased slightly in the Kazakh, Armenian and Estonian SSRs. In Azerbaidzhan it rose by 15%. The highest rates for rural population increase (23%-39%) were recorded in the Central Asian Republics, where the problem of employment is also acute.

Source: **Stat. Press-Byull.** 1989, 9, s. 96-9.

Migration of urban population: by Union Republic, 1988

	In-migrants	Out-migrants	In- per 1 000 out-migrants
USSR	**8 531 512**	**7 244 372**	**849**
Russian SFSR	5 007 677	4 250 701	849
Ukrainian SSR	1 573 648	1 292 473	821
Belorussian SSR	348 536	253 548	727
Uzbek SSR	279 278	266 896	956
Kazakh SSR	507 507	457 621	902
Georgian SSR	60 500	49 633	820
Azerbaidzhan SSR	119 692	123 073	1 028
Lithuanian SSR	115 310	87 721	761
Moldavian SSR	122 467	91 123	744
Latvian SSR	80 887	67 178	831
Kirgiz SSR	89 120	78 750	884
Tadzhik SSR	61 140	58 767	961
Armenian SSR	50 943	55 255	1 085
Turkmen SSR	71 362	71 436	1 001
Estonian SSR	43 445	40 197	925

Source: **Stat. Press-Byull.** 1989, 4, s. 49.

During the period 1979-1989 the main flow of migrants from various parts of the country was to the Republics of the Baltic and to the Russian SFSR. In the Lithuanian, Latvian and Estonian SSRs in-migration accounted for 34%-58% of the overall population increase, while in the Russian SFSR it accounted for 18% of the increase. In recent years a low level of migration into the Ukrainian and Belorussian SSRs has also been evident.

Within the Russian SFSR substantial in-migration has occurred in the Central and North-west economic regions, mainly to Moscow and Leningrad and to their respective oblasti. In these regions in-migration accounted for 69%-74% of the overall population growth. Migration also makes a noticeable impact on population size in the Far East and Siberia economic regions. There its contribution to the overall increase was 30%-40%.

Amongst the Republics which were net losers of population due to migration, the Kirgiz, Azerbaidzhan and Kazakh SSRs had the highest levels of out-migration. It stood at 40-50 persons per 10 000 population. In the case of Kirgizia and Kazakhstan the totals are influenced to some extent by emigration to beyond the Soviet Union's borders.

On average, roughly 65% of migration occurs within a single Republic - between urban and rural areas, and also between different oblasti. The closest interrepublic migratory contacts are found amongst the republics of the Russian SFSR and amongst republics of a given region.

The migratory process mainly involves people in the economically active age groups. In 1988 persons of working age made up 77% of the in-migrants to urban areas, and 79% of the out-migrants.

Amongst migrants over the age of 16 there is a majority of people with secondary general education (46%-43% [sic]) and secondary specialised education (24%-27%). The proportion of migrants with higher education is 12%-14%.

Source: **Stat. Press-Byull.** 1989, 9, s. 101-2.

Emigration from the USSR, 1973–1988

	To socialist countries	To capitalist countries	Total
1973	1 585	29 824	31 409
1974	1 861	21 419	23 280
1975	1 778	16 289	18 067
1976	2 104	19 347	21 451
1977	2 336	21 743	24 079
1978	2 637	28 935	31 572
1979	2 779	45 414	48 193
1980	2 526	12 052	33 657
1981	2 135	13 052	15 187
1982	2 182	5 095	7 277
1983	1 996	3 822	5 818
1984	1 757	2 523	4 280
1985	1 695	2 468	4 163
1986	1 718	2 614	4 332
1987	3 159	25 880	29 039
1988	3 014	72 158	75 172

In 1988 the right to leave the USSR was granted to 108 189
persons (and their children). As in the past, those leaving
are predominantly ethnic Germans, Jews and Armenians.

Source: **AiF** 1989, 40, s. 2.

Towns and urban settlements, 1979 and 1989

	Number 1979	1989	Population (millions) 1979	1989	% growth
Towns	**2 062**	**2 190**	**141.9**	**164.7**	**16**
with popn. of: below 50 000	1 568	1 611	29.5	31.4	6
50-99 900	221	283	14.8	19.1	29
100-249 900	163	164	24.5	25.3	3
250-499 900	65	75	22.6	25.6	14
500-999 900	27	34	18.6	22.0	18
over a million	18	23	31.9	41.3	29
Urban settlements	**3 852**	**4 026**	**21.7**	**24.1**	**11**
Total	5 914	6 216	163.6	188.8	15

Out of the total, urban settlements and small towns with a population of less than 50 000 account for the overwhelming majority (91%). However, only 29% of the urban population resides in them. The main body of town-dwellers (over 60%) is concentrated in large towns and cities with a population of over 100 000 persons.

The 23 cities which have over a million inhabitants are as follows: Moscow, Leningrad, Kiev, Tashkent, Kharkov, Minsk, Gorki, Novosibirsk, Sverdlovsk, Tbilisi, Kuibyshev, Erevan, Baku, Omsk, Chelyabinsk, Alma-Ata, Odessa, Donetsk, Kazan, Perm, Ufa, Dnepropetrovsk, and Rostov-na-Donu.

Source: **Stat. Press-Byull.** 1989, 9, 97-8.

Population of Union Republic capitals and towns with over 500 000 inhabitants, 1959-1989 (thousands)

	1959	1970	1979	1989
Alma-Ata	456	730	910	1 128
Astrakhan	306	410	461	509
Ashkhabad	170	253	312	398
Baku	968	1 266	1 550	1 757
less outlying popn.				
under city soviet	643	852	1 022	1 150
Barnaul	303	439	535	602
Vilnius	236	372	481	582
Vladivostok	291	441	550	648
Volgograd	591	815	929	999
Voronezh	447	660	783	887
Gomel	168	272	383	500
Gorki	941	1 170	1 344	1 438
Dnepropetrovsk	690	904	1 066	1 179
Donetsk	708	879	1 021	1 110
Dushanbe	227	374	494	595
Erevan	493	764	1 019	1 199
Zaporozhe	449	658	781	884
Izhevsk	285	422	549	635
Irkutsk	366	451	550	626
Kazan	667	869	993	1 094
Karaganda	383	523	572	614
Kemerovo	287	374	462	520
Kiev	1 104	1 624	2 133	2 587
Kishinev	212	349	503	665
Krasnodar	310	460	560	620
Krasnoyarsk	412	648	796	912
Krivoi Rog	408	581	650	713
Kuibyshev	806	1 038	1 206	1 257
Leningrad	3 367	4 027	4 588	5 020
less outlying popn.				
under city soviet	3 003	3 550	4 073	4 456
Lvov	411	553	667	790
Mariupol	284	417	503	517
Minsk	509	907	1 262	1 589

Table continues

	1959	1970	1979	1989
Moscow	6 130	7 190	8 137	8 967
less outlying popn.				
under city soviet	5 809	7 022	7 933	8 769
Naberezhnie Chelny	16	38	301	501
Nikolaev	251	362	440	503
Novokuznetsk	380	496	541	600
Novosibirsk	885	1 161	1 312	1 436
Odessa	664	892	1 046	1 115
Omsk	581	821	1 014	1 148
Orenburg	267	343	458	547
Penza	255	374	483	543
Perm	629	850	999	1 091
Riga	580	732	835	915
Rostov-na-Donu	600	789	934	1 020
Ryazan	214	350	453	515
Saratov	579	757	856	905
Sverdlovsk	779	1 025	1 211	1 367
Tallinn	282	361	430	482
Tashkent	927	1 385	1 780	2 073
Tbilisi	703	901	1 066	1 260
Tolyatti	72	251	502	630
Tomsk	249	338	421	502
Tula	351	462	514	540
Ulyanovsk	206	351	464	625
Ufa	547	780	978	1 083
Frunze	218	429	533	616
Khabarovsk	323	436	528	601
Kharkhov	953	1 223	1 444	1 611
Chelyabinsk	689	875	1 030	1 143
Yaroslavl	407	517	597	633

Source: **Nar. khoz. SSSR 1988**, s. 22-3.

Population of towns with over 100 000 inhabitants, 1979 and 1989

	Thousands 1979	1989	% increase
Abakan	128	154	20
Aktyubinsk	191	253	33
Aleksandriya	82	103	25
Alma-Ata	910	1 128	24
Almalyk	101	114	13
Almetevsk	110	129	18
Angarsk	239	266	11
Angren	106	131	24
Andizhan	230	293	27
Anzhero-Sudzhensk	105	108	3
Arzamas	93	109	17
Armavir	162	161	-0.3
Arkhangelsk	385	416	8
Astrakhan	461	509	10
Achinsk	117	122	4
Ashkhabad	312	398	28
Baku	1 550	1 757	13
less outlying popn.			
under city soviet	1 022	1 150	13
Balakovo	152	198	30
Balashikha	118	136	15
Baranovichi	131	159	22
Barnaul	535	602	12
Batumi	123	136	11
Belaya Tserkov	151	197	30
Belgorod	240	300	25
Beltsy	125	159	27
Bendery	101	130	28
Berdyansk	122	132	8
Berezhniki	185	201	9
Bisk	212	233	10
Blagoveshchensk			
(Amur oblast)	172	206	20
Bobruisk	192	223	16
Borisov	112	144	29
Bratsk	214	255	20
Brest	177	258	45
Bryansk	394	452	15
Bukhara	185	224	21
Velikie Luki	102	114	12
Vilnius	481	582	21
Vinnitsa	314	374	19
Vitebsk	297	350	18
Vladivostok	550	648	18
Vladimir	296	350	18

| | Thousands | | % increase |
	1979	1989	
Volgograd	929	999	8
Volgodonsk	91	176	92
Volzhski	209	269	28
Vologda	237	283	20
Vorkuta	100	116	16
Voronezh	783	887	13
Voroshilovgrad	463	497	7
Votkinsk	90	103	15
Glazov	81	104	28
Gomel	383	500	31
Gorlovka	336	337	0.3
Gorki	1 344	1 438	7
Grodno	195	270	39
Grozny	375	401	7
Gurev	131	149	14
Daugavpils	116	127	9
Dzhambul	264	307	16
Dzhezkazgan	89	109	22
Dzhizak	70	102	47
Dzerzhinsk (Gorki oblast)	257	285	11
Dimitrovgrad	106	124	17
Dneprodzerzhinsk	250	282	13
Dnepropetrovsk	1 066	1 179	11
Donetsk	1 021	1 110	9
Dushanbe	494	595	20
Evpatoriya	93	108	16
Elets	112	120	8
Enakievo	114	121	6
Erevan	1 019	1 199	18
Zhitomir	244	292	20
Zhukovski	90	101	12
Zagorsk	107	115	7
Zaporozhe	781	884	13
Zelenograd	140	158	13
Zlatoust	198	208	5
Ivanovo	465	481	4
Ivano-Frankovsk	150	214	43
Izhevsk	549	635	16
Irkutsk	550	626	14
Ioshkar-Ola	201	242	20

Table continues

	Thousands 1979	1989	% increase
Kazan	993	1 094	10
Kalinin	412	451	10
Kaliningrad	355	401	13
Kaliningrad (Moscow oblast)	133	160	20
Kaluga	265	312	18
Kamenets-Podolski	84	102	21
Kamensk-Uralski	187	209	12
Kamyshin	112	122	10
Kansk	101	110	9
Karaganda	572	614	7
Karshi	108	156	44
Kaunas	370	423	14
Kemerovo	462	520	13
Kerch	157	174	11
Kzyl-Orda	156	153	-2
Kiev	2 133	2 587	21
Kineshma	101	105	4
Kirov	390	441	13
Kirovabad	232	278	20
Kirovograd	237	269	14
Kiselevsk	122	128	5
Kislovodsk	101	114	13
Kishinev	503	665	32
Klaipeda	176	204	16
Kovrov	143	160	12
Kokand	153	182	19
Kokchetav	103	137	33
Kolomna	147	162	10
Kolpino	114	142	25
Kommunarsk	120	126	5
Komsomolsk-na-Amur	264	315	20
Konstantinovka	112	108	-4
Kostroma	255	278	9
Kramatorsk	178	198	11
Krasnodar	560	620	11
Krasnoyarsk	796	912	15
Krasny Luch	106	113	7
Kremenchug	210	236	13
Krivoi Rog	650	713	10
Kuibyshev	1 206	1 257	4
Kurgan	310	356	15
Kursk	375	424	13
Kustanai	165	224	36
Kutaisi	194	235	21

Table continues

| | Thousands | | % increase |
	1979	1989	
Leninabad	130	160	23
Leninakan	207	120	-42
Leningrad	4 588	5 020	9
less outlying popn.			
under city soviet	4 073	4 456	9
Leninsk-Kuznetski	158	165	5
Liepaya	108	114	6
Lipetsk	396	450	14
Lisichansk	119	127	6
Lutsk	141	198	40
Lvov	667	790	18
Lyubertsy	154	165	7
Magadan	121	152	25
Magnitogorsk	406	440	8
Maikop	128	149	16
Makeevka	436	430	-1
Margilan	110	125	14
Mariupol	503	517	3
Makhachkala	251	315	25
Mezhdurechensk	91	107	17
Melitopol	161	174	8
Miass	150	168	12
Minsk	1 262	1 589	26
Michurinsk	101	109	8
Mogilev	290	356	23
Mozyr	73	101	37
Moscow	8 137	8 967	10
less outlying popn.			
under city soviet	7 933	8 769	11
Murmansk	381	468	23
Murom	114	124	9
Mytishchi	141	154	10
Naberezhnie Chelny	301	501	66
Navoi	84	107	27
Nalchik	207	235	13
Namangan	227	308	36
Nakhodka	133	165	24
Nevinnomyssk	104	121	17
Neftekamsk	70	107	53
Nizhnevartovsk	109	242	122
Nizhnekamsk	134	191	42
Nizhni Tagil	398	440	11
Nikolaev	440	503	14
Nikopol	146	158	8
Novgorod	186	229	23

Table continues

	Thousands 1979	1989	% increase
Novokuznetsk	541	600	11
Novokuibyshevsk	109	113	4
Novomoskovsk			
(Tula oblast)	147	146	-0.3
Novorossisk	159	186	17
Novosibirsk	1 312	1 436	9
Novotroitsk	95	106	12
Novocheboksarsk	85	115	35
Novocherkassk	183	187	2
Novoshakhtinsk	104	106	2
Noginsk	119	123	4
Norilsk	180	174	-3
Nukus	109	169	55
Obninsk	73	100	36
Odessa	1 046	1 115	7
Odintsovo	101	125	23
Oktyabrski	88	105	19
Omsk	1 014	1 148	13
Ordzhonikidze			
(North Osetin ASSR)	279	300	8
Orel	305	337	10
Orenburg	458	547	20
Orekhovo-Zuevo	132	137	4
Orsk	246	271	10
Orsha	112	123	10
Osh	169	213	26
Pavlograd	107	131	22
Pavlodar	273	331	21
Panevezhis	102	126	25
Penza	483	543	12
Pervouralsk	129	142	10
Perm	999	1 091	9
Petrozavodsk	234	270	15
Petropavlovsk	207	241	17
Petropavlovsk-			
Kamchatski	215	269	25
Pinsk	90	119	32
Podolsk	202	210	4
Poltava	279	315	13
Prokopevsk	266	274	3
Pskov	176	204	16
Pyatigorsk	110	129	18

	Thousands		% increase
	1979	1989	
Riga	835	915	10
Rovno	179	228	27
Rostov-na-Donu	934	1 020	9
Rubtsovsk	157	172	9
Rudny	110	124	13
Rustavi	129	159	23
Rybinsk	239	252	5
Ryazan	453	515	14
Salavat	137	150	9
Samarkand	346	366	6
Saransk	263	312	18
Sarapul	107	111	4
Saratov	856	905	6
Sverdlovsk	1 211	1 367	13
Sevastopol	301	356	19
Severodvinsk	197	249	26
Severodonetsk	113	131	16
Semipalatinsk	283	334	18
Serov	101	104	2
Serpukhov	140	144	3
Simferopol	302	344	14
Slavyansk	140	135	-4
Smolensk	299	341	14
Solikamsk	101	110	9
Sochi	287	337	17
Stavropol	258	318	23
Stary Oskol	115	174	51
Stakhanov	108	112	4
Sterlitamak	220	248	13
Sumgait	190	231	22
Sumy	228	291	28
Surgut	107	248	131
Sukhumi	114	121	6
Syzran	166	174	5
Syktyvkar	183	233	27
Taganrog	276	291	5
Taldy-Kurgan	88	119	36
Tallinn	430	482	12
Tambov	270	305	13
Tartu	105	114	9
Tashauz	84	112	33
Tashkent	1 780	2 073	16
Tbilisi	1 066	1 260	18
Temirtau	213	212	-0.3
Ternopol	144	205	43
Tiraspol	139	182	31

Table continues

	Thousands 1979	1989	% increase
Tolyatti	502	630	26
Tomsk	421	502	19
Tula	514	540	5
Tyumen	359	477	33
Uzhgorod	91	117	29
Ulan-Ude	300	353	17
Ulyanovsk	464	625	35
Uralsk	167	200	20
Urgench	100	128	28
Usole-Sibirskoe	103	107	4
Ussurisk	147	162	10
Ust-Ilimsk	69	109	59
Ust-Kamenogorsk	274	324	18
Ufa	978	1 083	11
Ukhta	87	111	26
Fergana	176	200	14
Frunze	533	616	16
Khabarovsk	528	601	14
Kharkhov	1 444	1 611	12
Kherson	319	355	11
Khimiki	118	133	13
Khmelnitski	172	237	38
Tselinograd	232	277	19
Chardzhou	140	161	15
Cheboksary	308	420	36
Chelyabinsk	1 030	1 143	11
Cherepovets	266	310	17
Cherkassy	228	290	27
Cherkessk	91	113	24
Chernigov	238	296	24
Chernovtsy	219	257	17
Chimkent	322	393	22
Chirchik	132	156	19
Chita	303	366	21
Shakhty	209	224	7
Shevchenko	111	159	44
Shyaulyai	118	145	23
Shchelkovo	100	109	9

Table continues

	Thousands		% increase
	1979	1989	
Ekibastuz	66	135	105
Elektrostal	139	153	10
Engels	161	182	13
Yuzhno-Sakhalinsk	140	157	12
Yakutsk	152	187	23
Yaroslavl	597	633	6

At the beginning of 1989 the Soviet Union contained a total of 2 190 towns. Out of that total 57 had over half a million inhabitants and of those 23 had over one million inhabitants.

The proportion of the Soviet population living in towns with 100 000 to 500 000 persons increased by 9 per cent over the decade and the proportion living in cities with half a million to one million persons rose by 29 per cent.

Source: **Pravda** 1989, 29 aprelya, s. 2.

******

Between the censuses of 1979 and 1989 a total of 131 new towns were created, of which 28 are in the Ukraine, 34 in Uzbekistan and 39 in the Russian SFSR. Roughly half of the towns founded in the Russian SFSR are located in the East and West Siberia regions, as follows:

Tyumen oblast: Megion, Novy Urengoi, Noyarbsk, Langepas, Raduzhny, Nyagan, Kogalym, Beloyarski

Tomsk oblast: Kedrovy

Altai krai: Zarinsk, Belokurikha

Krasnoyarsk krai: Borodino, Sharypovo, Talnakh, Kaierkan, Sosnovoborsk

Irkutsk oblast: Sayansk

Buryat ASSR: Severobaikalsk

Number of administrative-territorial units, 1988 and 1989 (start of year)

	1988	1989
Autonomous republics	20	20
Kraya and oblasti*	129	120
Autonomous oblasti	8	8
Autonomous okruga	10	10
Districts	3 228	3 193
Towns	2 186	2 190
Districts within towns	665	628
Settlements of an urban type	4 014	4 026

* Includes six kraya.

In 1988 the administrative-territorial structure of the country was altered substantially in connection with restructuring of the management of the national economy, the improvement of organisational structures and a reduction in the number of administrative personnel.

A total of ten oblasti were abolished:

Dzhizak, Navoi	Uzbek SSR
Mangyshlak, Turgai	Kazakh SSR
Naryn, Talas	Kirgiz SSR
Kulyab, Kurgan-Tyube	Tadzhik SSR
Ashkhabad, Krasnovodsk	Turkmen SSR

The districts and towns of these oblasti became part of the neighbouring oblasti or were subordinated directly to republican organs. In the Tadzhik SSR Khatlon oblast was created from the oblasti which had been abolished.

During 1988 four new towns were designated:

South Sukhokumsk	Dagestan ASSR
Petrov Val	Volgograd oblast
Beloyarski	Khanty-Mansi autonomous okrug
Pustomyty	Lvov oblast

The number of settlements of an urban type rose by twelve.

District divisions were abolished in 16 towns with populations of less than 250 000 in the Russian SFSR, the Ukrainian SSR and the Kazakh SSR. The object was to bring about more effective resolution of problems relating to the construction of housing and socio-cultural facilities.

Source: **Stat. Press-Byull.** 1989, 4, s. 48.

Births: by Union Republic, 1988
(absolute numbers)

	Total	Urban	Rural
USSR	**5 381 056**	**3 171 588**	**2 209 468**
Russian SFSR	2 348 494	1 662 029	686 465
Ukrainian SSR	744 056	509 556	234 500
Belorussian SSR	163 193	116 005	47 188
Uzbek SSR	694 144	224 598	469 546
Kazakh SSR	407 166	209 889	197 227
Georgian SSR	91 905	49 096	42 809
Azerbaidzhan SSR	184 350	89 689	94 661
Lithuanian SSR	56 727	37 368	19 359
Moldavian SSR	88 568	39 836	48 732
Latvian SSR	41 275	27 506	13 769
Kirgiz SSR	133 710	40 803	92 907
Tadzhik SSR	201 864	48 491	153 373
Armenian SSR	74 707	47 639	27 068
Turkmen SSR	125 887	51 635	74 252
Estonian SSR	25 060	17 448	7 612

Source: **Stat. Press-Byull.** 1989, 10, s. 5-7.

Births: by Union Republic, 1988
per 1 000 population

	Total	Urban	Rural
USSR	**18.8**	**16.7**	**23.2**
Russian SFSR	16.0	15.3	18.0
Ukrainian SSR	14.5	14.6	14.1
Belorussian SSR	16.0	17.3	13.6
Uzbek SSR	35.1	26.9	41.0
Kazakh SSR	24.6	21.5	28.9
Georgian SSR	17.3	16.7	18.1
Azerbaidzhan SSR	26.5	23.7	29.7
Lithuanian SSR	15.3	14.9	16.3
Moldavian SSR	20.9	19.5	22.2
Latvian SSR	15.4	14.4	17.8
Kirgiz SSR	31.2	23.9	36.1
Tadzhik SSR	40.0	28.2	46.1
Armenian SSR	21.6	20.2	24.7
Turkmen SSR	36.0	31.0	40.6
Estonian SSR	15.9	15.4	17.2

Source: **Stat. Press-Byull.** 1989, 10, s. 5-7.

Number of births per 1 000 women of specifed age groups, 1978-1988

Ages	1978-1979	1982-1983	1984-1985	1985-1986	1986-1897	1988
15-49*	**69.9**	**76.0**	**76.9**	**78.2**	**79.7**	**76.8**
Under 20**	39.4	41.6	43.2	43.6	44.4	46.8
20-24	174.6	184.6	187.2	189.7	192.6	191.0
25-29	125.6	133.3	138.0	142.4	145.9	138.8
30-34	72.1	72.5	73.7	76.3	79.2	73.9
35-39	31.9	32.3	31.1	32.0	33.8	31.1
40-44	11.7	8.0	7.0	7.6	8.7	7.9
45-49	1.6	1.1	0.8	0.8	0.7	0.6

* Includes births to women under 15 and over 50.

** Calculation uses number of women in age group 15-19.

Source: **Nar. khoz. SSSR 1988**, s. 25.

38

Distribution of births: by birth order and age of mother, 1982 and 1988 (thousands)

	Total	1st birth	2nd	3rd + other
1982	5 100	2 228	1 708	1 164
1988	5 381	2 133	1 852	1 396
Mother aged below 20				
1982	442	407	33	2
1988	485	444	39	2
Mother aged 20-29				
1982	3 669	1 705	1 356	608
1988	3 658	1 533	1 422	703
Mother aged 30-44				
1982	977	115	318	544
1988	1 228	155	390	683

Percentage distribution of births: by birth order and age of mother, 1982 and 1988

	1st birth	2nd	3rd + other
1982	44	33	23
1988	40	34	26
Mother aged below 20			
1982	91	8	1
1988	92	8	0.4
Mother aged 20-29			
1982	46	37	17
1988	42	39	19
Mother aged 40-44			
1982	12	32	56
1988	13	31	56

Source of both tables: **Stat. Press-Byull.** 1989, 9, s. 115.

Number of births per 1 000 women*
and period fertility rate**: by Union Republic,
1987 and 1988

	1987	1988	Period rate 1987	1988
USSR	**79.7**	**76.8**	**2.528**	**2.452**
Russian SFSR	68.2	64.5	2.219	2.130
Ukrainian SSR	60.3	59.5	2.056	2.026
Belorussian SSR	65.0	65.1	2.025	2.031
Uzbek SSR	159.1	150.6	4.573	4.283
Kazakh SSR	102.4	99.8	3.187	3.126
Georgian SSR	72.0	70.4	2.301	2.261
Azerbaidzhan SSR	104.5	103.6	2.849	2.796
Lithuanian SSR	65.0	61.9	2.167	2.095
Moldavian SSR	85.6	82.3	2.734	2.635
Latvian SSR	64.1	62.7	2.155	2.114
Kirgiz SSR	139.6	133.9	4.195	4.000
Tadzhik SSR	186.7	179.2	5.662	5.348
Armenian SSR	88.5	84.7	2.544	2.512
Turkmen SSR	157.7	152.8	4.756	4.570
Estonian SSR	65.3	65.2	2.233	2.247

* Aged 15-49.

** The average number of children which would be born per woman if the age-specific fertility rates of the year in question were to apply through the child-bearing period.

Source: **Naselenie SSSR 1988**, s. 326-33.

Number of births per 1 000 women*
and period fertility rate: by Union Republic,**
1987 and 1988 in urban areas

	1987	1988	Period rate 1987	1988
USSR	**66.0**	**63.2**	**2.090**	**2.031**
Russian SFSR	61.4	57.8	1.974	1.896
Ukrainian SSR	56.4	55.8	1.894	1.892
Belorussian SSR	61.3	61.6	1.857	1.889
Uzbek SSR	112.9	106.6	3.197	3.027
Kazakh SSR	83.2	79.8	2.464	2.384
Georgian SSR	65.8	64.3	2.149	2.112
Azerbaidzhan SSR	95.6	93.1	2.641	2.595
Lithuanian SSR	58.3	54.6	1.859	1.764
Moldavian SSR	68.7	66.2	2.026	1.984
Latvian SSR	57.8	56.6	2.005	1.977
Kirgiz SSR	95.4	91.3	2.758	2.657
Tadzhik SSR	135.3	121.7	4.058	3.608
Armenian SSR	74.9	74.6	2.213	2.271
Turkmen SSR	128.8	126.0	3.761	3.667
Estonian SSR	61.1	60.7	2.116	2.113

* Aged 15-49.

** The average number of children which would be born per woman if the age-specific fertility rates of the year in question were to apply through the child-bearing period.

Source: **Naselenie SSSR 1988**, s. 333-8.

Number of births per 1 000 women*
and period fertility rate**: by Union Republic,
1987 and 1988 in rural areas

	1987	1988	Period rate 1987	1988
USSR	**113.8**	**111.2**	**3.686**	**3.556**
Russian SFSR	93.2	89.5	3.187	3.057
Ukrainian SSR	70.4	69.7	2.541	2.436
Belorussian SSR	75.7	75.8	2.593	2.523
Uzbek SSR	197.9	187.8	5.832	5.410
Kazakh SSR	136.2	136.1	4.732	4.745
Georgian SSR	80.6	78.9	2.497	2.448
Azerbaidzhan SSR	114.9	116.1	3.183	3.104
Lithuanian SSR	84.2	83.6	3.211	3.273
Moldavian SSR	106.0	102.7	3.808	3.667
Latvian SSR	81.9	79.7	2.606	2.528
Kirgiz SSR	175.2	168.3	5.514	5.242
Tadzhik SSR	215.2	210.8	6.683	6.417
Armenian SSR	123.0	111.2	3.290	3.074
Turkmen SSR	186.5	179.4	5.874	5.574
Estonian SSR	77.6	78.7	2.605	2.677

* Aged 15-49.

** The average number of children which would be born per woman if the age-specific fertility rates of the year in question were to apply through the child-bearing period.

Source: **Naselenie SSSR 1988**, s. 338-43.

Illegitimate births as percentage of all births, 1980-1988

	1980	1985	1988
Total	8.8	9.1	10.2
Urban areas	8.8	9.9	10.9
Rural areas	8.7	8.1	9.3

An average of 43% of these children are acknowledged by their fathers and are registered by their parents jointly. The proportion of children born to women who do not have a registered marriage varies between the Union Republics; it is lowest in the Azerbaidzhan, Uzbek, and Turkmen SSRs. In the USSR the frequency of illegitimate births is not great by comparison with developed countries, but it has reached a significant level in the rural areas of Latvia and particularly of Estonia.

Source: **Vestnik Statistiki** 1990, 1, s. 54.

Illegitimate births as percentage of all births: by Union Republic, 1980-1986

	1980	1985	1986
USSR	**8.78**	**9.14**	**9.46**
Russian SFSR	10.78	12.00	12.41
Ukrainian SSR	8.78	8.31	8.85
Belorussian SSR	6.43	7.12	6.62
Uzbek SSR	4.04	3.26	3.33
Kazakh SSR	10.34	10.12	10.63
Georgian SSR	4.69	10.52	11.18
Azerbaidzhan SSR	3.01	2.61	2.48
Lithuanian SSR	6.27	6.96	6.97
Moldavian SSR	7.44	8.82	9.41
Latvian SSR	12.48	14.40	15.04
Kirgiz SSR	10.96	9.88	10.03
Tadzhik SSR	7.25	4.83	4.54
Armenian SSR	4.33	6.53	7.26
Turkmen SSR	2.90	3.77	3.85
Estonian SSR	18.27	20.72	21.96

Source: **Naselenie SSSR 1987**, s. 217.

Illegitimate births:
by Union Republic, 1987 and 1988

	Number 1987	1988	% of all births 1987	1988
USSR	**548 730**	**550 234**	**9.8**	**10.2**
Russian SFSR	317 427	304 424	12.7	13.0
Ukrainian SSR	70 751	77 662	9.3	10.4
Belorussian SSR	12 185	12 813	7.5	7.9
Uzbek SSR	24 917	26 510	3.5	3.8
Kazakh SSR	46 215	45 774	11.1	11.2
Georgian SSR	11 282	15 167	11.9	16.5
Azerbaidzhan SSR	5 391	5 141	2.9	2.8
Lithuanian SSR	4 195	3 706	7.1	6.5
Moldavian SSR	9 268	9 081	10.1	10.3
Latvian SSR	6 523	6 405	15.5	15.5
Kirgiz SSR	14 194	15 521	10.4	11.6
Tadzhik SSR	10 658	12 980	5.2	6.4
Armenian SSR	4 629	5 574	5.9	7.5
Turkmen SSR	5 543	3 778	4.4	3.0
Estonian SSR	5 552	5 788	22.1	23.1

Source: **Naselenie SSSR 1988**, s. 344.

Illegitimate births: by Union Republic and urban and rural areas, 1987 and 1988

	Number 1987	1988	% of all births 1987	1988
Urban areas				
USSR	**351 118**	**345 063**	**10.6**	**10.8**
Russian SFSR	211 783	201 009	12.0	12.6
Ukrainian SSR	46 266	49 457	9.0	9.7
Belorussian SSR	7 754	7 913	6.8	6.8
Uzbek SSR	15 680	16 307	6.8	7.3
Kazakh SSR	28 010	26 695	12.9	12.7
Georgian SSR	6 898	8 292	13.8	16.9
Azerbaidzhan SSR	3 610	3 442	3.9	3.8
Lithuanian SSR	2 451	2 198	6.2	5.9
Moldavian SSR	4 581	4 512	11.4	11.3
Latvian SSR	3 714	3 708	13.2	13.5
Kirgiz SSR	5 690	5 867	13.6	14.4
Tadzhik SSR	4 001	5 080	7.6	10.3
Armenian SSR	3 448	4 167	7.2	8.7
Turkmen SSR	4 063	3 074	7.9	6.0
Estonian SSR	3 169	3 342	18.0	19.2
Rural areas				
USSR	**197 612**	**205 171**	**8.6**	**9.3**
Russian SFSR	105 644	103 415	14.5	15.1
Ukrainian SSR	24 485	28 205	10.0	12.0
Belorussian SSR	4 431	4 900	9.0	10.4
Uzbek SSR	9 237	10 203	1.9	2.2
Kazakh SSR	18 205	19 079	9.1	9.7
Georgian SSR	4 384	6 875	9.8	16.1
Azerbaidzhan SSR	1 781	1 699	1.9	1.8*
Lithuanian SSR	1 744	1 508	8.7	7.8
Moldavian SSR	4 687	4 569	9.1	9.4
Latvian SSR	2 809	2 697	19.9	19.6
Kirgiz SSR	8 504	9 654	9.0	10.4
Tadzhik SSR	6 657	7 810	4.4	5.1
Armenian SSR	1 181	1 407	3.8	5.2
Turkmen SSR	1 480	704	2.0	0.1
Estonian SSR	2 383	2 446	31.8	32.1

* This figure was recalculated by the editor.

Source: **Naselenie SSSR 1988**, s. 345.

Multiple births: by Union Republic, 1980-1986 per 1 000 total births

	1980	1985	1986
USSR	**78.5**	**78.8**	**80.0**
Russian SFSR	80.8	84.2	85.7
Ukrainian SSR	76.3	80.6	88.7
Belorussian SSR	67.3	68.9	67.8
Uzbek SSR	73.2	79.4	75.8
Kazakh SSR	76.1	71.7	71.0
Georgian SSR	28.3	42.2	42.8
Azerbaidzhan SSR	36.9	41.4	48.3
Lithuanian SSR	80.7	80.9	85.9
Moldavian SSR	70.9	83.1	85.1
Latvian SSR	78.4	73.6	84.6
Kirgiz SSR	77.3	82.5	69.5
Tadzhik SSR	161.9	68.3	69.2
Armenian SSR	119.8	118.3	112.4
Turkmen SSR	63.9	63.5	54.2
Estonian SSR	71.0	79.5	86.2

Infants born prematurely*: by Union Republic, 1980-1986 per 1 000 live-born infants

	1980	1985	1986
USSR	**49.1**	**49.2**	**49.1**
Russian SFSR	51.5	50.8	51.7
Ukrainian SSR	49.4	47.9	48.2
Belorussian SSR	43.0	44.2	40.9
Uzbek SSR	44.8	43.1	43.1
Kazakh SSR	46.9	53.1	49.9
Georgian SSR	48.9	30.3	50.2
Azerbaidzhan SSR	36.4	41.1	43.0
Lithuanian SSR	43.1	41.3	42.7
Moldavian SSR	52.5	56.2	52.9
Latvian SSR	40.7	37.6	37.1
Kirgiz SSR	48.6	48.7	49.9
Tadzhik SSR	58.1	71.1	54.5
Armenian SSR	53.8	60.5	55.6
Turkmen SSR	44.7	43.2	45.5
Estonian SSR	52.0	50.9	55.0

* Infants born between weeks 28 and 38 of gestation, less than 2 500 g. in weight and less than 45 cm. in height.

Source of both tables: **Naselenie SSSR 1987**, s. 317-8.

Infants born prematurely*: by Union Republic, 1987 and 1988 per 1 000 live-born infants

	1987	1988
USSR	**49.8**	**49.7**
Russian SFSR	51.3	52.2
Ukrainian SSR	48.2	46.8
Belorussian SSR	43.4	44.0
Uzbek SSR	44.7	44.7
Kazakh SSR	52.3	52.1
Georgian SSR	49.5	49.5
Azerbaidzhan SSR	46.0	39.4
Lithuanian SSR	42.6	43.9
Moldavian SSR	56.5	54.8
Latvian SSR	38.5	41.9
Kirgiz SSR	51.0	51.3
Tadzhik SSR	57.4	56.4
Armenian SSR	57.2	58.9
Turkmen SSR	46.4	44.5
Estonian SSR	54.5	57.2

* Infants born between weeks 28 and 38 of gestation, less than 2 500 g. in weight and less than 45 cm. in height.

Source: **Naselenie SSSR 1988**, s. 411.

Deaths per 1 000 population of specified age groups,
1978–1988

Ages	1978–1979	1982–1983	1984–1985	1985–1986	1986–1897	1988
All ages	9.9	10.2	10.7	10.2	9.9	10.1
Under 1	28.8	26.3	25.9	25.6	25.3	24.6
1–4	2.8	3.0	2.7	2.6	2.5	2.5
5–9	0.7	0.6	0.6	0.6	0.6	0.6
10–14	0.5	0.5	0.5	0.5	0.5	0.5
15–19	1.0	1.0	0.9	0.9	0.8	1.0
20–24	1.7	1.6	1.5	1.4	1.3	1.4
25–29	2.3	2.2	2.0	1.7	1.6	1.7
30–34	2.9	2.9	2.8	2.3	2.0	2.2
35–39	4.3	3.8	3.6	3.0	2.8	2.9
40–44	5.4	5.6	5.7	4.9	4.2	4.0
45–49	7.8	7.4	7.3	6.6	6.0	6.4
50–54	10.3	10.9	11.3	10.1	9.1	8.9
55–59	13.5	14.3	15.1	14.1	13.8	14.0
60–64	20.1	19.8	20.4	19.5	19.0	20.0
65–69	29.2	30.7	31.1	29.6	28.6	28.2
70 and over	76.5	74.0	78.7	77.6	76.7	80.2

Source: **Nar. khoz. SSSR 1988**, s. 27.

Deaths: by Union Republic, 1988
(absolute numbers)

	Total	Urban	Rural
USSR	2 888 753	1 747 052	1 141 701
Russian SFSR	1 569 112	1 062 515	506 597
Ukrainian SSR	600 725	335 538	265 187
Belorussian SSR	102 671	45 241	57 430
Uzbek SSR	134 688	55 507	79 181
Kazakh SSR	126 898	72 557	54 341
Georgian SSR	47 544	23 774	23 770
Azerbaidzhan SSR	47 485	24 750	22 735
Lithuanian SSR	37 649	19 581	18 068
Moldavian SSR	40 912	14 248	26 664
Latvian SSR	32 421	20 293	12 128
Kirgiz SSR	31 879	11 398	20 481
Tadzhik SSR	35 334	11 150	24 184
Armenian SSR	35 567	26 741	8 826
Turkmen SSR	27 317	12 151	15 166
Estonian SSR	18 551	11 608	6 943

Source: **Stat. Press-Byull.** 1989, 10, s. 5-7.

Deaths: by Union Republic, 1988
per 1 000 population

	Total	Urban	Rural
USSR	**10.1**	**9.2**	**12.0**
Russian SFSR	10.7	9.8	13.3
Ukrainian SSR	11.7	9.6	16.0
Belorussian SSR	10.1	6.7	16.5
Uzbek SSR	6.8	6.6	6.9
Kazakh SSR	7.7	7.4	8.0
Georgian SSR	9.0	8.1	10.0
Azerbaidzhan SSR	6.8	6.5	7.1
Lithuanian SSR	10.2	7.8	15.2
Moldavian SSR	9.7	7.0	12.2
Latvian SSR	12.1	10.6	15.7
Kirgiz SSR	7.4	6.7	8.0
Tadzhik SSR	7.0	6.5	7.3
Armenian SSR	10.3	11.3	8.1
Turkmen SSR	7.8	7.3	8.3
Estonian SSR	11.8	10.3	15.7

Source: **Stat. Press-Byull.** 1989, 10, s. 5-7.

Natural increase: by Union Republic, 1988
(absolute numbers)

	Total	Urban	Rural
USSR	2 492 303	1 424 536	1 067 767
Russian SFSR	779 382	599 514	179 868
Ukrainian SSR	143 331	174 018	-30 687
Belorussian SSR	60 522	70 764	-10 242
Uzbek SSR	559 456	169 091	390 365
Kazakh SSR	280 218	137 332	142 886
Georgian SSR	44 361	25 322	19 039
Azerbaidzhan SSR	136 865	64 939	71 926
Lithuanian SSR	19 078	17 787	1 291
Moldavian SSR	47 656	25 588	22 068
Latvian SSR	8 854	7 213	1 641
Kirgiz SSR	101 831	29 405	72 426
Tadzhik SSR	166 530	37 341	129 189
Armenian SSR	39 140	20 898	18 242
Turkmen SSR	98 570	39 484	59 086
Estonian SSR	6 509	5 840	669

Source: **Stat. Press-Byull.** 1989, 10, s. 5-7.

Natural increase: by Union Republic, 1988
per 1 000 population

	Total	Urban	Rural
USSR	**8.7**	**7.5**	**11.2**
Russian SFSR	5.3	5.5	4.7
Ukrainian SSR	2.8	5.0	-1.9
Belorussian SSR	5.9	10.6	-2.9
Uzbek SSR	28.3	20.3	34.1
Kazakh SSR	16.9	14.1	20.9
Georgian SSR	8.3	8.6	8.1
Azerbaidzhan SSR	19.7	17.2	22.6
Lithuanian SSR	5.1	7.1	1.1
Moldavian SSR	11.2	12.5	10.0
Latvian SSR	3.3	3.8	2.1
Kirgiz SSR	23.8	17.2	28.1
Tadzhik SSR	33.0	21.7	38.8
Armenian SSR	11.3	8.9	16.6
Turkmen SSR	28.2	23.7	32.3
Estonian SSR	4.1	5.1	1.5

Source: **Stat. Press-Byull.** 1989, 10, s. 5-7.

Births: by Union Republic, 1980-1987
per 1 000 population

	Total	Urban	Rural
USSR			
1980	18.3	17.0	20.4
1981	18.5	17.1	21.1
1982	18.9	17.3	21.6
1983	19.8	18.2	22.6
1984	19.6	17.8	22.8
1985	19.4	17.4	23.1
1986	20.0	17.9	24.1
1987	19.8	17.6	24.0
Russian SFSR			
1980	15.9	15.8	16.2
1981	16.0	15.7	16.7
1982	16.6	16.2	17.6
1983	17.5	17.1	18.7
1984	16.9	16.4	18.3
1985	16.5	15.9	18.2
1986	17.2	16.5	19.1
1987	17.1	16.4	19.1
Ukrainian SSR			
1980	14.8	15.5	13.7
1981	14.6	15.2	13.6
1982	14.8	15.3	13.9
1983	16.0	16.6	14.8
1984	15.6	16.1	14.6
1985	15.0	15.4	14.1
1986	15.5	15.8	15.0
1987	14.8	15.0	14.5
Belorussian SSR			
1980	16.0	18.8	12.4
1981	16.3	18.9	12.6
1982	16.3	18.8	12.8
1983	17.6	20.0	14.0
1984	17.0	19.1	13.7
1985	16.5	18.3	13.6
1986	17.1	18.7	14.3
1987	16.1	17.4	13.8
Uzbek SSR			
1980	33.8	25.4	38.9
1981	34.9	26.5	41.0
1982	35.0	27.2	40.7
1983	35.3	27.9	40.7
1984	36.2	28.6	41.7
1985	37.2	28.8	43.3
1986	37.8	28.8	44.3
1987	37.0	28.5	43.2

	Total	Urban	Rural
Kazakh SSR			
1980	23.8	22.0	26.0
1981	24.3	22.4	26.6
1982	24.3	22.0	27.3
1983	24.3	21.8	27.6
1984	25.4	22.7	28.9
1985	24.9	22.3	28.5
1986	25.5	22.3	29.8
1987	25.5	22.7	29.4
Georgian SSR			
1980	17.7	17.2	18.2
1981	18.2	17.5	19.0
1982	17.9	17.0	19.0
1983	18.0	17.1	19.1
1984	18.5	17.7	19.5
1985	18.7	17.8	19.8
1986	18.7	18.0	19.5
1987	17.9	17.3	18.7
Azerbaidzhan SSR			
1980	25.2	23.0	27.6
1981	26.3	24.1	28.9
1982	25.3	23.0	27.9
1983	26.1	23.5	29.2
1984	26.6	24.2	29.4
1985	26.7	24.2	29.6
1986	27.6	25.1	30.6
1987	26.9	24.6	29.6
Lithuanian SSR			
1980	15.1	15.9	13.7
1981	15.1	15.8	13.9
1982	15.2	15.7	14.3
1983	16.3	17.0	15.1
1984	16.2	16.7	15.3
1985	16.3	16.6	15.7
1986	16.5	16.6	16.2
1987	16.2	16.0	16.7
Moldavian SSR			
1980	20.0	19.3	20.4
1981	20.5	19.7	21.1
1982	20.6	19.5	21.4
1983	22.5	21.4	23.2
1984	21.9	20.8	22.8
1985	21.9	20.3	23.2
1986	22.7	21.1	24.1
1987	21.8	20.3	23.2

	Total	Urban	Rural
Latvian SSR			
1980	14.0	13.7	14.8
1981	14.0	13.9	14.4
1982	14.6	14.2	15.7
1983	15.7	15.5	16.4
1984	15.7	15.2	17.0
1985	15.2	14.7	16.4
1986	15.9	15.1	18.0
1987	15.8	14.8	18.3
Kirgiz SSR			
1980	29.6	24.5	32.8
1981	30.8	25.1	34.4
1982	31.2	24.3	35.6
1983	31.4	24.3	36.0
1984	32.1	25.4	36.5
1985	32.0	24.8	36.8
1986	32.6	25.1	37.6
1987	32.6	25.0	37.6
Tadzhik SSR			
1980	37.0	28.1	41.7
1981	38.3	28.9	43.1
1982	38.2	29.4	42.7
1983	38.3	29.0	43.0
1984	39.8	31.2	44.1
1985	39.9	30.3	44.8
1986	42.0	32.1	47.0
1987	41.8	32.5	46.5
Armenian SSR			
1980	22.7	21.5	25.1
1981	23.4	22.0	26.3
1982	23.2	21.5	26.8
1983	23.6	21.5	27.8
1984	24.2	22.1	28.6
1985	24.1	21.8	28.8
1986	24.0	21.8	28.7
1987	22.9	20.4	28.2
Turkmen SSR			
1980	34.3	29.3	38.8
1981	34.3	28.9	39.2
1982	34.7	30.1	38.9
1983	35.1	29.7	40.0
1984	35.2	30.4	39.6
1985	36.0	30.2	41.2
1986	36.9	31.8	41.5
1987	37.2	31.9	42.1

Table continues

	Total	Urban	Rural
Estonian SSR			
1980	15.0	14.9	15.2
1981	15.4	15.4	15.3
1982	15.4	15.4	15.5
1983	16.0	16.1	15.8
1984	15.9	15.9	15.8
1985	15.4	15.2	15.9
1986	15.6	15.3	16.3
1987	16.0	15.7	17.0

Source: **Naselenie SSSR 1987**, s. 128-43.

Deaths: by Union Republic, 1980-1987
per 1 000 population

	Total	Urban	Rural
USSR			
1980	10.3	9.3	12.1
1981	10.2	9.3	12.0
1982	10.1	9.1	11.8
1983	10.4	9.3	12.2
1984	10.8	9.7	12.8
1985	10.6	9.5	12.7
1986	9.8	8.9	11.5
1987	9.9	9.0	11.7
Russian SFSR			
1980	11.0	10.0	13.5
1981	10.9	9.9	13.4
1982	10.7	9.7	13.2
1983	11.0	10.0	13.7
1984	11.6	10.5	14.5
1985	11.3	10.2	14.3
1986	10.4	9.5	12.8
1987	10.5	9.6	13.0

	Total	Urban	Rural
Ukrainian SSR			
1980	11.4	9.5	14.4
1981	11.3	9.5	14.4
1982	11.3	9.5	14.4
1983	11.5	9.7	14.9
1984	12.0	10.0	15.8
1985	12.1	10.0	16.3
1986	11.1	9.2	14.7
1987	11.4	9.5	15.4
Belorussian SSR			
1980	9.9	6.5	14.4
1981	9.6	6.3	14.1
1982	9.6	6.4	14.3
1983	9.9	6.5	15.1
1984	10.5	6.9	16.2
1985	10.6	6.9	16.8
1986	9.7	6.5	15.3
1987	9.9	6.6	16.0
Uzbek SSR			
1980	7.4	7.3	7.5
1981	7.2	7.2	7.2
1982	7.4	7.3	7.4
1983	7.5	7.4	7.5
1984	7.4	7.4	7.5
1985	7.2	6.9	7.4
1986	7.0	6.7	7.3
1987	6.9	6.6	7.2
Kazakh SSR			
1980	8.0	8.1	7.8
1981	8.0	8.0	7.9
1982	7.8	7.8	7.9
1983	8.0	7.9	8.0
1984	8.2	8.2	8.3
1985	8.0	7.8	8.1
1986	7.4	7.2	7.6
1987	7.5	7.3	7.8
Georgian SSR			
1980	8.6	7.8	9.4
1981	8.6	7.7	9.7
1982	8.4	7.6	9.2
1983	8.4	7.6	9.3
1984	8.8	8.0	9.8
1985	8.8	8.1	9.8
1986	8.8	8.1	9.7
1987	8.8	7.9	9.8

	Total	Urban	Rural
Azerbaidzhan SSR			
1980	7.0	6.7	7.3
1981	6.9	6.9	6.9
1982	6.7	6.5	6.9
1983	6.7	6.5	6.9
1984	6.8	6.6	7.1
1985	6.8	6.6	7.0
1986	6.7	6.5	7.0
1987	6.7	6.4	7.0
Lithuanian SSR			
1980	10.5	7.7	14.9
1981	10.3	7.7	14.6
1982	10.0	7.5	14.5
1983	10.3	7.8	15.0
1984	10.9	8.1	16.1
1985	10.9	8.2	16.3
1986	9.9	7.5	14.7
1987	10.1	7.6	15.3
Moldavian SSR			
1980	10.2	8.0	11.6
1981	10.3	8.0	12.0
1982	10.2	7.7	11.9
1983	10.9	7.7	13.3
1984	11.1	7.8	13.7
1985	11.2	7.8	13.9
1986	9.7	6.9	12.1
1987	9.6	6.9	11.9
Latvian SSR			
1980	12.7	10.7	17.0
1981	12.6	10.8	16.8
1982	12.2	10.4	16.5
1983	12.5	10.8	16.7
1984	12.9	11.0	17.3
1985	13.1	11.4	17.2
1986	11.9	10.4	15.5
1987	12.1	10.6	15.6
Kirgiz SSR			
1980	8.4	7.6	8.9
1981	8.0	7.4	8.4
1982	7.8	7.2	8.1
1983	7.9	7.0	8.5
1984	8.3	7.5	8.8
1985	8.1	7.1	8.7
1986	7.1	6.3	7.6
1987	7.3	6.6	7.8

Table continues

	Total	Urban	Rural
Tadzhik SSR			
1980	8.0	7.7	8.2
1981	7.8	7.2	8.1
1982	7.7	7.5	7.7
1983	7.6	7.4	7.6
1984	7.4	7.3	7.5
1985	7.0	7.0	7.0
1986	6.8	6.5	6.9
1987	6.9	6.6	7.0
Armenian SSR			
1980	5.5	5.1	6.3
1981	5.3	5.0	6.0
1982	5.5	5.1	6.1
1983	5.7	5.3	6.4
1984	5.8	5.3	6.7
1985	5.9	5.3	7.0
1986	5.7	5.2	6.9
1987	5.7	5.3	6.7
Turkmen SSR			
1980	8.3	7.9	8.7
1981	8.5	8.0	8.9
1982	8.0	7.6	8.3
1983	8.4	8.2	8.7
1984	8.2	7.8	8.5
1985	8.1	7.3	8.7
1986	8.4	7.7	9.1
1987	7.9	7.4	8.3
Estonian SSR			
1980	12.3	10.1	17.5
1981	12.3	10.2	17.4
1982	11.9	10.0	16.5
1983	12.0	10.1	16.8
1984	12.5	10.7	17.1
1985	12.6	10.6	17.7
1986	11.6	10.0	15.8
1987	11.7	10.1	15.6

Source: **Naselenie SSSR 1987**, s. 128-43.

Natural increase: by Union Republic, 1980-1987
per 1 000 population

	Total	Urban	Rural
USSR			
1980	8.0	7.7	8.3
1981	8.3	7.8	9.1
1982	8.8	8.2	9.8
1983	9.4	8.9	10.4
1984	8.8	8.1	10.0
1985	8.8	7.9	10.4
1986	10.2	9.0	12.6
1987	9.9	8.6	12.3
Russian SFSR			
1980	4.9	5.8	2.7
1981	5.1	5.8	3.3
1982	5.9	6.5	4.4
1983	6.5	7.1	5.0
1984	5.3	5.9	3.8
1985	5.2	5.7	3.9
1986	6.8	7.0	6.3
1987	6.6	6.8	6.1
Ukrainian SSR			
1980	3.4	6.0	-0.7
1981	3.3	5.7	-0.8
1982	3.5	5.8	-0.5
1983	4.5	6.9	-0.1
1984	3.6	6.1	-1.2
1985	2.9	5.4	-2.2
1986	4.4	6.6	0.3
1987	3.4	5.5	-0.9
Belorussian SSR			
1980	6.1	12.3	-2.0
1981	6.7	12.6	-1.5
1982	6.7	12.4	-1.5
1983	7.7	13.5	-1.1
1984	6.5	12.2	-2.5
1985	5.9	11.4	-3.2
1986	7.4	12.2	-1.0
1987	6.2	10.8	-2.2
Uzbek SSR			
1980	26.4	18.1	32.3
1981	27.7	19.3	33.8
1982	27.6	19.9	33.3
1983	27.8	20.5	33.2
1984	28.8	21.2	34.2
1985	30.0	21.9	35.9
1986	30.8	22.1	37.0
1987	30.1	21.9	36.0

Table continues

	Total	Urban	Rural
Kazakh SSR			
1980	15.8	13.9	18.2
1981	16.3	14.4	18.7
1982	16.5	14.2	19.4
1983	16.3	13.9	19.6
1984	17.2	14.5	20.6
1985	16.9	14.5	20.4
1986	18.1	15.1	22.2
1987	18.0	15.4	21.6
Georgian SSR			
1980	9.1	9.4	8.8
1981	9.6	9.8	9.3
1982	9.5	9.4	9.8
1983	9.6	9.5	9.8
1984	9.7	9.7	9.7
1985	9.9	9.7	10.0
1986	9.9	9.9	9.8
1987	9.1	9.4	8.9
Azerbaidzhan SSR			
1980	18.2	16.3	20.3
1981	19.4	17.2	22.0
1982	18.6	16.5	21.0
1983	19.4	17.0	22.3
1984	19.8	17.6	22.3
1985	19.9	17.6	22.6
1986	20.9	18.6	23.6
1987	20.2	18.2	22.6
Lithuanian SSR			
1980	4.6	8.2	-1.2
1981	4.8	8.1	-0.7
1982	5.2	8.2	-0.2
1983	6.0	9.2	0.1
1984	5.3	8.6	-0.8
1985	5.4	8.4	-0.6
1986	6.6	9.1	1.5
1987	6.1	8.4	1.4
Moldavian SSR			
1980	9.8	11.3	8.8
1981	10.2	11.7	9.1
1982	10.4	11.8	9.5
1983	11.6	13.7	9.9
1984	10.8	13.0	9.1
1985	10.7	12.5	9.3
1986	13.0	14.2	12.0
1987	12.2	13.4	11.3

61

Table continues

		Total	Urban	Rural

Latvian SSR

		Total	Urban	Rural
1980		1.3	3.0	-2.2
1981		1.4	3.1	-2.4
1982		2.4	3.8	-0.8
1983		3.2	4.7	-0.3
1984		2.8	4.2	-0.3
1985		2.1	3.3	-0.8
1986		4.0	4.7	2.5
1987		3.7	4.2	2.7

Kirgiz SSR

		Total	Urban	Rural
1980		21.2	16.9	23.9
1981		22.8	17.7	26.0
1982		23.4	17.1	27.5
1983		23.5	17.3	27.5
1984		23.8	17.9	27.7
1985		23.9	17.7	28.1
1986		25.5	18.8	30.0
1987		25.3	18.4	29.8

Tadzhik SSR

		Total	Urban	Rural
1980		29.0	20.4	33.5
1981		30.5	21.7	35.0
1982		30.5	21.9	35.0
1983		30.7	21.6	35.4
1984		32.4	23.9	36.6
1985		32.9	23.3	37.8
1986		35.2	25.6	40.1
1987		34.9	25.9	39.5

Armenian SSR

		Total	Urban	Rural
1980		17.2	16.4	18.8
1981		18.1	17.0	20.3
1982		17.7	16.4	20.7
1983		17.9	16.2	21.4
1984		18.4	16.8	21.9
1985		18.2	16.5	21.8
1986		18.3	16.6	21.8
1987		17.2	15.1	21.5

Turkmen SSR

		Total	Urban	Rural
1980		26.0	21.4	30.1
1981		25.8	20.9	30.3
1982		26.7	22.5	30.6
1983		26.7	21.5	31.3
1984		27.0	22.6	31.1
1985		27.9	22.9	32.5
1986		28.5	24.1	32.4
1987		29.3	24.5	33.8

Table continues

	Total	Urban	Rural
Estonian SSR			
1980	2.7	4.8	-2.3
1981	3.1	5.2	-2.1
1982	3.5	5.4	-1.0
1983	4.0	6.0	-1.0
1984	3.4	5.2	-1.3
1985	2.8	4.6	-1.8
1986	4.0	5.3	0.5
1987	4.3	5.6	1.4

Source: **Naselenie SSSR 1987**, s. 128-43.

63

Births, deaths, natural increase, marriages and divorces: by Union Republic capitals and cities with over one million inhabitants, 1988 (absolute numbers)

	Births	Deaths	Natural increase	Marriages	Divorces
Alma-Ata	20 102	9 218	10 884	13 135	5 597
Ashkhabad	9 860	2 747	7 113	3 976	1 340
Baku*	35 933	13 431	22 502	15 362	5 002
Vilnius	8 043	4 222	3 821	6 248	2 089
Gorki	19 254	15 776	3 478	13 430	5 145
Dnepropetrovsk	16 262	12 440	3 822	11 604	5 476
Donetsk	13 822	11 294	2 528	10 649	5 272
Dushanbe	14 630	4 071	10 559	5 691	2 292
Erevan	21 978	7 392	14 586	9 069	2 315
Kazan	17 359	10 402	6 957	11 072	4 510
Kiev	38 010	21 255	16 755	25 886	12 550
Kishinev	12 926	4 346	8 580	7 893	3 254
Kuibyshev	17 153	13 790	3 363	11 961	5 880
Leningrad*	69 249	58 141	11 108	57 587	25 917
Minsk	27 022	9 792	17 230	15 821	6 470
Moscow*	117 310	107 320	9 990	90 043	40 533
Novosibirsk	21 098	13 961	7 137	15 413	7 431
Odessa	13 616	11 671	1 945	12 162	6 754
Omsk	18 870	9 480	9 390	12 967	6 475
Perm	16 891	9 736	7 155	10 840	4 189
Riga	12 315	10 045	2 270	9 597	4 427
Rostov-na-Donu	13 659	11 470	2 189	10 283	5 242
Sverdlovsk	20 473	12 715	7 758	13 761	5 737
Tallin	7 398	4 979	2 419	4 892	2 369
Tashkent	44 313	15 936	28 377	22 249	8 140
Tbilisi	17 925	9 996	7 929	10 724	2 888
Ufa	17 943	8 666	9 277	9 126	4 160
Frunze	11 737	4 618	7 119	6 382	2 502
Kharkov	22 225	16 203	6 022	16 928	7 898
Chelyabinsk	17 937	10 106	7 831	11 952	4 974

* The figure includes outlying settlements which are subordinated to the city.

Source: **Vestnik Statistiki** 1989, 11, s. 69.

Births, deaths, natural increase, marriages and divorces: by Union Republic capitals and cities with over one million inhabitants, 1988 per 1 000 population

	Births	Deaths	Natural increase	Marriages	Divorces
Alma-Ata	17.5	8.0	9.5	11.4	4.9
Ashkhabad	24.9	6.9	18.0	10.1	3.4
Baku*	20.1	7.5	12.6	8.6	2.8
Vilnius	13.8	7.2	6.6	10.7	3.6
Gorki	13.3	10.9	2.4	9.3	3.6
Dnepropetrovsk	13.5	10.3	3.2	9.6	4.5
Donetsk	12.5	10.2	2.3	9.6	4.8
Dushanbe	24.4	6.8	17.6	9.5	3.8
Erevan	18.5	6.2	12.3	7.6	2.0
Kazan	15.9	9.6	6.3	10.2	4.1
Kiev	14.7	8.2	6.5	10.0	4.8
Kishinev	18.6	6.3	12.3	11.4	4.7
Kuibyshev	13.2	10.6	2.6	9.2	4.5
Leningrad*	13.8	11.6	2.2	11.5	5.2
Minsk	16.9	6.1	10.8	9.9	4.0
Moscow*	13.1	12.0	1.1	10.1	4.5
Novosibirsk	14.6	9.7	4.9	10.7	5.2
Odessa	11.8	10.2	1.6	10.6	5.9
Omsk	16.4	8.2	8.2	11.3	5.6
Perm	15.5	8.9	6.6	9.9	3.8
Riga	13.4	10.9	2.5	10.5	4.8
Rostov-na-Donu	13.4	11.3	2.1	10.1	5.2
Sverdlovsk	15.1	9.4	5.7	10.2	4.2
Tallin	15.2	10.3	4.9	10.1	4.9
Tashkent	19.9	7.1	12.8	10.0	3.6
Tbilisi	14.7	8.2	6.5	8.8	2.4
Ufa	16.1	7.8	8.3	8.2	3.7
Frunze	17.9	7.0	10.9	9.7	3.8
Kharkov	13.8	10.0	3.8	10.5	4.9
Chelyabinsk	15.8	8.9	6.9	10.5	4.4

* The figure includes outlying settlements which are subordinated to the city.

Source: **Vestnik Statistiki** 1989, 11, s. 70.

Marital status of population: by age group, 1989*
(percentages)

Key: Column 1 Never married
                       2 Married
                       3 Widowers/widows
                       4 Divorced and separated

	Columns			
	1	2	3	4
Men				
All aged 16 and over	**20.6**	**71.5**	**2.6**	**4.7**
16-19	96.7	2.5	0.0	0.0
20-24	60.2	37.2	0.1	1.2
25-29	19.5	75.8	0.1	3.8
30-39	7.7	85.0	0.4	6.5
40-49	3.7	86.5	1.2	8.2
50-59	2.0	88.2	3.3	6.1
60 and over	1.1	82.8	12.9	2.7
Women				
All aged 16 and over	**14.0**	**60.6**	**17.4**	**7.5**
16-19	85.8	12.9	0.1	0.4
20-24	33.0	62.3	0.3	3.4
25-29	11.7	80.5	0.7	6.5
30-39	5.8	82.3	2.0	9.6
40-49	3.6	76.9	6.7	12.5
50-59	3.7	68.5	16.9	10.5
60 and over	5.1	34.1	54.9	5.4

* Census data.

At the 1989 census there were 68 million married couples.

Source: **Stat. Press-Byull.** 1990, 4, s. 45.

Marriages: by Union Republic, 1988

	Total	Urban	Rural
Absolute numbers			
USSR	2 673 056	1 825 017	848 039
Russian SFSR	1 397 445	1 054 372	343 073
Ukrainian SSR	455 770	327 767	128 003
Belorussian SSR	96 064	66 613	29 451
Uzbek SSR	193 856	79 313	114 543
Kazakh SSR	162 962	7 785	65 177
Georgian SSR	38 100	24 147	13 953
Azerbaidzhan SSR	68 887	34 708	34 179
Lithuanian SSR	34 906	24 396	10 510
Moldavian SSR	39 785	20 619	19 166
Latvian SSR	25 296	19 845	5 451
Kirgiz SSR	40 490	15 406	25 084
Tadzhik SSR	46 933	15 778	31 155
Armenian SSR	26 581	17 444	9 137
Turkmen SSR	33 008	15 787	17 221
Estonian SSR	12 973	11 037	1 936
Per 1 000 population			
USSR	9.4	9.6	8.9
Russian SFSR	9.5	9.7	9.0
Ukrainian SSR	8.9	9.4	7.7
Belorussian SSR	9.4	9.9	8.5
Uzbek SSR	9.8	9.5	10.0
Kazakh SSR	9.8	10.0	9.5
Georgian SSR	7.2	8.2	5.9
Azerbaidzhan SSR	9.9	9.2	10.7
Lithuanian SSR	9.4	9.7	8.9
Moldavian SSR	9.4	10.1	8.7
Latvian SSR	9.4	10.4	7.0
Kirgiz SSR	9.5	9.0	9.7
Tadzhik SSR	9.3	9.2	9.4
Armenian SSR	7.7	7.4	8.4
Turkmen SSR	9.4	9.5	9.4
Estonian SSR	8.2	9.7	4.4

Source: **Stat. Press-Byull.** 1989, 10, s. 5-7.

67

Persons entering marriage: by age group and marital status, 1988 (absolute numbers)

Key to sub-totals:
1 Never married
2 Widowers/widows
3 Divorced
4 Status unknown

	Total	Sub-totals 1	2	3	4
Men					
Total	**2 673 056**	**2 037 992**	**79 849**	**553 221**	**1 994**
Under 18	13 449	13 418	11	11	9
18-19	101 793	101 340	91	304	58
20-24	1 292 390	1 250 230	1 767	39 638	755
25-29	607 438	472 166	4 029	130 774	469
30-34	242 025	113 336	4 521	123 925	243
35-39	136 023	38 667	4 901	92 304	151
40-44	65 501	12 826	3 761	48 853	61
45-49	59 359	10 322	6 668	42 311	58
50-54	50 222	7 718	8 932	33 525	47
55-59	35 769	5 469	11 063	19 195	42
60 and over	68 817	12 287	34 088	22 344	98
age unknown	270	213	17	37	3
Women					
Total	**2 673 056**	**2 064 053**	**105 112**	**501 456**	**2 435**
Under 18	105 534	105 313	69	87	65
18-19	602 870	598 224	476	3 763	407
20-24	1 020 261	945 758	3 769	69 880	854
25-29	393 731	254 407	9 169	129 746	409
30-34	201 442	79 335	11 436	110 415	256
35-39	115 730	31 052	11 357	73 181	140
40-44	53 415	10 331	7 700	35 320	64
45-49	53 787	8 760	12 739	32 223	65
50-54	44 916	7 742	14 099	23 017	58
55-59	30 426	6 651	11 717	12 012	46
60 and over	50 645	16 230	22 575	11 771	69
age unknown	299	250	6	41	2

Source: **Naselenie SSSR 1988**, s. 153-4.

**Persons in urban population entering marriage:
by age group and marital status, 1988** (absolute numbers)

Key to sub-totals: 1 Never married
                     2 Widowers/widows
                     3 Divorced
                     4 Status unknown

	Total	Sub-totals 1	2	3	4
Men					
Total	1 825 017	1 310 638	55 418	457 677	1 284
Under 18	11 086	11 062	7	10	7
18-19	77 761	77 409	74	231	47
20-24	812 720	779 963	1 077	31 268	412
25-29	410 386	303 922	2 245	103 919	300
30-34	181 927	78 313	2 691	100 750	173
35-39	107 905	27 470	3 207	77 119	109
40-44	54 025	9 272	2 566	42 139	48
45-49	48 274	7 148	4 584	36 496	46
50-54	40 584	5 190	6 074	29 283	37
55-59	27 942	3 461	7 684	16 764	33
60 and over	52 300	7 357	25 201	19 672	70
age unknown	107	71	8	26	2
Women					
Total	1 825 017	1 336 505	76 892	410 063	1 557
Under 18	67 281	67 137	38	67	39
18-19	366 400	363 063	292	2 825	220
20-24	663 135	607 111	2 249	53 304	471
25-29	290 544	181 883	5 901	102 482	278
30-34	157 515	59 885	7 819	89 614	197
35-39	93 774	24 022	8 209	61 438	105
40-44	44 321	7 973	5 730	30 563	55
45-49	44 009	6 131	9 551	28 272	55
50-54	36 273	5 006	10 778	20 440	49
55-59	23 703	4 117	8 892	10 662	32
60 and over	37 929	10 076	17 429	10 369	55
age unknown	133	101	4	27	1

Source: **Naselenie SSSR 1988**, s. 153-4.

Persons in rural population entering marriage: by age group and marital status, 1988 (absolute numbers)

Key to sub-totals: 1 Never married
2 Widowers/widows
3 Divorced
4 Status unknown

	Total	Sub-totals 1	2	3	4
Men					
Total	848 039	727 354	24 431	95 544	710
Under 18	2 363	2 356	4	1	2
18-19	24 032	23 931	17	73	11
20-24	479 670	470 267	690	8 370	343
25-29	197 052	168 244	1 784	26 855	169
30-34	60 098	35 023	1 830	23 175	70
35-39	28 118	11 197	1 694	15 185	42
40-44	11 476	3 554	1 195	6 714	13
45-49	11 085	3 174	2 084	5 815	12
50-54	9 638	2 528	2 858	4 242	10
55-59	7 827	2 008	3 379	2 431	9
60 and over	16 517	4 930	8 887	2 672	28
age unknown	163	142	9	11	1
Women					
Total	848 039	727 548	28 220	91 393	878
Under 18	38 253	38 176	31	20	26
18-19	236 470	235 161	184	938	187
20-24	357 126	338 647	1 520	16 576	383
25-29	103 187	72 524	3 268	27 264	131
30-34	43 927	19 450	3 617	20 801	59
35-39	21 956	7 030	3 148	11 743	35
40-44	9 094	2 358	1 970	4 757	9
45-49	9 778	2 629	3 188	3 951	10
50-54	8 643	2 736	3 321	2 577	9
55-59	6 723	2 534	2 825	1 350	14
60 and over	12 716	6 154	5 146	1 402	14
age unknown	166	149	2	14	1

Source: **Naselenie SSSR 1988**, s. 153-4.

Men marrying under age 23: by Union Republic
per 1 000 men of specified age group*

	Year of birth:			
	1940-1944	1945-1949	1950-1954	1955-1959
USSR	**282**	**392**	**458**	**482**
Russian SFSR	289	407	471	489
Ukrainian SSR	289	398	469	506
Belorussian SSR	252	356	420	462
Uzbek SSR	285	377	487	541
Kazakh SSR	309	405	451	453
Georgian SSR	196	240	285	300
Azerbaidzhan SSR	191	210	225	255
Lithuanian SSR	220	294	372	402
Moldavian SSR	312	435	505	542
Latvian SSR	211	325	405	449
Kirgiz SSR	286	402	476	506
Tadzhik SSR	263	386	502	576
Armenian SSR	206	297	342	371
Turkmen SSR	350	419	546	553
Estonian SSR	222	314	370	410

*From a sample survey carried out in 1985.

Source: **Naselenie SSSR 1987**, s. 202.

Men marrying under age 23: by Union Republic per 1 000 men of specified age group, urban and rural areas*

	Year of birth: 1940–1944	1945–1949	1950–1954	1955–1959
Urban areas				
USSR	**268**	**389**	**455**	**480**
Russian SFSR	277	404	470	490
Ukrainian SSR	269	393	468	512
Belorussian SSR	225	359	435	487
Uzbek SSR	262	349	413	457
Kazakh SSR	286	413	460	463
Georgian SSR	183	242	285	300
Azerbaidzhan SSR	150	182	206	228
Lithuanian SSR	217	294	382	422
Moldavian SSR	258	395	485	532
Latvian SSR	223	318	411	465
Kirgiz SSR	303	398	455	487
Tadzhik SSR	262	386	451	501
Armenian SSR	185	282	320	352
Turkmen SSR	295	417	519	502
Estonian SSR	214	324	384	416
Rural areas				
USSR	**314**	**402**	**466**	**486**
Russian SFSR	323	420	473	481
Ukrainian SSR	328	413	467	492
Belorussian SSR	300	347	376	401
Uzbek SSR	306	406	549	601
Kazakh SSR	342	392	437	438
Georgian SSR	214	236	283	298
Azerbaidzhan SSR	259	273	263	298
Lithuanian SSR	226	292	348	358
Moldavian SSR	352	478	523	547
Latvian SSR	181	343	388	410
Kirgiz SSR	274	408	493	523
Tadzhik SSR	263	385	540	619
Armenian SSR	263	346	401	408
Turkmen SSR	390	420	572	597
Estonian SSR	242	287	334	396

*From a sample survey carried out in 1985.

Source: **Naselenie SSSR 1987**, s. 203.

Women marrying under age 20: by Union Republic
per 1 000 women of specified age group*

	Year of birth: 1940–1944	1945–1949	1950–1954	1955–1959	1960–1964
USSR	**297**	**302**	**321**	**332**	**340**
Russian SFSR	269	278	300	319	331
Ukrainian SSR	300	312	342	365	384
Belorussian SSR	240	250	264	283	299
Uzbek SSR	490	476	464	428	394
Kazakh SSR	372	337	318	300	301
Georgian SSR	276	304	318	319	332
Azerbaidzhan SSR	392	374	323	244	225
Lithuanian SSR	195	205	226	221	249
Moldavian SSR	362	335	337	364	374
Latvian SSR	184	197	231	261	295
Kirgiz SSR	458	437	415	384	375
Tadzhik SSR	545	582	574	525	491
Armenian SSR	389	434	397	340	362
Turkmen SSR	480	422	410	325	216
Estonian SSR	187	201	216	257	275

*From a sample survey carried out in 1985.

Source: **Naselenie SSSR 1987,** s. 200.

Women marrying under age 20: by Union Republic per 1 000 women of specified age group, urban and rural areas*

| | Year of birth: | | | | |
	1940– 1944	1945– 1949	1950– 1954	1955– 1959	1960– 1964
Urban areas					
USSR	**254**	**267**	**289**	**304**	**306**
Russian SFSR	238	256	279	297	301
Ukrainian SSR	267	280	310	335	348
Belorussian SSR	215	228	248	265	270
Uzbek SSR	390	372	361	351	343
Kazakh SSR	313	289	296	294	282
Georgian SSR	222	253	271	290	289
Azerbaidzhan SSR	332	314	299	242	230
Lithuanian SSR	199	191	214	203	227
Moldavian SSR	269	277	294	314	276
Latvian SSR	175	194	221	257	278
Kirgiz SSR	378	345	337	338	310
Tadzhik SSR	418	409	406	410	397
Armenian SSR	351	390	366	328	343
Turkmen SSR	429	386	399	332	232
Estonian SSR	181	194	203	239	255
Rural areas					
USSR	**389**	**408**	**410**	**398**	**413**
Russian SFSR	365	370	374	388	429
Ukrainian SSR	358	397	433	445	478
Belorussian SSR	288	325	333	350	404
Uzbek SSR	594	595	562	484	428
Kazakh SSR	459	420	354	313	331
Georgian SSR	345	386	384	356	376
Azerbaidzhan SSR	493	503	368	245	220
Lithuanian SSR	209	245	260	268	304
Moldavian SSR	429	397	381	411	482
Latvian SSR	208	205	262	276	342
Kirgiz SSR	525	532	481	426	430
Tadzhik SSR	651	739	711	599	535
Armenian SSR	491	570	493	366	399
Turkmen SSR	524	458	421	318	201
Estonian SSR	207	224	252	302	342

*From a sample survey carried out in 1985.

Source: **Naselenie SSSR 1987**, s. 201.

74

Men remarried within 10 years after divorce or death of wife: by Union Republic per 1 000 men divorced or widowers*

| | Previous marriage ended: | | | | |
	1950–1954	1955–1959	1960–1964	1965–1969	1970–1974
USSR	**667**	**650**	**591**	**593**	**566**
Russian SFSR	673	653	596	598	579
Ukrainian SSR	668	649	589	600	557
Belorussian SSR	722	690	629	614	553
Uzbek SSR	680	639	540	538	489
Kazakh SSR	656	646	599	614	587
Georgian SSR	587	532	485	412	362
Azerbaidzhan SSR	729	655	534	565	456
Lithuanian SSR	386	473	496	490	459
Moldavian SSR	749	712	681	659	636
Latvian SSR	497	591	554	571	545
Kirgiz SSR	692	752	639	606	628
Tadzhik SSR	712	775	603	623	595
Armenian SSR	640	672	563	578	414
Turkmen SSR	517	519	328	331	377
Estonian SSR	558	585	568	528	483

*From a sample survey carried out in 1985.

Source: **Naselenie SSSR 1987**, s. 207.

Women remarried within 10 years after divorce or death of husband: by Union Republic per 1 000 women divorced or widowed*

	Previous marriage ended:				
	1950–1954	1955–1959	1960–1964	1965–1969	1970–1974
USSR	**204**	**214**	**222**	**246**	**249**
Russian SFSR	219	234	243	266	274
Ukrainian SSR	177	179	199	230	231
Belorussian SSR	150	149	178	208	217
Uzbek SSR	193	207	181	180	147
Kazakh SSR	215	223	231	255	254
Georgian SSR	65	68	52	48	43
Azerbaidzhan SSR	129	138	102	83	74
Lithuanian SSR	145	135	164	186	193
Moldavian SSR	233	234	219	244	243
Latvian SSR	207	272	277	309	285
Kirgiz SSR	230	262	201	220	244
Tadzhik SSR	279	267	236	260	215
Armenian SSR	113	83	73	42	44
Turkmen SSR	167	164	148	128	149
Estonian SSR	285	265	250	275	251

*From a sample survey carried out in 1985.

Source: **Naselenie SSSR 1987,** s. 207.

Divorces: by Union Republic, 1988

	Total	Urban	Rural
Absolute numbers			
USSR	**949 796**	**797 554**	**152 242**
Russian SFSR	573 863	482 930	90 933
Ukrainian SSR	185 357	159 304	26 053
Belorussian SSR	32 111	26 307	5 804
Uzbek SSR	30 965	12 511	9 454
Kazakh SSR	45 942	38 120	7 822
Georgian SSR	7 082	6 588	494
Azerbaidzhan SSR	9 226	8 468	758
Lithuanian SSR	11 682	9 683	1 999
Moldavian SSR	12 085	10 625	1 460
Latvian SSR	10 890	8 883	2 007
Kirgiz SSR	8 207	5 177	3 030
Tadzhik SSR	7 509	6 104	1 405
Armenian SSR	3 997	3 657	340
Turkmen SSR	4 956	4 672	284
Estonian SSR	5 924	5 525	399
Per 1 000 population			
USSR	**3.3**	**4.2**	**1.6**
Russian SFSR	3.9	4.4	2.4
Ukrainian SSR	3.6	4.6	1.6
Belorussian SSR	3.2	3.9	1.7
Uzbek SSR	1.6	2.6	0.8
Kazakh SSR	2.8	3.9	1.1
Georgian SSR	1.3	2.2	0.2
Azerbaidzhan SSR	1.3	2.2	0.2
Lithuanian SSR	3.2	3.9	1.7
Moldavian SSR	2.9	5.2	0.7
Latvian SSR	4.1	4.6	2.6
Kirgiz SSR	1.9	3.0	1.2
Tadzhik SSR	1.5	3.6	0.4
Armenian SSR	1.2	1.5	0.3
Turkmen SSR	1.4	2.8	0.2
Estonian SSR	3.8	4.9	0.9

Source: **Stat. Press-Byull.** 1989, 10, s. 5-7.

Divorces: by Union Republic and size of family with children under 18, 1988
(absolute numbers)

	Divorces involving no. of children			
	0	1	2	3 + more
USSR	**376 777**	**402 188**	**148 766**	**22 065**
Russian SFSR	223 466	251 105	88 459	10 833
Ukrainian SSR	73 469	81 176	27 573	3 139
Belorussian SSR	11 449	13 901	5 980	781
Uzbek SSR	14 876	9 723	4 523	1 843
Kazakh SSR	17 321	18 448	8 407	1 766
Georgian SSR	4 322	1 500	1 034	226
Azerbaidzhan SSR	5 477	1 871	1 297	581
Lithuanian SSR	4 333	4 658	2 278	413
Moldavian SSR	4 559	5 099	2 098	329
Latvian SSR	4 289	4 434	1 832	335
Kirgiz SSR	3 420	3 076	1 348	363
Tadzhik SSR	3 218	2 596	1 133	562
Armenian SSR	2 065	829	831	272
Turkmen SSR	2 254	1 423	843	436
Estonian SSR	2 259	2 349	1 130	186

Source: **Naselenie SSSR 1988**, s. 324.

78

Children under 18 whose parents divorced:
by Union Republic, 1988

	Children left with one parent	Children per 1 000 divorces
USSR	**775 318**	**816.3**
Russian SFSR	465 143	810.5
Ukrainian SSR	146 485	790.3
Belorussian SSR	28 409	884.7
Uzbek SSR	25 376	819.5
Kazakh SSR	41 476	902.8
Georgian SSR	4 307	608.2
Azerbaidzhan SSR	6 476	701.9
Lithuanian SSR	10 666	913.0
Moldavian SSR	10 356	856.9
Latvian SSR	9 223	846.9
Kirgiz SSR	7 069	861.3
Tadzhik SSR	6 998	931.9
Armenian SSR	3 374	844.1
Turkmen SSR	4 738	956.0
Estonian SSR	5 222	881.5

Source: **Naselenie SSSR 1988**, s. 324.

Divorces: by number of children under 18 and age of wife, 1988

	Divorces	Children left with one parent	Children per 1 000 divorces
Total	**949 796**	**775 318**	**816.3**
Age			
Under 20	15 235	5 171	339.4
20-24	172 577	114 318	662.4
25-29	232 469	216 244	930.2
30-34	178 650	198 521	1 111.2
35-39	129 806	147 352	1 135.2
40-44	65 267	52 895	810.4
45-49	58 853	24 161	410.5
50 and over	90 943	11 604	127.6
age unknown	5 996	5 052	842.6

Source: **Naselenie SSSR 1988**, s. 325.

Divorces: by size of family with children under 18 and age of wife, 1988

	Divorces involving no. of children			
	0	1	2	3 + more
Total	**376 777**	**402 188**	**148 766**	**22 065**
Age				
Under 20	10 251	4 831	140	13
20-24	69 343	93 256	9 362	616
25-29	64 141	126 170	37 915	4 243
30-34	44 853	78 861	47 772	7 164
35-39	35 274	50 895	37 096	6 541
40-44	27 999	24 543	10 792	1 933
45-49	40 353	14 253	3 388	859
50 and over	82 357	6 631	1 404	551
age unknown	2 206	2 748	897	145

Source: **Naselenie SSSR 1988**, s. 325.

Divorces: by Union Republic and duration of marriage up to five years, 1988 (absolute numbers)

	Under 1	Years 1	2	3	4
USSR	**41 012**	**72 622**	**81 162**	**76 434**	**72 503**
Russian SFSR	22 048	42 828	47 017	44 829	43 029
Ukrainian SSR	8 640	14 838	16 975	15 439	14 564
Belorussian SSR	1 466	2 688	2 790	2 580	2 408
Uzbek SSR	1 669	2 773	3 589	3 259	2 791
Kazakh SSR	1 682	3 338	3 982	3 763	3 629
Georgian SSR	368	512	578	528	523
Azerbaidzhan SSR	1 130	875	772	718	606
Lithuanian SSR	389	689	803	862	853
Moldavian SSR	561	937	1 076	1 015	948
Latvian SSR	320	750	881	924	845
Kirgiz SSR	514	593	691	681	686
Tadzhik SSR	1 617	603	689	596	547
Armenian SSR	170	352	323	316	282
Turkmen SSR	255	471	525	465	370
Estonian SSR	183	375	471	459	422

Source: **Naselenie SSSR 1988**, s. 326-7.

Divorces: by Union Republic and duration of marriage over five years, 1988 (absolute numbers)

	5-9	Years 10-14	15-19	20+	unknown
USSR	**257 928**	**146 344**	**85 674**	**114 917**	**1 200**
Russian SFSR	157 461	91 436	53 606	71 181	428
Ukrainian SSR	48 511	26 928	16 519	22 895	48
Belorussian SSR	8 543	4 782	2 871	3 976	7
Uzbek SSR	8 572	3 861	1 907	2 280	264
Kazakh SSR	12 988	7 175	3 910	5 400	75
Georgian SSR	2 004	1 169	607	793	–
Azerbaidzhan SSR	2 191	1 168	669	1 097	–
Lithuanian SSR	3 369	1 905	1 181	1 623	8
Moldavian SSR	3 288	1 870	1 026	1 329	35
Latvian SSR	3 019	1 738	1 071	1 342	–
Kirgiz SSR	2 284	1 181	590	793	194
Tadzhik SSR	1 743	783	384	461	86
Armenian SSR	1 024	616	347	560	7
Turkmen SSR	1 345	736	338	404	47
Estonian SSR	1 586	996	648	783	1

Source: **Naselenie SSSR 1988**, s. 326-7.

Marriages and divorces: by Union Republic, 1980-1987

	Absolute numbers Marriages	Divorces	Per 1 000 population Marriages	Divorces
USSR				
1980	2 724 597	929 616	10.3	3.5
1981	2 788 075	929 537	10.4	3.5
1982	2 769 234	903 549	10.3	3.3
1983	2 834 806	944 791	10.4	3.5
1984	2 634 144	932 305	9.6	3.4
1985	2 717 805	933 097	9.8	3.4
1986	2 753 075	941 329	9.8	3.4
1987	2 776 568	950 709	9.8	3.4
Russian SFSR				
1980	1 464 579	580 720	10.6	4.2
1981	1 472 752	577 507	10.6	4.1
1982	1 460 198	557 623	10.4	4.0
1983	1 479 130	583 026	10.4	4.1
1984	1 367 827	573 705	9.6	4.0
1985	1 389 426	573 981	9.7	4.0
1986	1 417 544	579 387	9.8	4.0
1987	1 442 622	580 106	9.9	4.0
Ukrainian SSR				
1980	463 274	181 700	9.3	3.6
1981	510 496	185 818	10.2	3.7
1982	500 651	181 576	9.9	3.6
1983	537 399	190 061	10.6	3.8
1984	449 993	186 629	8.9	3.7
1985	489 910	183 373	9.6	3.6
1986	483 366	180 366	9.5	3.5
1987	512 985	184 720	10.0	3.6
Belorussian SSR				
1980	97 461	31 214	10.1	3.2
1981	99 734	30 848	10.3	3.2
1982	100 427	30 073	10.3	3.1
1983	102 178	30 061	10.4	3.1
1984	93 569	30 825	9.4	3.1
1985	98 673	31 197	9.9	3.1
1986	99 385	30 297	9.9	3.0
1987	102 053	30 507	10.1	3.0
Uzbek SSR				
1980	173 628	22 534	10.9	1.4
1981	177 215	22 543	10.8	1.4
1982	177 672	22 705	10.6	1.4
1983	185 660	23 760	10.8	1.4
1984	195 138	24 335	11.0	1.4
1985	200 799	26 146	11.0	1.4
1986	204 597	27 477	10.9	1.5
1987	189 557	29 169	9.8	1.5

83

	Absolute numbers		Per 1 000 population	
	Marriages	Divorces	Marriages	Divorces
Kazakh SSR				
1980	158 585	38 455	10.6	2.6
1981	160 083	38 729	10.6	2.6
1982	158 343	37 144	10.3	2.4
1983	160 893	40 206	10.3	2.6
1984	156 290	39 894	9.9	2.5
1985	159 449	41 263	10.0	2.6
1986	162 573	44 103	10.1	2.7
1987	160 909	46 466	9.8	2.8
Georgian SSR				
1980	50 547	6 788	10.0	1.3
1981	48 100	7 023	9.5	1.4
1982	49 688	7 114	9.7	1.4
1983	45 559	7 315	8.8	1.4
1984	41 775	7 117	8.1	1.4
1985	44 168	6 514	8.5	1.2
1986	44 485	6 667	8.5	1.3
1987	39 157	6 766	7.4	1.3
Azerbaidzhan SSR				
1980	60 134	7 116	9.8	1.2
1981	61 954	6 869	9.9	1.1
1982	62 143	6 789	9.8	1.1
1983	65 962	7 314	10.2	1.1
1984	67 368	7 119	10.3	1.1
1985	70 104	7 879	10.5	1.2
1986	71 371	8 199	10.6	1.2
1987	68 031	8 511	9.9	1.2
Lithuanian SSR				
1980	31 520	11 038	9.2	3.2
1981	31 338	10 906	9.1	3.2
1982	32 598	10 890	9.3	3.1
1983	33 417	11 087	9.5	3.1
1984	34 127	11 412	9.6	3.2
1985	34 211	11 464	9.5	3.2
1986	35 361	11 808	9.8	3.3
1987	35 122	11 726	9.6	3.2
Moldavian SSR				
1980	46 083	11 273	11.6	2.8
1981	44 306	10 971	11.0	2.7
1982	44 530	11 089	11.0	2.7
1983	44 351	11 449	10.9	2.8
1984	41 100	11 337	10.0	2.8
1985	40 901	11 176	9.9	2.7
1986	40 687	11 633	9.8	2.8
1987	39 084	11 598	9.3	2.8

| | Absolute numbers | | Per 1 000 population | |
	Marriages	Divorces	Marriages	Divorces
Latvian SSR				
1980	24 611	12 650	9.7	5.0
1981	24 767	12 228	9.7	4.8
1982	24 474	12 053	9.6	4.7
1983	24 284	12 469	9.4	4.8
1984	23 615	12 153	9.1	4.7
1985	24 032	11 670	9.2	4.5
1986	25 099	11 131	9.5	4.2
1987	25 477	10 709	9.6	4.0
Kirgiz SSR				
1980	38 719	6 671	10.7	1.8
1981	39 993	6 694	10.8	1.8
1982	39 525	6 616	10.5	1.8
1983	39 970	6 934	10.4	1.8
1984	39 959	6 521	10.2	1.7
1985	40 341	6 876	10.1	1.7
1986	42 253	8 003	10.3	2.0
1987	40 161	7 810	9.6	1.9
Tadzhik SSR				
1980	42 344	6 073	10.7	1.5
1981	43 593	6 131	10.7	1.5
1982	44 537	6 421	10.7	1.5
1983	44 825	6 894	10.4	1.6
1984	45 871	7 021	10.3	1.6
1985	48 079	7 029	10.5	1.5
1986	49 570	7 352	10.5	1.6
1987	46 233	7 344	9.5	1.5
Armenian SSR				
1980	32 147	3 387	10.4	1.1
1981	32 609	3 295	10.4	1.0
1982	33 473	3 329	10.5	1.0
1983	28 927	3 486	8.9	1.1
1984	34 479	3 536	10.5	1.1
1985	33 173	3 725	9.9	1.1
1986	31 465	3 966	9.3	1.2
1987	30 259	4 240	8.8	1.2
Turkmen SSR				
1980	28 001	3 870	9.8	1.4
1981	28 310	3 938	9.7	1.3
1982	28 712	4 225	9.6	1.4
1983	29 334	4 414	9.5	1.4
1984	30 503	4 507	9.7	1.4
1985	31 678	4 745	9.8	1.5
1986	32 346	4 901	9.8	1.5
1987	31 484	4 909	9.2	1.4

| | Absolute numbers | | Per 1 000 population | |
	Marriages	Divorces	Marriages	Divorces
Estonian SSR				
1980	12 964	6 127	8.8	4.1
1981	12 825	6 037	8.6	4.1
1982	12 263	5 902	8.2	3.9
1983	12 917	6 315	8.5	4.2
1984	12 530	6 194	8.2	4.1
1985	12 861	6 059	8.4	3.9
1986	13 000	6 039	8.4	3.9
1987	13 434	6 128	8.6	3.9

Source: **Naselenie SSSR 1987, s. 190-7.**

86

Number and average size of families:
by Union Republic, 1989*

	Thousands	Average size**
USSR	**73 078**	**3.5**
Russian SFSR	40 246	3.2
Ukrainian SSR	14 057	3.2
Belorussian SSR	2 796	3.2
Uzbek SSR	3 415	5.5
Kazakh SSR	3 824	4.0
Georgian SSR	1 244	4.1
Azerbaidzhan SSR	1 381	4.8
Lithuanian SSR	1 000	3.2
Moldavian SSR	1 144	3.4
Latvian SSR	732	3.1
Kirgiz SSR	856	4.7
Tadzhik SSR	799	6.1
Armenian SSR	559	4.7
Turkmen SSR	598	5.6
Estonian SSR	427	3.1

* Census data.

** Members of families who live together.

At the 1989 census there were 6.8 million (10%) more
families than in 1979. The average size for the country as
a whole has not altered, remaining at 3.5 persons - 3.3 in
urban areas and 3.8 in rural areas. However, certain
improvements have occurred in the distribution of family
size. In connection with changes in the marriage and birth
rates, the proportion of families with four persons has
increased and the proportion with three persons has
declined. A growth in the number of two member families has
been recorded.

At present 255.8 million persons - 89% of the total
population - live in families. Furthermore, 13 million
members of families live separately but share a common
budget with their families. Those who do not have a family
or have lost contact with it (single persons) number 16.4
million and represent 6% of the population. The proportion
of single persons and those living apart from their
families is low in the Republics of Central Asia, where it
is 4%-6%. The proportion is more significant in the Russian
SFSR, in the Ukraine, Belorussia and the Baltic Republics
(11%-15%).

Source: **Stat. Press-Byull.** 1990, 4, s. 46-7.

Families: by Union Republic and number of members, 1989* (thousands)

	Number of members**				
	2	3	4	5	6 and +
USSR	**22 918**	**18 880**	**17 801**	**6 984**	**6 495**
Russian SFSR	13 759	11 281	10 154	3 354	1 698
Ukrainian SSR	4 939	3 804	3 384	1 209	721
Belorussian SSR	972	766	748	212	98
Uzbek SSR	409	433	570	509	1 494
Kazakh SSR	866	852	972	520	614
Georgian SSR	265	242	314	200	223
Azerbaidzhan SSR	203	200	294	252	432
Lithuanian SSR	338	287	255	80	40
Moldavian SSR	351	292	306	127	68
Latvian SSR	277	210	165	55	25
Kirgiz SSR	146	148	178	131	253
Tadzhik SSR	89	91	115	103	401
Armenian SSR	70	78	147	116	148
Turkmen SSR	71	78	98	84	267
Estonian SSR	163	118	101	32	13

* Census data.

** Members of families living together.

Source: **Stat. Press-Byull.** 1990, 4, s. 46.

Sex composition of the population,
1959-1989

	Millions		Women per 1 000 men		
	Men	Women	Total	Urban	Rural
1959	94.0	114.8	1 220	1 211	1 229
1970	111.4	130.3	1 170	1 158	1 186
1979	122.3	140.1	1 145	1 144	1 148
1989	135.5	151.2	1 116	1 126	1 098

In 1959 women outnumbered men by 20.7 million. Subsequently
a gradual evening up of the sex ratio occurred and the
excess had fallen to 15.7 million by the 1989 census. Women
start to outnumber men from the age of 30, a phenemenon
which is related to the higher mortality rates among men.
The imbalance amongst the older age groups is particularly
influenced by the heavy losses of males during the years of
the Second World War.

Source: **Pravda** 1989, 29 aprelya, s. 2.

Percentage of women in total population:
by Union Republic, 1959-1989

	1959	1970	1979	1989
USSR	**55**	**54**	**53**	**53**
Russian SFSR	55	54	54	53
Ukrainian SSR	56	55	54	54
Belorussian SSR	56	54	54	53
Uzbek SSR	52	51	51	51
Kazakh SSR	53	52	52	52
Georgian SSR	54	53	53	53
Azerbaidzhan SSR	52	51	51	51
Lithuanian SSR	54	53	53	53
Moldavian SSR	54	53	53	53
Latvian SSR	56	54	54	53
Kirgiz SSR	53	52	51	51
Tadzhik SSR	51	51	51	50
Armenian SSR	52	51	51	51
Turkmen SSR	52	51	51	51
Estonian SSR	56	54	54	53

Source: **Vestnik Statistiki** 1990, 1, s. 46.

Population: by age group, 1979 and 1989*
(millions)

	1979	1989	1989 figs. as % of 1979
All ages	**262.1**	**285.7**	**109.0**
0-9	44.0	51.0	115.9
10-19	45.7	43.8	96.0
20-29	45.2	44.8	99.1
30-39	30.3	44.3	146.4
40-49	35.6	28.7	80.7
50-59	27.5	32.4	117.9
60-69	18.5	23.3	125.5
70-79	11.7	12.3	105.3
80 and over	3.5	5.0	140.6
under working age	69.6	77.9	111.9
of working age	151.9	158.9	104.6
over working age	40.5	48.8	120.5

* Permanently resident population at census dates.

Over the ten years the growth in the population of working age (16 to 59 for men and 16 to 54 for women) amounted to a total of 7 million persons. Of that growth almost 5 million (about 70%) occurred in the Republics of Central Asia and Kazakhstan. More than 25 million persons of working age are living there, out of the 159 million in the Union as a whole.

During the period which elapsed the number of persons over working age increased by 21%, while the total population grew by only 9%. In the country as a whole 17% of the population belongs to this age group; in the Russian SFSR, the Ukraine, Belorussia and the Baltic Republics the figure is 19%-21% but in the Republics of Central Asia it is 8%-10%.

Source: **AiF** 1990, 11, s. 49 (excerpt).

Male population: by Union Republic, 1959-1989
(thousands)

	1959	1969	1979	1989
USSR	**94 050**	**111 399**	**122 329**	**135 499**
Russian SFSR	52 425	59 325	63 483	69 122
Ukrainian SSR	18 575	21 305	22 744	23 959
Belorussian SSR	3 581	4 138	4 442	4 784
Uzbek SSR	3 897	5 744	7 558	9 820
Kazakh SSR	4 415	6 263	7 084	8 027
Georgian SSR	1 865	2 202	2 355	2 574
Azerbaidzhan SSR	1 757	2 483	2 939	3 421
Lithuanian SSR	1 245	1 468	1 603	1 750
Moldavian SSR	1 334	1 662	1 858	2 061
Latvian SSR	919	1 081	1 161	1 249
Kirgiz SSR	975	1 402	1 714	2 097
Tadzhik SSR	965	1 426	1 878	2 539
Armenian SSR	842	1 217	1 475	1 618
Turkmen SSR	730	1 063	1 358	1 741
Estonian SSR	525	620	677	737

Source: **Nar. khoz. SSSR 1988**, s. 20.

Female population: by Union Republic, 1959-1989
(thousands)

	1959	1969	1979	1989
USSR	**114 777**	**130 321**	**140 107**	**151 218**
Russian SFSR	65 109	70 754	74 068	78 264
Ukrainian SSR	23 294	25 821	27 011	27 745
Belorussian SSR	4 475	4 864	5 118	5 416
Uzbek SSR	4 222	6 055	7 833	10 086
Kazakh SSR	4 880	6 746	7 600	8 511
Georgian SSR	2 179	2 484	2 660	2 875
Azerbaidzhan SSR	1 941	2 634	3 089	3 608
Lithuanian SSR	1 466	1 660	1 795	1 940
Moldavian SSR	1 551	1 907	2 089	2 280
Latvian SSR	1 174	1 283	1 360	1 432
Kirgiz SSR	1 091	1 532	1 815	2 194
Tadzhik SSR	1 016	1 474	1 923	2 573
Armenian SSR	921	1 275	1 556	1 665
Turkmen SSR	786	1 096	1 401	1 793
Estonian SSR	672	736	789	836

Source: **Nar. khoz. SSSR 1988**, s. 20.

Population: by sex and age group, 1987*
(absolute numbers)

	Total	Men	Women
All ages	**281 337 791**	**132 043 477**	**149 294 314**
Under 5	26 142 845	13 340 277	12 802 568
5-9	23 226 189	11 812 417	11 413 772
10-14	22 262 212	11 275 206	10 987 006
15-19	20 635 971	10 441 517	10 194 454
20-24	22 166 892	11 220 015	10 946 877
25-29	24 676 706	12 554 221	12 122 485
30-34	22 227 719	11 047 694	11 180 025
35-39	19 449 811	9 610 903	9 838 908
40-44	11 038 637	5 344 836	5 693 801
45-49	19 572 889	9 231 397	10 341 492
50-54	15 123 737	7 046 118	8 077 619
55-59	16 567 674	7 402 169	9 165 505
60-64	12 745 156	4 593 216	8 151 940
65-69	7 366 485	2 352 824	5 013 661
70 and over	18 134 868	4 770 667	13 364 201
under working age	75 918 220	38 601 574	37 316 646
of working age	158 007 557	81 725 196	76 282 361
over working age	47 412 014	11 716 707	35 695 307

* Permanently resident population.

Source: **Naselenie SSSR 1987**, s. 49.

93

Population of Russian SFSR: by sex and age group, 1987*
(absolute numbers)

	Total	Men	Women
All ages	**145 170 146**	**67 388 233**	**77 781 913**
Under 5	11 811 386	6 027 987	5 783 399
5-9	10 680 306	5 433 677	5 246 629
10-14	10 278 254	5 214 940	5 063 314
15-19	9 365 653	4 716 662	4 648 991
20-24	10 761 179	5 393 718	5 367 461
25-29	13 246 135	6 831 238	6 414 897
30-34	12 394 657	6 222 311	6 172 346
35-39	10 958 160	5 461 979	5 496 181
40-44	5 733 035	2 801 757	2 931 278
45-49	10 877 739	5 129 709	5 748 030
50-54	8 300 843	3 825 604	4 475 239
55-59	9 447 430	4 173 771	5 273 659
60-64	7 093 370	2 470 750	4 622 620
65-69	4 050 917	1 244 026	2 806 891
70 and over	10 171 082	2 440 104	7 730 978
under working age	34 722 599	17 667 454	17 055 145
of working age	83 858 519	43 565 899	40 292 620
over working age	26 589 028	6 154 880	20 434 148

* Permanently resident population.

Source: **Naselenie SSSR 1987**, s. 51.

Population of Ukrainian SSR: by sex and age group, 1987*
(absolute numbers)

	Total	Men	Women
All ages	**51 055 719**	**23 513 771**	**27 541 948**
Under 5	3 901 525	1 997 030	1 904 495
5-9	3 660 425	1 865 867	1 794 558
10-14	3 657 740	1 853 359	1 804 381
15-19	3 571 245	1 823 631	1 747 614
20-24	3 746 246	1 919 851	1 826 395
25-29	3 972 352	1 982 532	1 989 820
30-34	3 685 093	1 803 075	1 882 018
35-39	3 506 342	1 697 683	1 808 659
40-44	2 365 069	1 111 242	1 253 827
45-49	4 075 403	1 886 976	2 188 427
50-54	2 942 927	1 369 383	1 573 544
55-59	3 370 112	1 494 920	1 875 192
60-64	2 843 326	1 034 872	1 808 454
65-69	1 674 114	544 410	1 129 704
70 and over	4 083 800	1 128 940	2 954 860
under working age	11 948 028	6 086 988	5 861 040
of working age	28 631 259	14 718 561	13 912 698
over working age	10 476 432	2 708 222	7 768 210

* Permanently resident population.

Source: **Naselenie SSSR 1987**, s. 55.

Population of Belorussian SSR: by sex and age group, 1987*
(absolute numbers)

	Total	Men	Women
All ages	**10 049 856**	**4 699 029**	**5 350 827**
Under 5	844 354	430 964	413 390
5-9	782 117	399 533	382 584
10-14	735 751	375 575	360 176
15-19	750 109	372 706	377 403
20-24	822 564	416 266	406 298
25-29	866 269	438 585	427 684
30-34	762 430	378 535	383 895
35-39	685 319	339 499	345 820
40-44	424 352	204 650	219 702
45-49	654 595	306 655	347 940
50-54	623 834	282 741	341 093
55-59	633 688	284 395	349 293
60-64	503 550	182 338	321 212
65-69	268 936	91 115	177 821
70 and over	691 988	195 472	496 516
under working age	2 511 204	1 281 025	1 230 179
of working age	5 724 885	2 949 079	2 775 806
over working age	1 813 767	468 925	1 344 842

* Permanently resident population.

Source: **Naselenie SSSR 1987**, s. 57.

Population of Uzbek SSR: by sex and age group, 1987*
(absolute numbers)

	Total	Men	Women
All ages	**19 023 841**	**9 384 960**	**9 638 881**
Under 5	3 059 610	1 554 793	1 504 817
5-9	2 466 177	1 246 654	1 219 523
10-14	2 220 681	1 117 473	1 103 208
15-19	1 969 351	995 843	973 508
20-24	1 869 799	952 734	917 065
25-29	1 663 507	817 881	845 626
30-34	1 236 599	608 031	628 568
35-39	891 364	442 200	449 164
40-44	491 277	249 554	241 723
45-49	750 667	374 705	375 962
50-54	606 576	303 197	303 379
55-59	567 427	269 862	297 565
60-64	407 258	168 724	238 534
65-69	246 285	83 557	162 728
70 and over	577 263	199 752	377 511
under working age	8 160 772	4 128 339	4 032 433
of working age	9 334 698	4 804 588	4 530 110
over working age	1 528 371	452 033	1 076 338

* Permanently resident population.

Source: **Naselenie SSSR 1987**, s. 61.

Population of Kazakh SSR: by sex and age group, 1987*
(absolute numbers)

	Total	Men	Women
All ages	**16 244 063**	**7 863 140**	**8 380 923**
Under 5	1 850 741	943 292	907 449
5-9	1 644 480	834 515	809 965
10-14	1 610 979	814 821	796 158
15-19	1 419 550	722 241	697 309
20-24	1 390 231	721 151	669 080
25-29	1 430 772	736 211	694 561
30-34	1 285 404	644 840	640 564
35-39	1 090 589	540 474	550 115
40-44	573 896	280 316	293 580
45-49	1 014 731	487 713	527 018
50-54	703 936	337 994	365 942
55-59	700 867	316 154	384 713
60-64	520 907	191 144	329 763
65-69	290 691	96 019	194 672
70 and over	716 289	196 255	520 034
under working age	5 412 072	2 747 722	2 664 350
of working age	8 919 391	4 632 000	4 287 391
over working age	1 912 600	483 418	1 429 182

* Permanently resident population.

Source: **Naselenie SSSR 1987**, s. 63.

Population of Georgian SSR: by sex and age group, 1987*
(absolute numbers)

	Total	Men	Women
All ages	**5 244 289**	**2 475 519**	**2 768 770**
Under 5	461 548	236 277	225 271
5-9	427 192	217 776	209 416
10-14	424 831	213 826	211 005
15-19	398 077	205 354	192 723
20-24	431 306	217 919	213 387
25-29	430 525	214 447	216 078
30-34	386 296	183 765	202 531
35-39	331 377	157 261	174 116
40-44	216 354	99 731	116 623
45-49	374 732	172 677	202 055
50-54	319 408	153 548	165 860
55-59	315 974	150 129	165 845
60-64	243 750	99 600	144 150
65-69	150 322	49 133	101 189
70 and over	332 597	104 076	228 521
under working age	1 397 087	710 294	686 793
of working age	2 954 688	1 512 416	1 442 272
over working age	892 514	252 809	639 705

* Permanently resident population.

Source: **Naselenie SSSR 1987**, s. 67.

Population of Azerbaidzhan SSR: by sex and age group, 1987*
(absolute numbers)

	Total	Men	Women
All ages	6 808 813	3 321 868	3 486 945
Under 5	835 392	428 658	406 734
5-9	711 792	363 398	348 394
10-14	666 001	337 036	328 965
15-19	697 083	357 955	339 128
20-24	744 866	382 028	362 838
25-29	688 650	339 821	348 829
30-34	486 405	230 976	255 429
35-39	345 480	166 167	179 313
40-44	182 936	87 459	95 477
45-49	341 260	161 361	179 899
50-54	328 879	160 897	167 982
55-59	272 289	131 225	141 064
60-64	175 199	72 957	102 242
65-69	97 240	31 897	65 343
70 and over	235 341	70 033	165 308
under working age	2 347 866	1 197 155	1 150 711
of working age	3 812 103	1 949 826	1 862 277
over working age	648 844	174 887	473 957

* Permanently resident population.

Source: **Naselenie SSSR 1987**, s. 69.

Population of Lithuanian SSR: by sex and age group, 1987*
(absolute numbers)

	Total	Men	Women
All ages	3 634 889	1 713 909	1 920 980
Under 5	290 544	148 302	142 242
5-9	272 259	138 989	133 270
10-14	272 846	138 279	134 567
15-19	265 929	135 075	130 854
20-24	265 773	133 823	131 950
25-29	311 504	160 097	151 407
30-34	272 203	136 724	135 479
35-39	246 329	121 037	125 292
40-44	213 675	101 120	112 555
45-49	233 878	110 245	123 633
50-54	223 123	100 869	122 254
55-59	212 910	94 338	118 572
60-64	171 795	63 888	107 907
65-69	107 680	39 633	68 047
70 and over	274 441	91 490	182 951
under working age	892 096	454 276	437 820
of working age	2 070 305	1 064 622	1 005 683
over working age	672 488	195 011	477 477

* Permanently resident population.

Source: **Naselenie SSSR 1987**, s. 73.

Population of Moldavian SSR: by sex and age group, 1987*
(absolute numbers)

	Total	Men	Women
All ages	**4 187 614**	**1 996 054**	**2 191 560**
Under 5	441 368	225 708	215 660
5-9	380 538	195 053	185 485
10-14	366 304	184 956	181 348
15-19	357 438	178 799	178 639
20-24	344 096	174 209	169 887
25-29	333 852	164 784	169 068
30-34	319 680	152 195	167 485
35-39	299 683	144 284	155 399
40-44	173 774	79 305	94 469
45-49	251 813	115 472	136 341
50-54	224 218	102 684	121 534
55-59	211 697	96 669	115 028
60-64	170 812	67 054	103 758
65-69	118 366	47 216	71 150
70 and over	193 975	67 666	126 309
under working age	1 262 030	642 896	619 134
of working age	2 327 403	1 171 222	1 156 181
over working age	598 181	181 936	416 245

* Permanently resident population.

Source: **Naselenie SSSR 1987**, s. 75.

Population of Latvian SSR: by sex and age group, 1987*
(absolute numbers)

	Total	Men	Women
All ages	**2 629 199**	**1 221 094**	**1 408 105**
Under 5	200 188	102 837	97 351
5-9	180 798	93 238	87 560
10-14	179 127	91 909	87 218
15-19	172 451	87 908	84 543
20-24	194 457	97 203	97 254
25-29	220 911	114 212	106 699
30-34	193 816	97 300	96 516
35-39	178 751	87 627	91 124
40-44	149 612	70 817	78 795
45-49	191 023	90 275	100 748
50-54	164 619	74 975	89 644
55-59	165 143	73 256	91 887
60-64	135 089	46 002	89 087
65-69	84 753	29 333	55 420
70 and over	218 461	64 202	154 259
under working age	596 334	306 293	290 041
of working age	1 502 675	775 264	727 411
over working age	530 190	139 537	390 653

* Permanently resident population.

Source: **Naselenie SSSR 1987**, s. 79.

Population of Kirgiz SSR: by sex and age group, 1987*
(absolute numbers)

	Total	Men	Women
All ages	**4 137 316**	**2 022 634**	**2 114 682**
Under 5	599 745	305 228	294 517
5-9	493 819	250 823	242 996
10-14	457 412	230 082	227 330
15-19	422 265	209 943	212 322
20-24	384 898	196 485	188 413
25-29	340 647	176 358	164 289
30-34	284 813	140 246	144 567
35-39	219 967	108 760	111 207
40-44	104 403	51 817	52 586
45-49	186 892	91 358	95 534
50-54	157 629	76 774	80 855
55-59	160 075	73 608	86 467
60-64	114 648	46 125	68 523
65-69	65 696	22 068	43 628
70 and over	144 407	42 959	101 448
under working age	1 638 451	830 375	808 076
of working age	2 087 647	1 081 107	1 006 540
over working age	411 218	111 152	300 066

* Permanently resident population.

Source: **Naselenie SSSR 1987**, s. 81.

Population of Tadzhik SSR: by sex and age group, 1987*
(absolute numbers)

	Total	Men	Women
All ages	**4 811 637**	**2 382 531**	**2 429 106**
Under 5	827 437	420 527	406 910
5-9	643 506	324 179	319 327
10-14	571 217	288 436	282 781
15-19	509 761	258 693	251 068
20-24	461 463	232 858	228 605
25-29	386 879	185 290	201 589
30-34	286 061	139 405	146 656
35-39	209 469	104 110	105 359
40-44	121 322	65 002	56 320
45-49	183 293	93 589	89 704
50-54	156 931	78 018	78 913
55-59	144 422	70 896	73 526
60-64	102 762	43 636	59 126
65-69	64 615	23 099	41 516
70 and over	142 499	54 793	87 706
under working age	2 152 025	1 088 404	1 063 621
of working age	2 276 210	1 172 599	1 103 611
over working age	383 402	121 528	261 874

* Permanently resident population.

Source: **Naselenie SSSR 1987**, s. 85.

Population of Armenian SSR: by sex and age group, 1987*
(absolute numbers)

	Total	Men	Women
All ages	**3 418 465**	**1 674 311**	**1 744 154**
Under 5	377 453	192 994	184 459
5-9	331 947	170 255	161 692
10-14	310 608	157 872	152 736
15-19	280 091	144 896	135 195
20-24	317 393	163 543	153 850
25-29	363 471	181 026	182 445
30-34	286 257	137 233	149 024
35-39	206 403	100 183	106 220
40-44	111 197	53 584	57 613
45-49	194 736	92 647	102 089
50-54	169 272	82 409	86 863
55-59	166 793	81 699	85 094
60-64	112 178	48 335	63 843
65-69	50 940	18 211	32 729
70 and over	139 726	49 424	90 302
under working age	1 077 639	550 669	526 970
of working age	1 952 888	1 007 672	945 216
over working age	387 938	115 970	271 968

* Permanently resident population.

Source: **Naselenie SSSR 1987**, s. 87.

Population of Turkmen SSR: by sex and age group, 1987*
(absolute numbers)

	Total	Men	Women
All ages	**3 367 248**	**1 658 921**	**1 708 327**
Under 5	524 862	266 070	258 792
5-9	438 111	220 416	217 695
10-14	400 005	200 257	199 748
15-19	355 049	179 704	175 345
20-24	323 555	163 644	159 911
25-29	294 603	145 615	148 988
30-34	224 703	110 187	114 516
35-39	166 941	83 140	83 801
40-44	93 391	47 806	45 585
45-49	132 041	65 857	66 184
50-54	105 990	53 009	52 981
55-59	101 108	47 844	53 264
60-64	72 199	29 450	42 749
65-69	46 060	15 774	30 286
70 and over	88 630	30 148	58 482
under working age	1 438 119	724 360	713 759
of working age	1 668 976	859 189	809 787
over working age	260 153	75 372	184 781

* Permanently resident population.

Source: **Naselenie SSSR 1987**, s. 91.

Population of Estonian SSR: by sex and age group, 1987*
(absolute numbers)

	Total	Men	Women
All ages	1 554 696	727 503	827 193
Under 5	116 692	59 610	57 082
5-9	112 722	58 044	54 678
10-14	110 456	56 385	54 071
15-19	101 919	52 107	49 812
20-24	109 066	54 583	54 483
25-29	126 629	66 124	60 505
30-34	123 302	62 871	60 431
35-39	113 637	56 499	57 138
40-44	84 344	40 676	43 668
45-49	110 086	52 158	57 928
50-54	95 552	44 016	51 536
55-59	97 739	43 403	54 336
60-64	78 313	28 341	49 972
65-69	49 870	17 333	32 537
70 and over	124 369	35 353	89 016
under working age	361 898	185 324	176 574
of working age	885 910	461 152	424 758
over working age	306 888	81 027	225 861

* Permanently resident population.

Source: **Naselenie SSSR 1987**, s. 93.

Ethnic composition of the population and percentage who consider the language of their ethnic group as their mother tongue, 1979 and 1989

	Ethnic group (thousands)		Language %	
	1979	1989	1979	1989
Total	262 085	285 743	93.1	92.7
Russians	137 397	145 162	99.9	99.8
Ukrainians	42 347	44 183	82.8	81.1
Belorussians	9 463	10 036	74.2	70.9
Uzbeks	12 456	16 698	98.5	98.3
Kazakhs	6 556	8 136	97.5	97.0
Georgians	3 571	3 981	98.3	98.2
Azeris	5 477	6 770	97.9	97.7
Lithuanians	2 851	3 067	97.9	97.7
Moldavians	2 968	3 352	93.2	91.6
Latvians	1 439	1 459	95.0	94.8
Kirgiz	1 906	2 529	97.9	97.8
Tadzhiks	2 898	4 215	97.8	97.7
Armenians	4 151	4 623	90.7	91.7
Turkmenians	2 028	2 729	98.7	98.5
Estonians	1 020	1 027	95.3	95.5
Abazas	29	34	95.3	93.4
Abkhazians	91	105	94.3	93.5
Avars	483	601	97.7	97.2
Austrians	0.6	0.5	24.2	29.6
Aguls	12	19	98.3	94.9
Adygeians	109	125	95.7	94.7
Albanians	4.3	4.0	54.5	52.1
Altais	60	71	86.4	84.3
Americans	0.1	0.3	65.8	63.2
English	0.2	0.3	49.8	57.8
Arabs	6.8	7.7	66.3	61.5
Assyrians	25	26	54.9	59.6
Afghans	4.0	6.7	65.8	63.1
Balkars	66	85	96.9	93.6
Bashkirs	1 371	1 449	67.0	72.3
Belu	19	29	98.1	96.9
Bulgarians	361	373	68.0	67.6
Buryats	353	421	90.2	86.3
Hungarians	171	171	95.4	93.9
Veps	8.1	13	38.4	50.8
Vietnamese	2.8	3.4	97.8	96.4
Gagauz	173	198	89.3	87.5
Dutch	0.7	0.8	36.5	31.5
Greeks	344	358	38.0	44.5
Darghins	287	365	98.3	97.5
Dungans	52	69	94.8	94.8
Jews	1 762	1 378	12.5	11.1
Mountain Jews	9.4	19	69.5	75.8
Georgian Jews	8.5	16	91.5	90.9
Central Asian Jews	28	36	76.9	65.1

Ethnic group (thousands)		Language %	
1979	1989	1979	1989
Izhora	0.7	0.8	32.6	36.8
Ingush	186	237	97.4	96.9
Indians and Pakistanis	0.5	1.7	75.4	71.5
Spaniards	3.0	3.2	49.7	46.1
Italians	1.0	1.3	22.8	39.7
Kabardians	322	391	97.9	97.2
Kalmyks	147	174	91.3	90.0
Karaites	3.3	2.6	16.0	19.3
Karakalpaks	303	424	95.9	94.1
Karachais	131	156	97.7	96.8
Karelians	138	131	55.6	47.8
Chinese	12	11	37.8	32.9
Komi	327	345	76.2	70.4
Komi-Permyaks	151	152	77.1	70.1
Koreans	389	439	55.4	49.4
Krymchaki	3.0	1.4	53.6	34.9
Cubans	2.6	2.8	70.9	71.9
Kumyks	228	282	98.2	97.4
Kurds	116	153	83.6	80.5
Laks	100	118	95.0	93.6
Lezghians	383	466	90.9	91.6
Livs	0.1	0.2	...	43.8
Mari	622	671	86.7	80.8
Mordovians	1 192	1 154	72.6	67.1
Germans	1 936	2 038	57.0	48.8
Nogai	60	75	90.3	89.9
Ossets	542	598	88.2	87.0
Persians	31	40	30.7	33.2
Poles	1 151	1 126	29.1	30.5
Romanians	129	146	41.1	60.9
Rutuls	15	20	99.1	94.8
Peoples of the North	158	184	61.7	52.2
Aleuts	0.5	0.7	17.7	26.6
Dolgan	5.1	6.9	90.0	81.9
Itelmeny	1.4	2.5	24.4	19.6
Ket	1.1	1.1	61.0	48.3
Koryaks	7.9	9.2	69.1	52.4
Mansi	7.6	8.5	49.5	37.1
Nanai	10.5	12.0	55.8	44.1
Nganasany	0.9	1.3	90.2	83.2
Negidal	0.5	0.6	44.4	28.3
Nenets	29.9*	34.7	80.4	77.1
Nivkh	4.4	4.7	30.6	23.3
Oroki	...	0.2	...	44.7
Orochi	1.2	0.9	40.6	18.8
Saami	1.9	1.9	53.0	42.2
Selkups	3.6	3.6	56.6	47.6
Tofalary	0.8	0.7	62.1	43.0

	Ethnic group (thousands)		Language %	
	1979	1989	1979	1989
Udegei	1.6	2.0	31.0	26.3
Ulchi	2.6	3.2	38.8	30.8
Khanty	20.9	22.5	67.8	60.5
Chuvantsy	...	1.5	...	21.4
Chukchi	14.0**	15.2	78.3	70.3
Evenki	27.3	30.2	42.8	29.6
Eveny	12.5	17.2	56.9	43.9
Entsy	...	0.2	...	45.5
Eskimos	1.5	1.7	60.7	51.6
Yukaghir	0.8	1.1	37.5	32.8
Serbs	1.7	2.7	44.2	40.8
Slovaks	9.4	9.1	41.7	37.9
Tabasarans	75	98	97.4	95.9
Talysh	1.4	22	...	90.4
Tatars	6 185	6 648	86.1	83.2
Crimean Tatars	132	272	78.1	92.6
Tats	22	31	67.4	71.9
Tuvans	166	207	98.8	98.5
Turks	93	208	84.7	91.1
Udins	6.9	8.0	89.9	85.7
Udmurts	714	747	76.5	69.6
Uighurs	211	263	86.1	86.6
Finns	77	67	40.9	34.6
French	0.8	0.7	49.1	46.6
Khakass	71	80	80.9	76.1
Khalkha-Mongols	3.2	2.9	91.3	87.8
Khorvat	0.2	0.8	41.8	49.7
Tsakhurs	13	20	95.2	95.2
Gypsies	209	262	74.1	77.4
Cherkess	46	52	91.4	90.4
Czechs	18	16	32.7	35.3
Chechens	756	957	98.6	98.1
Chuvash	1 751	1 842	81.7	76.4
Shors	16	17	61.2	56.7
Yakuts	328	382	95.3	93.8
Japanese	0.8	0.7	49.2	46.0
Others***	25	30	66.8	31.0

* Includes Entsy, who are separately recorded in the 1989
census. ** Includes Chuvantsy, who are separately recorded
in the 1989 census. *** Includes persons whose ethnic group
is not shown on the census list.

Note: Ascription to a ethnic group at the census reflects
an individual's own statement based on self-awareness.
Parents decide for their children.
Source: **Stat. Press-Byull.** 1990, 4, s. 49-52.

Persons fluent in a second language of the USSR: by ethnic group, 1979 and 1989 (percentages)

| | Russian | | Other languages | |
	1979	1989	1979	1989
Total	**23.4**	**24.2**	**4.7**	**5.3**
Russians	0.1	0.2	3.5	4.0
Ukrainians	49.8	56.2	7.1	8.5
Belorussians	57.0	54.7	11.7	11.7
Uzbeks	49.3	23.8	2.8	3.7
Kazakhs	52.3	60.4	2.1	2.9
Georgians	26.7	33.1	0.9	1.0
Azeris	29.5	34.3	2.0	2.2
Lithuanians	52.1	37.9	1.5	1.6
Moldavians	47.4	53.8	3.9	4.4
Latvians	56.7	64.4	2.2	2.5
Kirgiz	29.4	35.2	4.1	4.6
Tadzhiks	29.6	27.7	10.6	12.2
Armenians	38.6	47.1	5.7	5.0
Turkmenians	25.4	27.7	1.6	2.0
Estonians	24.2	33.9	1.9	1.8
Abazas	75.4	78.1	4.6	4.3
Abkhazians	73.3	78.8	3.0	3.5
Avars	59.3	60.8	6.0	6.7
Austrians	28.3	28.8	6.1	11.5
Aguls	62.9	68.4	8.0	6.5
Adygeians	76.7	81.7	1.3	1.5
Albanians	49.5	49.8	9.9	8.8
Altais	68.7	65.1	2.4	2.3
Americans	55.0	45.8	6.7	11.9
English	37.7	48.3	8.8	7.2
Arabs	49.1	51.0	11.9	17.7
Assyrians	41.7	43.7	21.4	19.9
Afghans	27.4	30.0	40.1	30.1
Balkars	77.4	78.6	1.4	2.0
Bashkirs	64.9	71.8	2.8	3.6
Belu	4.9	4.6	53.0	56.3
Bulgarians	58.2	60.3	7.9	8.8
Buryats	71.9	72.1	2.5	2.7
Hungarians	34.2	43.3	9.4	11.7
Veps	35.8	49.0	15.4	16.7
Vietnamese	80.7	53.1	0.6	0.8
Gagauz	68.0	71.1	7.3	6.9
Dutch	39.2	30.7	4.9	6.0
Greeks	34.1	39.5	17.7	16.5
Darghins	64.1	68.0	2.0	1.8
Dungans	62.8	70.8	3.9	2.9
Jews	12.5	10.1	28.1	29.2
Mountain Jews	65.1	54.6	11.5	16.8
Georgian Jews	44.1	46.4	4.5	4.6
Central Asian Jews	65.2	50.6	10.3	17.0

Table continues

	Russian 1979	1989	Other languages 1979	1989
Izhora	32.4	37.8	25.6	24.1
Ingush	79.6	80.0	0.6	1.0
Indians and Pakistanis	57.4	43.6	4.3	5.1
Spaniards	47.2	42.8	5.3	7.9
Italians	17.2	25.7	11.4	9.9
Kabardians	76.7	77.7	0.6	0.7
Kalmyks	84.1	85.3	1.0	1.5
Karaites	13.3	14.4	17.9	22.4
Karakalpaks	45.1	20.6	10.8	11.4
Karachais	75.5	79.2	0.9	1.0
Karelians	51.3	45.5	13.2	14.8
Chinese	32.4	30.5	3.6	5.1
Komi	64.5	62.2	5.7	6.1
Komi-Permyaks	64.3	61.3	6.0	8.0
Koreans	47.7	43.3	2.2	3.7
Krymchaki	15.0	30.2	10.5	13.4
Cubans	69.6	73.0	0.9	2.2
Kumyks	72.6	74.5	0.8	1.1
Kurds	25.4	28.7	40.7	40.4
Laks	73.0	76.4	2.5	2.9
Lezghians	47.6	54.3	21.3	19.9
Livs	...	34.1	...	35.0
Mari	69.9	68.8	5.5	5.8
Mordovians	65.5	62.5	7.7	8.9
Germans	51.7	45.0	1.1	1.6
Nogai	75.6	79.3	1.4	1.4
Ossets	64.9	68.9	12.2	12.2
Persians	57.1	45.9	10.6	18.3
Poles	44.7	43.9	13.1	17.3
Romanians	48.4	50.8	14.0	11.6
Rutuls	52.0	63.1	12.3	8.3
Peoples of the North	54.0	49.9	5.2	5.6
Aleuts	15.0	24.5	9.6	4.8
Dolgan	72.9	66.5	1.6	2.5
Itelmeny	20.7	17.2	4.0	5.9
Ket	53.5	44.3	4.2	6.6
Koryaks	60.8	46.6	5.0	6.4
Mansi	40.7	32.9	4.8	4.4
Nanai	49.4	40.1	7.4	6.3
Nganasany	71.3	56.5	2.2	4.0
Negidal	37.7	23.6	5.2	7.9
Nenets	64.2	61.7	3.0	3.1
Nivkh	26.9	19.9	8.1	3.9
Oroki	...	40.0	...	3.2
Orochi	20.4	14.0	7.2	3.2
Saami	49.7	40.8	9.9	9.4
Selkups	46.6	42.6	4.4	4.1
Tofalary	51.4	39.1	6.0	3.7

Table continues

	Russian 1979	1989	Other languages 1979	1989
Udegei	26.5	18.7	7.3	9.1
Ulchi	33.2	24.0	8.5	8.0
Khanty	52.8	50.6	3.6	3.0
Chuvantsy	...	26.7	...	8.1
Chukchi	61.3	61.2	2.9	3.9
Evenki	54.5	52.3	4.8	8.8
Eveny	51.9	52.5	13.5	9.6
Entsy	...	47.8	...	9.6
Eskimos	53.7	48.4	5.8	4.5
Yukaghirs	34.3	37.5	20.4	16.7
Serbs	46.6	50.8	10.1	8.7
Slovaks	48.5	51.9	26.2	25.8
Tabasarans	59.0	62.5	7.8	5.3
Talysh	...	5.5	...	73.5
Tatars	68.6	70.8	4.9	5.3
Crimean Tatars	82.0	76.1	4.2	8.0
Tats	61.3	64.1	13.5	13.3
Tuvans	59.2	59.2	0.2	0.4
Turks	46.4	40.3	22.3	30.6
Udins	52.2	51.3	29.5	27.3
Udmurts	64.4	61.3	6.4	7.1
Uighurs	52.1	58.3	9.0	10.8
Finns	39.9	35.4	9.0	10.8
French	39.4	44.2	13.1	14.6
Khakass	68.3	66.8	3.0	3.6
Khalkha-Mongols	61.4	75.0	0.8	1.1
Khorvat	44.2	42.6	6.4	7.7
Tsakhurs	22.4	23.5	48.7	54.3
Gypsies	59.1	63.3	14.3	13.8
Cherkess	69.6	76.3	2.3	2.2
Czechs	34.6	36.8	20.9	22.9
Chechens	76.0	74.0	0.7	0.8
Chuvash	64.8	65.1	5.5	5.9
Shors	52.6	52.7	6.3	7.1
Yakuts	55.6	64.9	1.1	1.5
Japanese	38.0	38.9	2.4	3.1
Others	31.3	23.5	27.5	14.6

At the 1989 census 92.7% of the population regarded the language of their ethnic group as their mother tongue and 7.3% the languages of other peoples; the corresponding figures for 1979 were 93.1% and 6.9%. In 1989 Russian was named as their mother tongue by 163.5 million persons (and by 153.5 million in 1979). Of those, 144.8 million were Russians. Moreover, 69 million were fluent in Russian as a second language; 61.3 million were fluent in it in 1979.
Source: **Stat. Press-Byull.** 1990, 4, s. 49-53.

Inter-ethnic marriages in 1988 as percentages of all marriages by specified ethnic groups (incomplete data)

	Men	Women
in USSR as a whole		
Russians	16.0	stated to be about the same
Ukrainians	33.4	ditto
Belorussians	38.6	ditto
Uzbeks	6.6	5.0
Kirgiz	6.9	6.1
Turkmenians	9.0	3.9
Russians outside the Russian SFSR		
in Ukraine	57.2	n. a.
in Belorussia	74.5	73.4
in Georgia	39.6	53.2
in Lithuania	56.5	n. a.
in Moldavia	61.9	59.9
in Azerbaidzhan	n. a.	40.3
in Armenia	n. a.	70.6

Inter-ethnic marriages of men as percentages of all marriages by specified ethnic groups

	in USSR	within homeland SSR
Azeris	11.5	2.8
Moldavians	28.2	14.4
Armenians	20.2	2.3
Latvians	25.3	19.7

Source: **Pravda** 1989, 12 oktyabrya, s. 2.

115

Married persons and persons married within their own ethnic group: by Union Republic, 1988
(absolute numbers)

	Men	within own group	Women	within own group
RUSSIAN SFSR				
Russians	1 101 638	994 241	1 118 016	994 241
Urban	876 956	793 754	893 202	793 754
Rural	224 682	200 487	224 814	200 487
Ukrainians	51 680	6 257	47 245	6 257
Urban	41 860	4 642	37 075	4 642
Rural	9 820	1 615	10 170	1 615
Tatars	59 436	36 564	60 511	36 564
Urban	35 302	18 047	36 468	18 047
Rural	24 134	18 517	24 043	18 517
Belorussians	14 303	927	12 881	927
Urban	11 781	736	10 471	736
Rural	2 522	191	2 410	191
Jews	4 676	1 254	3 373	1 254
Urban	4 566	1 240	3 301	1 240
Rural	110	14	72	14
Kazakhs	7 341	5 542	7 336	5 542
Urban	3 009	1 904	2 957	1 904
Rural	4 332	3 638	4 379	3 638
Armenians	7 165	2 620	4 612	2 620
Urban	5 667	1 771	3 462	1 771
Rural	1 498	849	1 150	849
UKRAINIAN SSR				
Ukrainians	315 241	249 429	321 241	249 429
Urban	208 625	153 215	213 966	153 215
Rural	106 616	96 214	107 275	96 214
Russians	111 791	47 897	110 706	47 897
Urban	98 323	43 041	97 525	43 041
Rural	13 468	4 856	13 181	4 856
Jews	4 375	2 006	3 626	2 006
Urban	4 329	1 999	3 587	1 999
Rural	46	7	39	7

	Men	within own group	Women	within own group
Belorussians	4 827	297	4 190	297
Urban	3 830	175	3 311	175
Rural	997	122	879	122
Moldavians	3 292	1 210	3 400	1 210
Urban	1 432	203	1 363	203
Rural	1 860	1 007	2 037	1 007

BELORUSSIAN SSR

	Men	within own group	Women	within own group
Belorussians	70 668	56 482	72 124	56 482
Urban	46 370	35 549	47 861	35 549
Rural	24 298	20 933	24 263	20 933
Russians	15 583	3 980	14 960	3 980
Urban	12 977	3 479	12 327	3 479
Rural	2 606	501	2 633	501
Ukrainians	3 373	314	3 064	314
Urban	2 666	235	2 388	235
Rural	707	79	676	79
Jews	940	486	809	486
Urban	919	484	782	484
Rural	21	2	27	2

UZBEK SSR

	Men	within own group	Women	within own group
Uzbeks	143 377	137 251	141 912	137 251
Urban	45 155	41 707	44 276	41 707
Rural	98 222	95 544	97 636	95 544
Russians	14 732	11 196	15 909	11 196
Urban	14 067	10 761	15 151	10 761
Rural	665	435	758	435
Tatars	5 851	3 656	6 110	3 656
Urban	5 109	3 160	5 267	3 160
Rural	742	496	843	496
Kazakhs	7 694	6 488	7 827	6 488
Urban	3 128	2 434	3 211	2 434
Rural	4 566	4 054	4 616	4 054

Table continues

	Men	within own group	Women	within own group
Tadzhiks	6 935	4 925	7 056	4 925
Urban	2 522	1 519	2 355	1 519
Rural	4 413	3 406	4 701	3 406
Ukrainians	1 340	116	1 337	116
Urban	1 266	107	1 234	107
Rural	74	9	103	9
Kirgiz	1 683	1 278	1 666	1 278
Urban	229	130	239	130
Rural	1 454	1 148	1 427	1 148

KAZAKH SSR

	Men	within own group	Women	within own group
Kazakhs	69 545	66 570	68 992	66 570
Urban	30 275	28 426	29 931	28 426
Rural	39 270	38 144	39 061	38 144
Russians	56 460	42 768	58 661	42 768
Urban	45 442	35 317	46 780	35 317
Rural	11 018	7 451	11 881	7 451
Ukrainians	9 239	1 757	9 140	1 757
Urban	6 290	1 038	6 280	1 038
Rural	2 949	719	2 860	719
Tatars	3 167	984	3 316	984
Urban	2 520	822	2 618	822
Rural	647	162	698	162
Uzbeks	3 775	3 249	3 668	3 249
Urban	1 586	1 241	1 509	1 241
Rural	2 189	2 008	2 159	2 008
Belorussians	1 958	107	1 819	107
Urban	1 329	53	1 189	53
Rural	629	54	630	54

GEORGIAN SSR

	Men	within own group	Women	within own group
Georgians	25 896	23 703	25 081	23 703
Urban	16 466	14 728	15 860	14 728
Rural	9 430	8 975	9 221	8 975

	Men	within own group	Women	within own group
Russians	2 278	1 375	2 941	1 375
Urban	2 033	1 232	2 553	1 232
Rural	245	143	388	143
Armenians	3 432	2 620	3 345	2 620
Urban	2 174	1 464	2 087	1 464
Rural	1 258	1 156	1 258	1 156
Azeris	2 593	2 459	2 546	2 459
Urban	660	560	628	560
Rural	1 933	1 899	1 918	1 899

AZERBAIDZHAN SSR

	Men	within own group	Women	within own group
Azeris	59 719	58 045	58 863	58 045
Urban	28 177	26 831	27 415	26 831
Rural	31 542	31 214	31 448	31 214
Russians	2 486	1 875	3 140	1 875
Urban	2 374	1 781	3 003	1 781
Rural	112	94	137	94
Armenians	3 029	2 524	3 045	2 524
Urban	2 358	1 879	2 379	1 879
Rural	671	645	666	645

LITHUANIAN SSR

	Men	within own group	Women	within own group
Lithuanians	27 557	25 808	27 992	25 808
Urban	18 407	17 092	18 888	19 092
Rural	9 150	8 716	9 104	8 716
Russians	3 287	1 430	2 962	1 430
Urban	2 976	1 328	2 606	1 328
Rural	311	102	356	102

MOLDAVIAN SSR

	Men	within own group	Women	within own group
Moldavians	24 960	21 366	25 714	21 366
Urban	9 711	7 324	10 335	7 324
Rural	15 249	14 042	15 379	14 042
Russians	5 573	2 121	5 294	2 121
Urban	4 773	1 929	4 483	1 929
Rural	800	192	811	192

	Men	within own group	Women	within own group
Ukrainians	5 772	2 155	5 550	2 155
Urban	3 996	1 349	3 884	1 349
Rural	1 776	806	1 666	806

LATVIAN SSR

	Men	within own group	Women	within own group
Latvians	11 900	9 561	11 961	9 561
Urban	8 262	6 529	8 359	6 529
Rural	3 638	3 032	3 602	3 032
Russians	9 143	5 747	9 214	5 747
Urban	8 088	5 205	8 121	5 205
Rural	1 055	542	1 093	542
Belorussians	1 255	197	1 336	197
Urban	1 036	166	1 097	166
Rural	219	31	239	31
Ukrainians	1 227	178	1 113	178
Urban	1 038	141	921	141
Rural	189	37	192	37

KIRGIZ SSR

	Men	within own group	Women	within own group
Kirgiz	21 052	20 282	20 907	20 282
Urban	4 820	4 514	4 765	4 514
Rural	16 232	15 768	16 142	15 768
Russians	7 827	6 310	8 196	6 310
Urban	5 609	4 616	5 836	4 616
Rural	2 218	1 694	2 360	1 694
Uzbeks	6 108	5 429	5 956	5 429
Urban	2 214	1 902	2 087	1 902
Rural	3 894	3 527	3 869	3 527
Ukrainians	950	146	962	146
Urban	586	78	609	78
Rural	364	68	353	68

TADZHIK SSR

	Men	within own group	Women	within own group
Tadzhiks	28 329	26 451	28 012	26 451
Urban	7 821	6 884	7 609	6 884
Rural	20 508	19 567	20 403	19 567

Table continues

	Men	within own group	Women	within own group
Russians	3 489	2 582	3 789	2 582
Urban	3 346	2 482	3 594	2 482
Rural	143	100	195	100
Uzbeks	11 866	10 270	11 759	10 270
Urban	2 417	1 698	2 347	1 698
Rural	9 449	8 572	9 412	8 572

ARMENIAN SSR

	Men	within own group	Women	within own group
Armenians	24 328	23 779	23 969	23 779
Urban	16 776	16 338	16 492	16 338
Rural	7 552	7 441	7 477	7 441
Azeris	1 228	1 208	1 223	1 208
Urban	146	135	147	135
Rural	1 082	1 073	1 076	1 073

TURKMEN SSR

	Men	within own group	Women	within own group
Turkmenians	24 645	23 198	23 770	23 198
Urban	9 300	8 331	8 769	8 331
Rural	15 345	14 867	15 001	14 867
Russians	2 672	1 944	2 987	1 944
Urban	2 615	1 910	2 896	1 910
Rural	57	34	91	34
Tatars	283	114	375	114
Urban	264	109	343	109
Rural	19	5	32	5

ESTONIAN SSR

	Men	within own group	Women	within own group
Estonians	6 914	6 318	6 936	6 318
Urban	5 362	4 859	5 397	4 859
Rural	1 552	1 459	1 539	1 459
Russians	4 526	3 440	4 727	3 440
Urban	4 270	3 273	4 452	3 273
Rural	256	167	275	167

Source: **Naselenie SSSR 1988,** s. 205-321.

Managers from titular ethnic group of Republics as percentage of all managers of enterprises and organisations in various economic sectors*, 1 January 1989

	Ethnic group	% of all managers
Russian SFSR	Russians	77.3
Karelian ASSR	Karelians	9.0
Komi ASSR	Komi	18.3
Mari ASSR	Mari	26.4
Mordvin ASSR	Mordovians	37.9
Chuvash ASSR	Chuvash	59.2
Kalmyk ASSR	Kalmyks	48.1
Tatar ASSR	Tatars	64.1
Dagestan ASSR	Natives of ASSR	83.8
Kabardino-Balkar ASSR	Peoples of the title	69.8
North Osetin ASSR	Ossets	75.5
Chechen-Ingush ASSR	Peoples of the title	71.5
Bashkir ASSR	Bashkirs	24.2
Udmurt ASSR	Udmurts	30.8
Buryat ASSR	Buryats	36.7
Tuva ASSR	Tuvans	39.6
Yakut ASSR	Yakuts	38.2
Ukrainian SSR	Ukrainians	79.0
Belorussian SSR	Belorussians	77.7
Uzbek SSR	Uzbeks	67.6
Karakalpak ASSR	Karakalpaks	35.5
Kazakh SSR	Kazakhs	39.5
Georgian SSR	Georgians	89.3
Azerbaidzhan SSR	Azeris	93.8
Lithuanian SSR	Lithuanians	91.5
Moldavian SSR	Moldavians	49.8
Latvian SSR	Latvians	63.1
Kirgiz SSR	Kirgiz	55.1
Tadzhik SSR	Tadzhiks	66.3
Armenian SSR	Armenians	99.4
Turkmen SSR	Turkmenians	71.8
Estonian SSR	Estonians	82.2

* Industry, agriculture, transport, communications and construction.

Source: AiF 1989, 2, s. 5.

Employees from titular ethnic group of Union Republics as percentage of all employees in various economic sectors, 1 June 1987

Key: Column 1 Industry
                 2 Agriculture (excluding collective farms)
                 3 Transport and communications
                 4 Construction
                 5 Trade and public catering

| | Sectors | | | | |
	1	2	3	4	5
Russian SFSR	83	75	85	78	84
Ukrainian SSR	68	79	71	69	73
Belorussian SSR	77	89	78	76	81
Uzbek SSR	53	76	55	50	66
Kazakh SSR	21	52	28	21	29
Georgian SSR	61	77	68	70	70
Azerbaidzhan SSR	69	90	74	73	78
Lithuanian SSR	71	84	67	81	79
Moldavian SSR	48	79	54	52	55
Latvian SSR	38	69	38	46	49
Kirgiz SSR	25	69	35	26	34
Tadzhik SSR	48	63	57	48	61
Armenian SSR	93	85	96	95	94
Turkmen SSR	53	81	48	54	65
Estonian SSR	43	84	47	61	62

Table continues on next page.

Table continues

Column   6 Housing, community provisions and non-productive
          services for the population
        7 Health care, physical culture and social security
        8 Education
        9 Culture and art
       10 Science and scientific services

| | Sectors | | | | |
	6	7	8	9	10
Russian SFSR	85	83	81	83	85
Ukrainian SSR	68	68	74	70	59
Belorussian SSR	77	76	74	72	58
Uzbek SSR	55	64	69	63	39
Kazakh SSR	23	38	43	42	25
Georgian SSR	77	77	85	84	77
Azerbaidzhan SSR	76	88	80	79	60
Lithuanian SSR	80	80	84	83	64
Moldavian SSR	51	62	58	56	37
Latvian SSR	45	53	59	75	42
Kirgiz SSR	30	46	43	46	27
Tadzhik SSR	56	50	58	56	31
Armenian SSR	89	97	94	97	94
Turkmen SSR	53	62	67	70	48
Estonian SSR	67	67	71	84	67

Table continues on next page.

Table continues

Column   11 Apparatus of government
         12 Titular ethnic group as percentage of Union
            Republic's population

	Column 11	12
Russian SFSR	83	82.6
Ukrainian SSR	73	73.6
Belorussian SSR	74	79.4
Uzbek SSR	57	68.7
Kazakh SSR	40	36.0
Georgian SSR	78	68.8
Azerbaidzhan SSR	78	78.1
Lithuanian SSR	86	80.0
Moldavian SSR	51	63.9
Latvian SSR	56	53.7
Kirgiz SSR	42	47.9
Tadzhik SSR	51	58.8
Armenian SSR	96	89.7
Turkmen SSR	51	68.4
Estonian SSR	72	64.7

Source: **Vestnik Statistiki** 1990, 1, s. 8.

Permanent pre-school units: by language of tuition in Union Republics, at end of 1988 (percentages)

Key: Column   1 Russian
                2 Non-Russian
                3 Russian and non-Russian

	Columns 1	2	3
USSR	**74.0**	**23.2**	**2.8**
Russian SFSR	95.8	2.8	1.4
Ukrainian SSR	40.2	58.2	1.6
Belorussian SSR	72.7	19.3	8.0
Uzbek SSR	27.7	68.1	4.2
Kazakh SSR	86.4	11.9	1.7
Georgian SSR	8.8	81.6	9.6
Azerbaidzhan SSR	17.5	63.0	19.5
Lithuanian SSR	9.1	85.9	5.0
Moldavian SSR	31.7	53.4	14.9
Latvian SSR	38.8	43.7	17.5
Kirgiz SSR	61.3	36.5	2.2
Tadzhik SSR	51.0	39.4	9.6
Armenian SSR	5.7	78.2	16.1
Turkmen SSR	39.7	59.0	1.3
Estonian SSR	27.1	67.3	5.6

Source: **Narodnoe obrazovanie, s. 41.**

Permanent pre-school units where non ethnic Russian children study in the Russian language: by Union Republic, at end of 1988

Key: Column   1 Number of units
                   2 As % of all pre-school units
                   3 Non ethnic Russian children (thousands)

	Columns 1	2	3
USSR	**25 136**	**17.2**	**1 152**
Russian SFSR	4 409	5.2	147
Ukrainian SSR	12 284	52.0	592
Belorussian SSR	-	-	-
Uzbek SSR	2 164	24.0	111
Kazakh SSR	1 313	15.8	68
Georgian SSR	816	34.7	32
Azerbaidzhan SSR	764	36.8	29
Lithuanian SSR	35	1.9	1
Moldavian SSR	1 397	61.4	65
Latvian SSR	425	39.8	15
Kirgiz SSR	160	10.2	7
Tadzhik SSR	225	25.2	20
Armenian SSR	748	60.9	41
Turkmen SSR	379	25.4	24
Estonian SSR	17	2.3	0.5

Source: **Narodnoe obrazovanie**, s. 41.

Pupils taught in Russian and other languages in day general education schools: by Union Republic, 1980/81 and 1988/89*

Language	Thousands 1980	1988	% of all pupils 1980	1988
RUSSIAN SFSR				
Russian	16 832	18 881	97.0	98.2
Bashkir	68	44	0.4	0.2
Buryat	6	14	0.04	0.1
Languages of peoples of Dagestan	59	51	0.3	0.3
Komi-Permyak	1	–	0.00	–
Mari	14	12	0.1	0.1
Mordva	12	4	0.1	0.02
Tatar	217	98	1.3	0.5
Tuva	38	29	0.2	0.1
Udmurt	2	2	0.01	0.01
Chechen	1	–	0.01	–
Chuvash	58	37	0.3	0.2
Yakut	46	54	0.3	0.3
UKRAINIAN SSR				
Ukrainian	3 544	3 228	54.6	47.5
Russian	2 895	3 521	44.5	51.8
Moldavian	41	34	0.6	0.5
Hungarian	19	17	0.3	0.2
Polish	0.3	0.3	0.01	0.00
BELORUSSIAN SSR				
Belorussian	488	298	35.0	20.8
Russian	907	1 140	65.0	79.2
UZBEK SSR				
Uzbek	2 964	3 422	77.7	76.8
Russian	519	668	13.6	15.0
Karakalpak	96	108	2.5	2.4
Kazakh	117	130	3.0	2.9
Tadzhik	98	102	2.6	2.3
Turkmen	14	16	0.4	0.4
Kirgiz	6	7	0.2	0.2

Language	Thousands		% of all pupils	
	1980	1988	1980	1988

KAZAKH SSR

Language				
Kazakh	965	931	33.0	30.2
Russian	1 879	2 079	64.2	67.4
Uzbek	62	60	2.1	1.9
Uighur	17	14	0.6	0.4
Tadzhik	2	2	0.1	0.1

GEORGIAN SSR

Language				
Georgian	599	574	67.6	66.6
Russian	187	204	21.1	23.6
Azeri	54	46	6.0	5.4
Armenian	40	31	4.5	3.6
Abkhaz	4	5	0.5	0.6
Ossete	2	2	0.3	0.2

AZERBAIDZHAN SSR

Language				
Azeri	1 180	1 062	83.4	79.5
Russian	202	247	14.2	18.5
Armenian	31	25	2.2	1.9
Georgian	2	2	0.2	0.1

LITHUANIAN SSR

Language				
Lithuanian	444	420	84.6	82.2
Russian	67	81	12.8	15.8
Polish	13	10	2.6	2.0

MOLDAVIAN SSR

Language				
Moldavian	407	416	63.1	59.1
Russian	239	288	36.9	40.9

LATVIAN SSR

Language				
Latvian	172	174	55.9	52.4
Russian	136	157	44.1	47.6

Language	Thousands 1980	1988	% of all pupils 1980	1988
KIRGIZ SSR				
Kirgiz	433	474	52.7	52.4
Russian	279	323	34.0	35.7
Uzbek	107	106	13.1	11.7
Tadzhik	2	2	0.2	0.2
TADZHIK SSR				
Tadzhik	659	793	64.4	66.0
Russian	103	117	10.0	9.7
Uzbek	246	274	24.1	22.9
Kirgiz	11	13	1.1	1.1
Turkmen	4	4	0.4	0.3
Kazakh	0.03	0.05	0.00	0.00
ARMENIAN SSR				
Armenian	446	474	79.8	80.5
Russian	66	88	11.8	15.1
Azeri	47	26	8.4	4.4
TURKMEN SSR				
Turkmen	548	621	78.0	76.9
Russian	107	130	15.2	16.0
Uzbek	39	49	5.6	6.1
Kazakh	8	7	1.2	1.0
ESTONIAN SSR				
Estonian	129	138	67.5	63.5
Russian	62	79	32.5	36.5

* At start of academic year, excluding pupils in schools for mentally and physically handicapped children.

In the general education schools of the country there were 46 languages of tuition in 1980 and 44 in 1988.

Source: **Narodnoe obrazovanie,** s. 88-91.

Students in specialised secondary education from titular ethnic group of Union Republics, 1984/85

(Start of academic year)	Thousands	% of all students
Russian SFSR Russians	2 003.2	80
Ukrainian SSR Ukrainians	583.5	72
Belorussian SSR Belorussians	124.8	77
Uzbek SSR Uzbeks	177.6	65
Kazakh SSR Kazakhs	129.2	46
Georgian SSR Georgians	46.6	87
Azerbaidzhan SSR Azeris	66.4	85
Lithuanian SSR Lithuanians	52.9	85
Moldavian SSR Moldavians	37.5	62
Latvian SSR Latvians	19.5	47
Kirgiz SSR Kirgiz	29.4	57
Tadzhik SSR Tadzhiks	22.0	54
Armenian SSR Armenians	46.2	97
Turkmen SSR Turkmenians	25.8	70
Estonian SSR Estonians	13.1	58

Source: **Narodnoe obrazovanie**, s. 175.

Students in higher education from titular ethnic group of Union Republics, 1984/85 (start of academic year)

	Thousands	% of all students
Russian SFSR Russians	2 463.3	81
Ukrainian SSR Ukrainians	576.3	66
Belorussian SSR Belorussians	130.3	70
Uzbek SSR Uzbeks	195.1	67
Kazakh SSR Kazakhs	152.5	54
Georgian SSR Georgians	78.0	88
Azerbaidzhan SSR Azeris	91.1	84
Lithuanian SSR Lithuanians	59.2	86
Moldavian SSR Moldavians	34.1	64
Latvian SSR Latvians	23.3	51
Kirgiz SSR Kirgiz	37.4	63
Tadzhik SSR Tadzhiks	35.9	61
Armenian SSR Armenians	56.6	98
Turkmen SSR Turkmenians	30.3	78
Estonian SSR Estonians	18.0	73

Source: **Narodnoe obrazovanie,** s. 226.

Students in specialised secondary education by titular ethnic group of Republics and autonomous oblasti, 1974/75 and 1984/85* (thousands)

	1974/75	1984/85
Total	**4 477.8**	**4 512.4**
Russians	2 719.7	2 409.6
Ukrainians	656.0	702.3
Belorussians	157.0	158.7
Uzbeks	106.7	197.2
Kazakhs	86.0	169.2
Georgians	44.8	52.7
Azeris	60.6	77.9
Lithuanians	59.4	54.9
Moldavians	33.7	44.8
Latvians	20.5	20.3
Kirgiz	17.7	36.0
Tadzhiks	20.8	30.6
Armenians	66.9	63.9
Turkmenians	16.4	30.4
Estonians	15.4	13.8
Abkhazians	1.0	1.4
Balkars	1.2	1.1
Bashkirs	20.1	30.0
Buryats	8.1	9.6
Ingush	2.4	3.5
Kabardians	4.5	6.4
Kalmyks	3.6	4.4
Karakalpaks	5.3	10.2
Karelians	2.5	1.6
Komi, Komi-Permyaks	9.3	7.2
Mari	8.0	10.1
Mordovians	18.5	18.7
Peoples of Dagestan	21.8	31.7
Ossets	7.9	9.2
Tatars	114.1	132.2
Tuvans	2.0	4.0
Udmurts	10.1	11.1
Chechen	7.5	9.8
Chuvash	24.2	32.0
Yakuts	6.1	7.9
Adygeians	2.3	2.9
Altais	1.4	1.5
Jews	35.5	17.9
Karachais	1.5	2.2
Khakass	1.4	1.3
Cherkess	0.7	1.0

* At start of academic year.

Source: **Narodnoe obrazovanie**, s. 174.

Students in higher education by titular ethnic group of Republics and autonomous oblasti, 1974/75 and 1984/85* (thousands)

	1974/75	1984/85
Total	4 751.1	5 280.0
Russians	2 834.8	2 949.3
Ukrainians	640.0	710.7
Belorussians	141.2	175.9
Uzbeks	158.8	216.1
Kazakhs	114.2	183.0
Georgians	82.7	99.9
Azeris	86.4	110.5
Lithuanians	54.1	62.6
Moldavians	31.6	40.5
Latvians	22.7	25.3
Kirgiz	29.2	45.2
Tadzhiks	32.4	45.3
Armenians	79.7	91.2
Turkmenians	22.8	36.0
Estonians	17.8	19.6
Abkhazians	1.8	2.8
Balkars	1.8	2.2
Bashkirs	17.2	24.8
Buryats	13.2	17.0
Ingush	2.1	4.3
Kabardians	5.8	7.1
Kalmyks	3.8	5.5
Karakalpaks	4.1	7.1
Karelians	1.9	1.7
Komi, Komi-Permyaks	6.2	6.8
Mari	6.1	8.5
Mordovians	12.5	14.8
Peoples of Dagestan	22.0	33.6
Ossets	13.0	15.5
Tatars	99.8	124.2
Tuvans	1.9	3.6
Udmurts	7.4	10.2
Chechens	5.9	12.5
Chuvash	18.9	26.6
Yakuts	6.6	11.1
Adygeians	2.6	2.9
Altais	1.0	1.5
Jews	76.2	41.0
Karachais	3.0	3.3
Khakass	1.2	1.8
Cherkess	1.2	1.2

* At start of academic year.

Source: **Narodnoe obrazovanie, s. 225.**

Level of educational attainment, 1970–1989
per 1 000 population*, (census data)

	1970	1979	1989
Population aged 10 and over			
Higher and secondary	483	638	738
Higher	42	68	98
Secondary (full and incomplete)	441	570	640
Employed population			
Higher and secondary	653	805	921
Higher	65	100	143
Secondary (full and incomplete)	588	705	778

* With higher and secondary education.

Source: **Narodnoe obrazovanie**, s. 9.

Level of educational attainment of urban and rural
population, 1970–1989

	1970	1979	1989
Per 1 000 urban population aged 10 and over*			
Higher and secondary	592	723	792
Higher	62	93	126
Secondary (full and incomplete)	530	630	666
Per 1 000 rural population aged 10 and over*			
Higher and secondary	332	492	629
Higher	14	25	41
Secondary (full and incomplete)	318	467	588

* With higher and secondary education.

Source: **Narodnoe obrazovanie**, s. 9.

Level of educational attainment of men and women, 1970-1989 per 1 000 population aged ten and over*

	1970	1979	1989
Men			
Higher and secondary	522	685	775
Higher	48	75	102
Secondary (full and incomplete)	474	610	673
Women			
Higher and secondary	452	597	706
Higher	37	62	94
Secondary (full and incomplete)	415	535	612

* With higher and secondary education.

Source: **Narodnoe obrazovanie, s. 9.**

Level of educational attainment of employed men and women, 1970-1989 per 1 000 population*

	1970	1979	1989
Employed men			
Higher and secondary	654	810	914
Higher	68	102	138
Secondary (full and incomplete)	586	708	776
Employed women			
Higher and secondary	651	801	927
Higher	62	98	148
Secondary (full and incomplete)	589	703	779

* With higher and secondary education.

Source: **Narodnoe obrazovanie, s. 9.**

Level of educational attainment: by Union Republic, 1989

Key: Column 1 Higher and secondary education
                   2 Completed higher
                   3 Full secondary
                   4 Incomplete secondary

Columns	1	2	3	4
Per 1 000 persons over 15 with education				
USSR	812	108	504	200
Russian SFSR	806	113	483	210
Ukrainian SSR	794	104	506	184
Belorussian SSR	770	108	494	168
Uzbek SSR	867	92	577	198
Kazakh SSR	838	99	541	198
Georgian SSR	877	151	574	152
Azerbaidzhan SSR	878	105	581	192
Lithuanian SSR	753	106	466	181
Moldavian SSR	755	87	464	204
Latvian SSR	838	115	489	234
Kirgiz SSR	842	94	564	184
Tadzhik SSR	837	75	551	211
Armenian SSR	901	138	577	186
Turkmen SSR	864	83	568	213
Estonian SSR	801	117	474	210
Per 1 000 employed persons with education				
USSR	921	143	617	161
Russian SFSR	915	146	591	178
Ukrainian SSR	928	139	648	141
Belorussian SSR	899	144	623	132
Uzbek SSR	948	127	694	127
Kazakh SSR	926	131	648	147
Georgian SSR	942	199	639	104
Azerbaidzhan SSR	943	148	666	129
Lithuanian SSR	879	145	588	146
Moldavian SSR	884	114	584	186
Latvian SSR	925	146	584	195
Kirgiz SSR	930	128	686	116
Tadzhik SSR	916	111	662	143
Armenian SSR	953	192	627	134
Turkmen SSR	935	114	682	139
Estonian SSR	892	150	564	178

Source: **Ekonomika i zhizn** 1990, 10, s. 16.

**Level of educational attainment among working youth
up to age 30, 1980–1987** (percentages)

	1980	1985	1987
Higher	8.5	9.7	10.2
Incomplete higher	1.8	1.7	1.8
Specialised secondary	17.4	19.3	19.6
General secondary	52.6	60.3	61.3
Incomplete secondary	19.7	9.0	7.1

Source: **Nar. khoz. SSSR 1988**, s. 46.

**Level of educational attainment among working youth
up to age 30: by Union Republic, November 1987**
(percentages)

Key: Column 1 Higher
2 Incomplete higher
3 Specialised secondary
4 General secondary
5 Without full secondary

	Columns				
	1	2	3	4	5
USSR	**10.2**	**1.8**	**19.6**	**61.3**	**7.1**
Russian SFSR	10.4	1.8	20.8	58.8	8.2
Ukrainian SSR	9.9	1.8	19.6	64.0	4.7
Belorussian SSR	10.7	1.7	19.4	64.9	3.3
Uzbek SSR	9.7	2.3	16.0	64.7	7.3
Kazakh SSR	9.5	1.8	19.2	62.1	7.4
Georgian SSR	13.8	3.2	16.9	62.7	3.4
Azerbaidzhan SSR	10.3	3.0	12.4	68.6	5.7
Lithuanian SSR	11.8	1.8	23.5	58.5	4.4
Moldavian SSR	8.6	1.4	17.4	64.7	7.9
Latvian SSR	10.7	2.0	19.8	56.9	10.6
Kirgiz SSR	9.4	1.6	16.2	68.5	4.3
Tadzhik SSR	9.1	1.3	12.4	69.6	7.6
Armenian SSR	13.2	1.9	15.3	62.3	7.3
Turkmen SSR	8.1	1.4	14.8	67.1	8.6
Estonian SSR	11.4	1.5	20.9	53.7	12.5

Source: **Narodnoe obrazovanie**, s. 10.

Specialists* with higher and specialised secondary education employed in the national economy: by Union Republic, 1987 (thousands)

	Total	Higher	Specialised secondary
All specialists			
USSR	35 692.5	15 530.9	20 161.6
Russian SFSR	20 157.8	8 468.5	11 689.3
Ukrainian SSR	6 639.2	2 868.7	3 770.5
Belorussian SSR	1 360.2	604.0	756.2
Uzbek SSR	1 536.0	743.3	792.7
Kazakh SSR	1 787.9	753.1	1 034.8
Georgian SSR	618.8	367.7	251.1
Azerbaidzhan SSR	624.8	336.1	288.7
Lithuanian SSR	537.7	228.2	309.5
Moldavian SSR	472.7	206.2	266.5
Latvian SSR	369.3	166.0	203.3
Kirgiz SSR	367.5	172.0	195.5
Tadzhik SSR	327.0	169.3	157.7
Armenian SSR	393.2	218.6	174.6
Turkmen SSR	268.8	127.0	141.8
Estonian SSR	231.6	102.2	129.4
Women specialists			
USSR	21 617.2	8 470.4	13 146.8
Russian SFSR	12 576.6	4 768.6	7 808.0
Ukrainian SSR	4 000.2	1 544.9	2 455.3
Belorussian SSR	840.6	337.1	503.5
Uzbek SSR	787.0	344.8	442.2
Kazakh SSR	1 113.4	426.7	686.7
Georgian SSR	338.2	185.7	152.5
Azerbaidzhan SSR	282.1	141.6	140.5
Lithuanian SSR	331.1	131.5	199.6
Moldavian SSR	292.1	115.5	176.6
Latvian SSR	229.6	97.4	132.2
Kirgiz SSR	215.9	95.9	120.0
Tadzhik SSR	139.0	62.6	76.4
Armenian SSR	207.5	106.4	101.1
Turkmen SSR	124.9	53.3	71.6
Estonian SSR	139.0	58.4	80.6

* Russian: **spetsialisty.**

Source: **Nar. khoz. SSSR 1988**, s. 48-9.

139

Specialists* with higher and specialised secondary education working as blue-collar workers: by Union Republic, 1980-1987** (thousands)

	1980	1985	1987
With higher education			
USSR	**203.3**	**484.2**	**578.8**
Russian SFSR	126.4	286.4	350.0
Ukrainian SSR	39.4	101.2	116.2
Belorussian SSR	6.3	15.5	18.4
Uzbek SSR	4.2	12.8	13.5
Kazakh SSR	10.0	22.8	29.9
Georgian SSR	1.1	3.2	4.4
Azerbaidzhan SSR	3.3	8.5	7.0
Lithuanian SSR	1.8	5.5	7.2
Moldavian SSR	1.7	4.5	5.9
Latvian SSR	1.8	6.4	7.7
Kirgiz SSR	2.1	4.3	4.3
Tadzhik SSR	1.4	3.8	3.4
Armenian SSR	1.2	2.5	3.1
Turkmen SSR	0.8	2.5	2.6
Estonian SSR	1.8	4.3	5.2
With specialised secondary education			
USSR	**1 890.2**	**3 831.6**	**4 161.2**
Russian SFSR	1 149.0	2 279.2	2 485.6
Ukrainian SSR	395.1	835.2	900.2
Belorussian SSR	72.3	148.3	161.8
Uzbek SSR	35.4	84.2	87.0
Kazakh SSR	74.0	155.2	179.4
Georgian SSR	5.0	19.9	20.8
Azerbaidzhan SSR	21.0	35.0	32.0
Lithuanian SSR	30.6	66.2	77.4
Moldavian SSR	20.1	38.2	45.1
Latvian SSR	18.5	42.1	45.8
Kirgiz SSR	17.3	28.6	26.6
Tadzhik SSR	12.7	26.0	20.1
Armenian SSR	13.0	24.5	27.6
Turkmen SSR	8.7	15.5	14.9
Estonian SSR	17.5	33.5	36.9

* Russian: **spetsialisty.**   ** At mid-November.

Source: **Nar. khoz. SSSR 1988**, s. 52-3.

Students in higher and specialised secondary education: by Union Republic, 1970–1989* per 10 000 population

	1970/1	1980/1	1985/6	1988/9
Higher education				
USSR	**188**	**196**	**185**	**174**
Russian SFSR	204	219	206	190
Ukrainian SSR	170	176	167	166
Belorussian SSR	154	183	182	175
Uzbek SSR	192	172	154	154
Kazakh SSR	151	173	171	166
Georgian SSR	189	169	169	161
Azerbaidzhan SSR	191	173	158	141
Lithuanian SSR	180	206	181	178
Moldavian SSR	124	128	128	125
Latvian SSR	171	186	167	164
Kirgiz SSR	162	152	144	132
Tadzhik SSR	149	142	118	114
Armenian SSR	214	186	163	166
Turkmen SSR	131	124	119	112
Estonian SSR	161	172	153	153
Specialised secondary education				
USSR	**180**	**173**	**161**	**152**
Russian SFSR	199	190	172	163
Ukrainian SSR	168	160	159	154
Belorussian SSR	161	168	160	146
Uzbek SSR	134	147	152	145
Kazakh SSR	165	176	173	161
Georgian SSR	112	105	103	90
Azerbaidzhan SSR	135	127	114	96
Lithuanian SSR	206	198	170	150
Moldavian SSR	143	147	146	130
Latvian SSR	163	166	156	148
Kirgiz SSR	139	135	126	114
Tadzhik SSR	118	100	86	82
Armenian SSR	185	166	143	135
Turkmen SSR	129	118	113	101
Estonian SSR	175	161	144	130

* At start of academic year.

Source: **Nar. khoz. SSSR 1988**, s. 198.

Students completing higher and specialised secondary education: by Union Republic, 1970–1988 per 10 000 population

	1970	1980	1985	1988
Higher education				
USSR	**26**	**31**	**31**	**27**
Russian SFSR	28	33	33	30
Ukrainian SSR	25	30	30	27
Belorussian SSR	23	32	32	30
Uzbek SSR	28	28	27	21
Kazakh SSR	21	26	28	24
Georgian SSR	26	29	31	25
Azerbaidzhan SSR	27	29	31	25
Lithuanian SSR	23	30	32	25
Moldavian SSR	19	21	22	19
Latvian SSR	20	27	27	23
Kirgiz SSR	21	23	25	20
Tadzhik SSR	20	23	22	16
Armenian SSR	31	35	34	27
Turkmen SSR	20	20	22	17
Estonian SSR	21	25	23	17
Specialised secondary education				
USSR	**43**	**48**	**45**	**43**
Russian SFSR	46	52	46	44
Ukrainian SSR	44	46	47	45
Belorussian SSR	40	49	46	44
Uzbek SSR	35	40	44	47
Kazakh SSR	37	47	51	47
Georgian SSR	29	32	31	30
Azerbaidzhan SSR	35	37	37	36
Lithuanian SSR	41	56	47	42
Moldavian SSR	33	43	41	40
Latvian SSR	37	43	39	37
Kirgiz SSR	32	35	37	34
Tadzhik SSR	27	28	25	25
Armenian SSR	38	52	48	48
Turkmen SSR	29	30	34	31
Estonian SSR	35	39	35	32

Source: **Nar. khoz. SSSR 1988**, s. 204.

142

Students admitted to higher and specialised secondary education: by type of study, 1970-1988 (thousands)

	1970	1980	1985	1988
Higher education				
Total	911.5	1 051.9	1 104.0	1 075.8
Day divisions	500.5	639.9	649.9	661.9
Evening	127.4	134.3	137.5	108.7
Distance learning	283.6	277.7	316.6	305.2
Specialised secondary education				
Total	1 338.4	1 457.0	1 513.0	1 459.6*
Day divisions	837.0	946.2	979.9	952.4
Evening	159.7	136.9	122.3	101.6
Distance learning	341.7	373.9	410.8	405.6

* Includes 533 700 persons with incomplete secondary education and 925 900 persons with general secondary education.

Source: **Nar. khoz. SSSR 1988**, s. 200.

Students completing higher and specialised secondary education: by type of study, 1970-1988 (thousands)

	1970	1980	1985	1988
Higher education				
Total	630.8	817.3	858.9	775.2
Day divisions	334.8	518.0	549.1	447.1
Evening	82.1	85.3	83.1	77.7
Distance learning	213.9	214.0	226.7	250.4
Specialised secondary education				
Total	1 033.3	1 274.7	1 246.6	1 237.3
Day divisions	602.7	834.1	801.8	789.3
Evening	161.5	113.4	96.4	88.5
Distance learning	269.1	327.2	348.4	359.5

Source: **Nar. khoz. SSSR 1988**, s. 202.

143

Students admitted to higher and specialised secondary education: by sectoral affiliation of their institutions, 1970-1988 (thousands)

	1970	1980	1985	1988
Higher education				
Total	911.5	1 051.9	1 104.0	1 075.8
Industry and construction	367.9	421.8	437.0	407.4
Agriculture	85.0	103.2	110.1	105.8
Transport and communications	48.1	56.9	59.1	55.7
Economics and law	72.6	80.1	81.0	69.4
Health care, physical culture and sport	60.5	69.3	69.7	72.8
Education	269.0	310.7	337.2	354.7
Art and cinematography	8.4	9.9	9.9	10.0
Specialised secondary education				
Total	1 338.4	1 457.0	1 513.0	1 459.6
Industry and construction	548.0	547.3	550.7	511.7
Agriculture	215.3	245.9	242.8	216.0
Transport and communications	109.6	115.0	113.4	105.3
Economics and law	175.0	199.7	193.3	183.6
Health care, physical culture and sport	142.7	169.4	191.4	213.3
Education	117.1	148.1	193.8	203.3
Art and cinematography	30.7	31.6	27.6	26.4

Source: **Nar. khoz. SSSR 1988**, s. 201.

Students completing higher and specialised secondary education: by sectoral affiliation of their institutions, 1970-1988 (thousands)

	1970	1980	1985	1988
Higher education				
Total	630.8	817.3	858.9	775.2
Industry and construction	214.2	303.0	313.8	263.7
Agriculture	68.7	75.3	83.4	77.4
Transport and communications	28.2	40.6	42.4	39.2
Economics and law	50.9	66.3	71.3	69.6
Health care, physical culture and sport	42.9	60.4	65.1	63.2
Education	219.2	263.3	273.7	253.3
Art and cinematography	6.7	8.4	9.2	8.8
Specialised secondary education				
Total	1 033.3	1 274.7	1 246.6	1 237.3
Industry and construction	418.2	472.1	436.2	419.6
Agriculture	144.4	209.5	198.7	190.4
Transport and communications	78.9	104.4	95.7	82.3
Economics and law	132.8	187.4	184.7	171.9
Health care, physical culture and sport	135.6	151.8	163.4	172.0
Education	105.3	122.4	142.1	177.1
Art and cinematography	18.1	27.1	25.8	24.0

Source: **Nar. khoz. SSSR 1988**, s. 203.

The Environment

The item which follows consists of extracts from a special report published in **Pravda**.

There exists a "black book" - if one may call it that - in which are listed the cities which have high levels of pollution. Until recently all this information was kept on the "secret" list so that the ecological crisis situation could be rectified without causing panic. Instead of the situation improving, however, huge obstructions piled up...

The Minister of Health of the Russian SFSR and corresponding member of the USSR Academy of Medical Science, A. I. Potapov, opened a safe and took out formerly classified material on the actual ecological situation in the territory of Russia (comparable documents on other republics exist in the Union Republic Ministries of Health). He said:

The ecological situation in various regions of the country is taking on a threatening character. We will never have any success in the prevention of disease if pollution of the environment does not cease. In a number of regions of the country clean air is becoming a rarity. And while we medical staff do not tire of repeating 'in order to live longer you must eat less', it is hardly likely that any amongst us will risk saying 'in order to live longer you must breathe less'.

The ecological "black book" for the Russian SFSR lists 36 towns:

Angarsk, Arkhangelsk, Astrakhan, Barnaul, Berezniki, Blagoveshchensk, Bratsk, Volgograd, Volzhski (Volgograd oblast), Grozny, Gorki, Irkutsk, Kaliningrad (city of the oblast), Kemerovo, Komsomolsk-na-Amur, Krasnoyarsk, Kuibyshev, Kurgan, Lipetsk, Magnitogorsk, Nizhni Tagil, Novokuznetsk, Novotroitsk, Norilsk, Omsk, Perm, Saratov, Sverdlovsk, Tolyatti, Tyumen, Usole-Sibirskoe, Ufa, Khabarovsk, Chelyabinsk, Shelekhov, Yuzhno-Sakhalinsk.

The atmosphere in the residential zones of these towns is full of noxious substances in concentrations which exceed the permitted levels by from 4 to 46 times.

As in the past, untreated waste water from domestic-communal and industrial sources is discharged into open reservoirs of water. In the Russian SFSR as a whole, 8.1% of water samples from municipal mains and 14.2% of samples from industrial ministries' mains exceeded the all-Union level permitted for bacteria and 19.2% and 20.4% of samples, respectively, exceeded the level permitted for chemical substances. This applies particularly to Astrakhan, Arkhangelsk, Krasnodar, Kemerov, Sverdlovsk, Perm, Krasnoyarsk and Murmansk.

In towns and urban settlements about 27 million tonnes of
solid household waste accumulate each year. The position
has deteriorated in Smolensk, Klin and Saransk, where
electric light bulb factories, for as long as they have
been functioning, have taken waste containing mercury to
the dump or to disused quarries. Now mercury is being
discovered in water, in soil and in the air.

In the diet of the Republic's population there is a high
proportion of bread, potatoes and sugar. A shortage of
meat, fish, dairy products and fruit leads to the dietary
calory intake exceeding the calories expended in activity.
As a consequence, 30% of the population is overweight, and
the number of cases of atherosclerosis, ischaemic heart
disease and diabetes mellitus has doubled. [The base year
is not given.]

The low quality of food products gives cause for alarm.
11.7% of samples of food failed to meet the standards
required; the proportions were 3.7% for dairy products,
12.8% for fish and 12.2% for confectioneries. In 1988, to
give an example, beetroots, carrots and cabbages contained
nitrates in amounts several times higher than the
prescribed limits. These are the norms which, with the
blessing of the USSR's Chief Medical Officer for
Environmental Health, were raised by two to three times on
30 May.

Source: **Pravda** 1989, 1 sentyabrya, s. 8.

******

In the USSR during the first half of 1989 discharges of
noxious substances into the atmosphere from stationary
sources amounted to 29 million tonnes. By comparison with
the corresponding period of the previous year discharges
decreased by 1.8 million tonnes. The entry of pollutants
into the atmosphere declined in Novokuznetsk, Lipetsk,
Nizhni Tagil, Dneprodzerzhinsk and a number of other towns.

Over nine thousand industrial enterprises increased their
discharges of noxious substances by 1.2 million tonnes.
Thus in Grozny thirteen works increased discharges by 9 000
tonnes despite an overall reduction of 3 000 tonnes, and
similarly in Donetsk sixty works increased their discharges
by 2 000 tonnes despite an overall reduction of 14 000
tonnes. The entry of noxious substances into the atmosphere
from industrial enterprises rose in Arkhangelsk, Bratsk and
Chimkent.

Some reduction in the discharge of noxious substances in 1988 did not improve the ecological situation of certain towns. The annual average concentration of benzpyrene exceeded the maximum permitted norms in Frunze by 14 times, in Novokuznetsk by 12 times, in Magnitogorsk by 11 times, in Donetsk by 8 times, and in Kemerovo and Alma-Ata by 7 times. The concentration of formaldehyde exceeded the norm in Dushanbe by 4 times, in Grozny by 9 times and in Zaporozhe it was twice the norm. The concentration of ammonia was 5 times higher than the norm in Rustavi and 4 times higher in Nizhni Tagil.

Towns with a critical level of atmospheric pollution by industry, 1988 and first half of 1989

	1st ½ of 1989 0 000 tonnes	1988 0 000 tonnes	1988 figs as % of 1987
Alma-Ata	24	46	96
Arkhangelsk	52	85	102
Bratsk	93	158	91
Grozny	138	298	97
Donetsk	86	178	92
Dushanbe	13	31	82
Erevan	27	51	71
Zaporozhe	127	267	93
Irkutsk	43	94	105
Kemerovo	60	122	91
Kiev	29	70	75
Magnitogorsk	412	849	97
Nizhni Tagil	310	641	94
Novokuznetsk	399	833	93
Rustavi	58	130	97
Fergana	73	140	91
Frunze	40	74	85
Chelyabinsk	192	427	96
Chimkent	56	109	103

Industrial pollution of atmosphere in USSR

	29 016	61 716	96

Source: **Stat. Press-Byull.** 1989, 10, s. 50-1.

Effluent discharged into natural reservoirs after purification to the norm: by Union Republic, 1985–1988

	1985	1986	1987	1988
Million cubic metres				
USSR	**22 374**	**22 968**	**18 470**	**12 208**
Russian SFSR	13 986	14 331	9 561	4 576
Ukrainian SSR	4 536	4 749	4 858	3 975
Belorussian SSR	728	812	850	895
Uzbek SSR	892	936	1 012	482
Kazakh SSR	327	292	316	278
Georgian SSR	279	265	230	309
Azerbaidzhan SSR	173	206	199	252
Lithuanian SSR	88	95	116	123
Moldavian SSR	223	155	171	197
Latvian SSR	118	125	113	109
Kirgiz SSR	183	152	171	177
Tadzhik SSR	187	190	186	206
Armenian SSR	359	352	352	313
Turkmen SSR	21	14	12	13
Estonian SSR	274	294	323	303
As percentage of all purified effluent discharged				
USSR	**58**	**60**	**47**	**30**
Russian SFSR	54	56	36	16
Ukrainian SSR	78	80	81	62
Belorussian SSR	89	91	91	93
Uzbek SSR	68	70	72	58
Kazakh SSR	54	50	50	45
Georgian SSR	45	44	38	49
Azerbaidzhan SSR	28	33	33	42
Lithuanian SSR	21	22	28	27
Moldavian SSR	84	58	63	69
Latvian SSR	32	35	31	30
Kirgiz SSR	94	95	97	92
Tadzhik SSR	76	74	70	69
Armenian SSR	67	60	59	51
Turkmen SSR	95	95	96	100
Estonian SSR	58	60	61	60

In 1988 the volume of polluted effluent discharged into reservoirs was 28.4 million cubic kilometres. In 1987-1988 the reduction in the indicator for the discharge into reservoirs of effluent purified to the norm is mainly linked to raised quality demands by the water-protection organs.

Source: **Nar. khoz. SSSR 1988, s.** 247.

Effluent discharged into various seas and rivers after purification to the norm, 1985-1988

	1985	1986	1987	1988
Cubic kilometres				
Baltic Sea				
total	1.76	2.02	1.84	1.0
incl. Lake Ladoga	0.20	0.20	0.04	0.0
Black Sea, Sea of Azov				
total	6.66	6.93	6.62	5.78
incl. Dnieper	2.40	2.51	2.61	2.34
Don	1.67	1.78	1.53	1.02
Caspian Sea				
total	8.77	8.87	5.0	2.45
incl. Volga	7.66	7.72	3.78	1.23
Ural	0.16	0.16	0.18	0.08
As percentage of all purified effluent discharged				
Baltic Sea				
total	39	45	41	23
incl. Lake Ladoga	43	44	10	0.0
Black Sea, Sea of Azov				
total	65	67	64	51
incl. Dnieper	72	74	75	62
Don	78	80	66	41
Caspian Sea				
total	71	72	39	18
incl. Volga	76	78	36	11
Ural	80	81	82	39

Source: **Nar. khoz. SSSR 1988**, s. 247.

Effluent discharged into the Baltic Sea, Black Sea and Sea of Azov in areas of mass leisure, 1985-1988
(millions of cubic metres per year)

	1985	1987	1988
Yurmala (Latvian SSR)			
Town sewerage system	2.4	2.9	3.2
Slokski cellulose and paper-making factory	15.0	14.7	14.8
Palanga (Lithuanian SSR)			
Town sewerage system	3.0	4.1	4.8
Pryanu (Estonian SSR)			
Town sewerage system	5.1	5.7	5.5
Odessa			
Town sewerage system	201.3	123.4	99.1
Mariupol			
Town sewerage system	-	0.8	0.5
Ilich metallurgical combine	35.9	21.9	14.4

In connection with the critical sanitary situation, caused to a significant degree by the continuing discharge of polluted effluent, bathing from many seaside beaches of the towns listed was forbidden in the summer of 1988.

Source: **Nar. khoz. SSSR 1988**, s. 248.

******

Reducing the negative consequences of atmospheric pollution by noxious substances is achieved through the construction of gas-cleansing installations and equipment, removal of sources of pollution, introduction of low-emission technology, utilisation of noxious substances from gaseous emissions and the use of ecologically clean forms of energy. As a result of the introduction of measures for the protection of the atmosphere when industrial production is growing, the volume of noxious substances emitted into the atmosphere during the years 1985-1988 fell by 10%. In 1988 it amounted to 62 million tonnes.

The total of emitted pollutants consisted of 15 million tonnes of solids and 47 million tonnes of gaseous and acid substances. The latter total contained 18 million tonnes of sulphur oxides, 5 million tonnes of nitrous oxide and 15 million tonnes of carbon monoxide.

Source: **Nar. khoz. SSSR 1988**, s. 249.

Noxious substances removed or neutralised from emissions from stationary sources of air pollution: by Union Republic, 1985-1988

	1985	1986	1987	1988
Million tonnes				
USSR	**209.3**	**207.7**	**212.3**	**209.1**
Russian SFSR	123.6	123.3	123.2	122.2
Ukrainian SSR	38.4	33.8	35.5	33.8
Belorussian SSR	3.2	3.3	3.6	3.6
Uzbek SSR	2.9	3.0	3.6	3.0
Kazakh SSR	27.9	28.2	30.3	30.4
Georgian SSR	0.6	0.5	0.5	0.5
Azerbaidzhan SSR	1.0	1.0	1.0	1.0
Lithuanian SSR	1.5	1.5	1.5	1.5
Moldavian SSR	2.2	2.2	2.4	2.5
Latvian SSR	0.5	0.5	0.5	0.5
Kirgiz SSR	1.1	1.1	1.1	1.1
Tadzhik SSR	0.5	0.6	0.6	0.7
Armenian SSR	0.7	0.7	0.7	0.7
Turkmen SSR	0.3	0.3	0.3	0.4
Estonian SSR	8.5	7.7	7.5	7.2
As percentage of total noxious substances emitted from stationary sources				
USSR	**76**	**76**	**77**	**77**
Russian SFSR	76	76	76	76
Ukrainian SSR	74	74	75	75
Belorussian SSR	68	70	72	73
Uzbek SSR	65	67	73	70
Kazakh SSR	82	82	84	85
Georgian SSR	55	50	49	50
Azerbaidzhan SSR	54	51	53	56
Lithuanian SSR	77	76	75	77
Moldavian SSR	82	82	82	84
Latvian SSR	71	71	71	73
Kirgiz SSR	83	84	84	85
Tadzhik SSR	80	81	80	83
Armenian SSR	74	73	74	76
Turkmen SSR	30	32	33	40
Estonian SSR	93	93	93	93

Source: **Nar. khoz. SSSR 1988**, s. 249.

Noxious substances removed or neutralised from emissions from stationary sources of air pollution in Union Republic capitals and Leningrad, 1985-1988

	1985	1986	1987	1988
Thousand tonnes				
Moscow	647	648	656	517
Leningrad	529	537	434	419
Kiev	176	134	208	189
Minsk	184	182	192	197
Tashkent	55	61	109	98
Alma-Ata	152	155	161	158
Tbilisi	20	25	26	25
Baku	374	337	372	392
Vilnius	22	22	18	18
Kishinev	37	37	39	39
Riga	170	162	126	110
Frunze	558	538	546	454
Dushanbe	326	411	388	475
Erevan	35	44	45	41
Ashkhabad	14	12	15	12
Tallinn	194	210	221	212
As percentage of total emissions of noxious substances				
Moscow	62	62	64	62
Leningrad	67	67	63	64
Kiev	64	60	69	73
Minsk	62	61	63	64
Tashkent	48	52	68	66
Alma-Ata	74	76	77	77
Tbilisi	31	38	39	37
Baku	43	41	44	48
Vilnius	47	44	32	35
Kishinev	43	42	48	55
Riga	80	79	75	75
Frunze	86	86	86	86
Dushanbe	91	92	91	94
Erevan	36	34	38	44
Ashkhabad	39	37	45	64
Tallinn	82	82	84	84

Source: **Nar. khoz. SSSR 1988**, s. 250.

**Emissions into the atmosphere of noxious solids,
gaseous and acid substances from stationary sources
in various cities, 1988** (thousand tonnes)

Key to sub-totals: Column 1 Sulphur oxides
                           2 Nitrous oxide
                           3 Carbon monoxide

	Total	Gases, acids	Types of gases, acids 1	2	3
Alma-Ata	47	37	16	3	15
Arkhangelsk	85	65	45	5	13
Ashkhabad	7	3	0.5	0.5	1.5
Baku	421	258	18	16	49
Bratsk	158	117	21	6	85
Volgograd	228	186	38	19	60
Vilnius	34	32	19	4	5
Dzhambul	107	75	52	13	3
Donetsk	178	156	31	7	110
Dushanbe	31	19	6	4	8
Erevan	52	47	15	9	11
Zaporozhe	267	197	25	14	147
Irkutsk	94	65	29	8	26
Kiev	70	58	19	22	5
Kemerovo	122	85	26	28	21
Kishinev	31	27	11	6	5
Krasnoyarsk	259	181	39	13	115
Leningrad	236	190	74	47	41
Magnitogorsk	849	679	84	34	548
Mariupol	777	664	54	30	573
Minsk	112	102	30	17	41
Moscow	312	282	70	99	28
Mogilev	115	108	67	7	22
Novokuznetsk	833	697	90	34	562
Odessa	88	69	15	5	27
Riga	37	28	9	2	9
Tallinn	41	34	20	4	6
Tashkent	50	34	2	5	19
Tbilisi	42	35	4	3	22
Ust-Kamenogorsk	143	119	69	12	36
Ufa	304	295	72	25	36
Frunze	74	54	36	8	9
Chelyabinsk	427	333	60	29	210

One fifth of the country's urban population live in the 68
towns which have a critical level of atmospheric pollution.

Source: **Nar. khoz. SSSR 1988**, s. 251.

154

Number of recorded crimes, 1985-1988
(thousands)

	1985	1986	1987	1988
Total	**2 080.0**	**1 987.3**	**1 798.5**	**1 867.2**
Embezzlement of state or public property	317.3	269.9	254.6	280.3
Pilfering of state or public property	61.7	51.3	46.5	36.4
Crimes against personal property:	555.0	478.6	483.6	655.7
Theft	453.9	394.3	401.6	548.5
Robbery with violence	67.2	50.5	52.2	76.4
Speculation	38.2	41.0	43.4	45.2
Fraud	27.7	35.6	38.2	39.0
Illegal distillation of spirits for sale	2.7	6.2	9.8	8.2
Premeditated murder, attempted murder	18.7	14.8	14.6	16.7
Premeditated bodily harm*	73.9	56.3	54.0	66.2
Rape, attempted rape	19.4	18.5	16.8	17.7
Drug offences	30.0	40.8	32.0	23.8
Hooliganism	193.9	165.4	133.1	116.0
Public transport and motoring offences	120.1	122.9	116.4	129.0

* Grievous and less grievous bodily harm.

Source: **Nar. khoz. SSSR 1988**, s. 253.

Note on translation:

embezzlement	**khishcheniya**
pilfering	**melkie khishcheniya**
theft	**krazhi**
robbery with violence	**grabezh i razboi**

Number of persons convicted of various crimes, 1985-1988
(thousands)

	1985	1986	1987	1988
Total	**1 269.5**	**1 217.5**	**907.0**	**679.2**
Embezzlement of state or public property	192.1	166.7	115.1	89.4
Pilfering of state or public property	32.0	25.9	24.5	17.5
Crimes against personal property:				
Theft	178.2	161.3	123.4	113.9
Robbery with violence	56.8	42.5	33.2	32.0
Speculation	20.5	24.1	17.8	15.0
Fraud	13.6	18.3	15.8	13.9
Illegal distillation of spirits for sale	2.0	5.4	6.1	6.2
Premeditated murder, attempted murder	18.7	14.6	12.2	11.2
Premeditated g. b. h.*	34.8	26.4	21.4	21.1
Rape, attempted rape	22.6	20.5	18.3	16.3
Drug offences	25.6	33.6	26.8	14.4
Hooliganism	161.1	133.9	94.5	63.7
Motoring offences with serious consequences	29.4	26.5	21.9	20.3

* Grievous bodily harm.

Source: **Nar. khoz. SSSR 1988**, s. 254.

156

Number of persons convicted by the courts: by Union Republic, 1985–1988
(thousands)

	1985	1986	1987	1988
USSR	**1 269.5**	**1 217.5**	**907.0**	**679.2**
Russian SFSR	837.3	797.3	580.1	427.0
Ukrainian SSR	173.9	167.6	124.9	91.0
Belorussian SSR	38.7	33.8	25.1	21.7
Uzbek SSR	41.2	41.3	34.9	28.6
Kazakh SSR	68.7	71.6	59.4	43.9
Georgian SSR	14.1	14.6	11.3	9.4
Azerbaidzhan SSR	13.8	12.9	9.3	7.5
Lithuanian SSR	11.6	11.7	9.4	8.0
Moldavian SSR	15.4	14.9	10.8	9.1
Latvian SSR	13.0	11.2	9.0	7.9
Kirgiz SSR	10.8	10.8	8.5	6.7
Tadzhik SSR	9.0	8.5	7.2	5.5
Armenian SSR	7.2	6.9	5.7	3.8
Turkmen SSR	8.1	7.7	6.4	5.6
Estonian SSR	6.7	6.7	5.0	3.5

Source: **Nar. khoz. SSSR 1988**, s. 253.

Breakdown of persons convicted: by age group and key categories, 1985–1988
(percentages)

	1985	1986	1987	1988
Ages:				
14–17	8.7	8.7	9.7	11.7
18–24	23.1	20.9	21.6	23.7
25–29	20.3	19.8	20.9	22.0
30–49	39.4	39.1	37.6	35.8
50 plus	8.5	11.5	10.2	6.8
Women	13.7	19.2	15.9	10.8
Previous offenders	34.7	31.8	32.2	37.0
Unemployed	22.3	16.8	15.5	17.6

Source: **Nar. khoz. SSSR 1988**, s. 255.

Murder, 1980-1988

	Thousands	Per 100 000 population
1980	26	10
1984	24	9
1985	21	8
1986	16	6
1987	17	6
1988	21	7

Source: **Nar. khoz. SSSR 1988**, s. 28.

Premeditated murder, 1979-1988

	Thousands	Per 100 000 population
1979	20.9	8.0
1980	21.4	8.1
1981	21.3	8.0
1982	21.5	7.9
1983	21.3	7.8
1984	20.5	7.5
1985	18.7	6.8
1986	14.8	5.3
1987	14.7	5.2
1988	16.7	5.9

Source: **AiF** 1990, 11, s. 3.

Crime in 1988

In 1988 there were 1 867 223 cases of recorded crime, an increase of 68 700 or 3.8% over the previous year. Growth in recorded crime occurred in 59 out of the total of SSRs, ASSRs, kraya and oblasti. Particular figures follow:

Moldavian SSR	56.2%
Kirgiz SSR	32.2%
Tuva ASSR	23.7%
Kurgan oblast	19.0%
North Osetin ASSR	18.3%
Irkutsk oblast	17.8%

```
Rostov oblast        17.0%
Gorki oblast         14.9%
Altai krai           13.2%
```

In 1988 the crime rate was 657.1 cases per 100 000 population. That represents an increase of 17.8% over the previous year. In the following areas the indicator was above the average for the USSR as a whole:

```
Latvian SSR          864.9
Russian SFSR         833.8
Estonian SSR         775.3
Moldavian SSR        767.8
```

Within the Russian SFSR the incidence of crime rose in a total of 30 ASSRs, kraya and oblasti.

In towns and settlements of an urban type the number of recorded crimes increased by 9.5% in 1988. A rise occurred in 70 areas, including the Moldavian and Kirgiz SSRs, the Tuva and North Osetin ASSRs, Primorski krai, Rostov, Irkutsk and Kurgan oblasti.

Street crime increased in all the Union Republics with the exception of Georgia, and in 67 regions of the Russian SFSR. It rose substantially in the Moldavian and Kirgiz SSRs, in the North Osetin ASSR and in Sverdlovsk and Magadan oblasti. In 1988 street murder was up by 35.6%, grievous bodily harm by 67.0%, rape by 17.3%, attacks by thieves by 48.5%, robbery by 61.2% and hooliganism by 4.4%.

Juveniles were responsible for a total of 183 953 recorded crimes. Crimes committed under the influence of alcohol numbered 362 096. Previous offenders were responsible for 302 802 crimes.

The number of persons who were reported as missing in 1988 totalled 87 252. Of these, 69 835 were found following searches.

Source: **Izvestiya** 1989, 14 fevralya, s. 6 (extract, with minor simplification of the text).

                            ******

In 1988 the number of criminals apprehended was 1 286 000, a reduction of 12% on the previous year.

Juvenile crime increased by 11%. Alarmingly, a total of 88 thousand crimes were committed by teenagers in groups. There was a 25% increase in crimes committed by juveniles under the influence of alcohol, and crimes by juveniles with previous convictions rose by 19%. For every 10 000 juveniles 107 crimes are committed.

An explanation of the growth in juvenile crime can be adduced from the example of Kazan. There 200 people took part in fighting but only one or two appeared in court. A total of 7 400 complaints were received from persons who had sustained bodily injuries; in Kazan they were simply not investigated. One young man who had an eye knocked out eventually got a form stating that he had struck himself against a tree.

In 1988 the number of unsolved crimes stood at 463 000. Of these, murders accounted for 1 558 (from the previous year alone). The backlog for the entire country may be two million unsolved cases.

In 1988 the number of people killed on the roads was 47 000 while 297 000 sustained injuries. An official check revealed that one in three traffic inspectors are not familiar with the traffic regulations.

Cases of bribery decreased by 37%, and cases of embezzlement fell by 10%. However, these figures probably reflect the passivity of the services rather than an improvement in the position. Experts take the view that the proportion of bribery which comes to light is only about 2%, and that the figures for embezzlement are 46% in trade, 25% in local industry, and 6% in meat and dairy production.

The police service received a total of two million complaints during the year. Half of the complaints which alleged cover-ups were substantiated.

Over a three year period 600 policemen were found guilty of complicity in criminal acts. Embezzlement within the system of the Ministry of Internal Affairs costs five million roubles each year. Of that total, embezzlement valued at 3.5 million roubles occurs within the Chief Administration for Corrective Labour Institutions, which is responsible for the re-education of criminals.

As for unemployment among former prisoners, 33 000 persons who had completed their sentences failed to find jobs. It is mainly they who are responsible for the 10% increase in recidivist crime.

Over a period of six months 88 brawls involving 45 000 persons occurred at treatment and work rehabilitation Centres. In 1988 there were 66 assaults and cases of hostage-taking in corrective labour institutions and investigation cell blocks.

The currently 'fashionable' form of crime is racketeering; in 1988 a total of 600 cases involving racketeers came to light. Only 139 complaints were received from the victims. The criminals do not stop at extorting money from members of cooperatives or leasees, or at threats, arson and the destruction of equipment. Racketeers are seeking ways into cooperatives whose activities involve foreign currency, and they are attempting to penetrate enterprises which conduct joint undertakings with foreign firms.

Source: **Izvestiya** 1989, 8 fevralya, s. 8 (extracts, with minor simplification of the text).

******

Economic crimes of various types, 1986-1988
(thousands)

	1986	1987	1988
Embezzlement of socialist property	269.9	254.5	280.3
Pilfering	51.3	46.5	36.4
Embezzlement of personal property	459.5	467.9	644.2
incl. extortion	1.7	1.9	2.3
Bribery	11.4	7.8	4.9
Speculation	41.0	43.4	45.2
Fraud	35.6	38.2	39.0
Receipt of illegal payments in the service sphere	2.6	2.4	1.9
Infringement of trading rules	15.9	15.1	17.5
Drug offences	39.9	31.2	23.0
Handling stolen goods	12.5	11.1	9.5

Source: **Stat. Press-Byull.** 1989, 9, s. 144-5.

Economic crimes: by Union Republic, 1986-1988 (thousands)

	1986	1987	1988
USSR	**1 204.3**	**1 089.7**	**1 147.8**
Russian SFSR	809.8	710.1	734.9
Ukrainian SSR	145.3	145.0	152.7
Belorussian SSR	35.4	32.1	30.2
Uzbek SSR	42.9	38.6	42.7
Kazakh SSR	63.0	62.5	67.9
Georgian SSR	10.4	9.6	9.6
Azerbaidzhan SSR	9.1	8.7	8.7
Lithuanian SSR	13.3	12.9	14.3
Moldavian SSR	12.7	12.8	22.8
Latvian SSR	14.3	14.1	15.5
Kirgiz SSR	7.9	8.6	12.2
Tadzhik SSR	8.8	8.4	9.0
Armenian SSR	4.3	4.3	3.4
Turkmen SSR	7.3	6.8	7.6
Estonian SSR	8.0	7.5	8.7

Source: **Stat. Press-Byull.** 1989, 9, s. 144.

Crime in 1989

The item which follows consists of extracts from an article published in **Izvestiya,** with minor simplification of the text.

During the first six months of 1989 the Internal Affairs organs and offices of the Procuracy recorded a total of 1 102 509 crimes, which is an increase of 267 650 or 32.1% over the same period in the previous year.

The number of serious crimes was 169 575, which accounts for 15.4% of the total of all crimes. This is lower than the level for 1985, when such cases numbered 175 744, representing 17.8% of the total.

There has been a sharp increase in street crime. With almost 60 000 additional cases, this category is now 84.3% above the 1988 level.

Murders and attempted murders numbered 10 161. In the past, as a rule, these crimes were committed under the influence of alcohol during family quarrels or fights in apartments and were soon solved by the police. Today the picture has changed. When the background to a murder is established increasingly the words 'mafia' and 'organised crime' are heard. The occurrence of hired killings has been substantiated.

Cases of premeditated grievous bodily harm numbered 25 558. There were 10 298 reported cases of rape and intended rape, and 9 155 of attacks by thieves.

Having to deal with criminal acts which involve the use of firearms is becoming almost normal for the police force. Furthermore, each year sees an increase in the number of policemen who are killed; in 1988 the figure was 263.

Property crimes have shown an increase but there has been a reduction of 2.6% in crimes in the economic sphere.

Data on racketeering are available. In the first five months of 1989 there came light 1 849 cases of extortion involving state, public, cooperatives' or personal property. A total of 1 057 persons were called to account in connection with these crimes.

In the first five months of 1989 the involvement of 10 263 persons in gambling-related offences came to light. The total is composed as follows:

card sharpers	5 283
thimble-riggers	3 844
roulette operators	316
others	820

The number of persons called to account in various ways was
9 610. It is known that in some card games hundreds of
thousands of roubles have been lost in one evening - and
human lives as well.

Unsolved crimes, first half of 1988 and 1989

	1988	1989	% increase
Total	**168 262**	**350 790**	**180.5**
Premeditated murder incl. attempts	556	941	69.2
Grievous bodily harm (premeditated)	2 273	5 592	146.0
Rape, attempted rape	693	1 089	61.8
Attacks by thieves*	1 160	2 885	148.7
Robbery*	11 125	26 914	141.9
Theft of state or public property	28 278	58 952	108.5
Theft of personal property	93 941	196 988	109.7

* Involving state or private property.

Unsolved crimes include those regarding which investigation
was discontinued for the first time in the current year
(irrespective of when they were committed or recorded) on
account of unsuccessful searches or failure to identify the
guilty persons.

Source: **Izvestiya** 1989, 11 iyuliya, s. 8.

Recorded crimes: by Union Republic, first half of years 1987-1989

	Thousands 1987	1988	1989	As % of prior ½ year 1988	1989
USSR	**908.1**	**834.9**	**1 102.5**	**91.9**	**132.1**
Russian SFSR	600.5	546.4	718.4	91.0	131.5
Ukrainian SSR	119.9	105.9	144.4	88.4	136.3
Belorussian SSR	24.1	21.4	29.4	88.7	137.3
Uzbek SSR	34.6	33.6	39.4	97.0	117.3
Kazakh SSR	49.5	45.8	60.5	92.6	132.0
Georgian SSR	8.4	8.1	8.4	97.2	102.9
Azerbaidzhan SSR	7.3	6.7	7.9	92.8	117.2
Lithuanian SSR	9.6	9.3	14.6	96.9	156.9
Moldavian SSR	9.5	14.0	19.3	147.5	138.3
Latvian SSR	10.5	10.3	13.2	98.1	128.3
Kirgiz SSR	7.0	8.1	11.8	116.2	145.4
Tadzhik SSR	6.6	6.6	8.3	100.9	125.0
Armenian SSR	3.7	2.9	4.3	77.8	149.0
Turkmen SSR	6.2	6.1	8.1	98.6	133.4
Estonian SSR	5.5	4.6	8.7	83.2	188.6

During the first half of 1989 the number of serious crimes recorded in the USSR was 39.9% above the figure for the same period of the previous year. The highest rates of increase occurred in Belorussia (57.6%), Estonia (53.5%), Armenia (52.7%), Kirgizia (45.6%), and in the Russian SFSR (42.3%).

Serious crime as a proportion of recorded crime rose from 14.5% in the first half of 1988 to 15.4% in the first half of 1989. This is connected with a significant rise in premeditated murder (up by 26.8%), rape (up by 21.8%), premeditated grievous bodily harm (up by 47.3%), assault with intent to rob (up by 73.4%), robbery (up by 87.2) and in a range of other dangerous crimes.

During the first six months of 1989 a total of 113 800 crimes were committed by persons in groups; this was an increase of 13.2% on the same period of the previous year.

The number of crimes committed by juveniles, or with their involvement, was 97 500, which is 22% higher than the figure for the first half of 1988. The largest increases in juvenile crime occurred in Armenia (55.6%), Lithuania (47.3%), Belorussia (40.6%), and also in the Kazakh, Georgian, Ukrainian, and Azerbaidzhan SSRs (26%-29%). In the Russian SFSR, juvenile crime showed a fall in only 15 out of 73 kraya, oblasti and ASSRs. It rose significantly in: Altai krai, Tatar ASSR, Kursk, Murmansk, Novgorod and Novosibirsk oblasti (50%-57%); in Kaliningrad, Kemerovo and Tambov oblasti (63%-65%); in Belgorod oblast (72.3%) and in the city of Moscow (85.8%).

Increasingly crime is committed on the streets, in squares and in parks. Every 8th recorded crime came into that category, compared to every 12th crime in the first half of 1988. Street crime rose by two to three times in twenty one regions of the Russian SFSR, and in the Belorussian, Kazakh, Lithuanian, and Estonian SSRs.

The number of crimes committed under the influence of alcohol rose by 14%.

After a reduction during recent years in the number of cases of hooliganism which received criminal sentences, the figure rose from 59 000 to 68 700. That represents an increase of 16.4%.

During the first six months of 1989 there was a sharp upturn (of 54.6%) in incidents of arson with the intention of destroying state, public or personal property. The organs of the USSR Ministry of Internal Affairs recorded a total of 3 900 such crimes. More than two thirds of them took place in regions of the Russian SFSR, in the following areas particularly: Krasnodar krai (129), Irkutsk oblast (102) and Moscow oblast (101). Cases of arson also increased in other Union Republics, rising from 363 to 470 in the Ukraine, from 106 to 182 in Uzbekistan, from 73 to 127 in Belorussia and from 74 to 107 in Kazakhstan.

Source: **Stat. Press-Byull.** 1989, 9, s. 57-8.

******

Lawbreaking among youth

In 1988 the number of persons identified as having committed a crime was 1.3 million and amongst these more than a half - 710 000 - were under the age of 30. For the most part they fell into the age group 18-29. Juveniles made up 26.1% of the total.

166

Amongst the persons who had committed crimes, there was a total of 63 100 pupils at occupational-technical schools, 47 400 pupils at secondary general schools and 14 200 students of higher and secondary specialised educational establishments. Those who were members of the Young Communist League numbered 127 000.

The most common crimes of young people were embezzlement of state, public or personal property, drug offences, hooliganism, resisting the police, attempts on the lives of policemen, theft of firearms, military supplies and explosives, and sexual offences. The proportion of youth amongst those who have committed such offences ranges from 60% to 87%. Persons under the age of 30 remain a significant proportion of those who have committed premeditated grievous bodily harm (41.4%), premeditated murder (42.0%) and gangsterism (56.4%).

Criminal recidivism among juveniles increased by 19.2%. Nearly 23 000 boys and girls were guilty of repeated offences.

The prevalence of crime among young people has a direct connection with vagrancy and other forms of deviation from the socialist way of life. Out of those identified as having committed crimes in 1988 every 6th person aged 16-17 and every 5th person aged 18-24 had no employment and was not engaged in studies. In 1988 official warnings for following a parasitic way of life were delivered to 82 000 persons aged 18-29. Although the number of those identified as refusing to undertake work useful to society has declined in recent years the proportion of young people among them remains significant and stands at 37%.

In 1988 reception centres accommodated more than 34 000 vagrants under the age of 30, an increase of 2.7% on 1987. Every fourth person amongst them was female.

In 1988 the Internal Affairs organs identified a total of 12 300 juvenile prostitutes, homosexuals, drug addicts and other persons belonging to a group at risk of contracting and transmitting AIDS. A total of 113 girls were sentenced under the administrative code for the practice of prostitution.

At the end of 1988 a total of 526 900 teenagers were on registers of the Internal Affairs organs as potential lawbreakers: 44 100 juveniles had received a conditional discharge or a suspended sentence. Moreover, in the course of the year 957 700 juveniles were taken to the police for illegal acts, being drunk in public places or using drugs and other narcotising substances.

In 1988 a total of 2 200 juveniles were sentenced under the administrative code for offences connected with drugs, half for taking drugs. Almost every second person - 5 000 - who had been sentenced under the administrative code for approaching foreigners with the intent of obtaining things was a juvenile.

On average each year 45 000 teenagers are detained for minor hooliganism.

Inreasingly teenagers are banding together in groups with antisocial tendencies. In 1988 the number of teenagers who committed crimes in a group by themselves or with adults was 122 600, which is 14.2% more than in 1987. The names of 17 700 members of various unofficial groups were put on the register; they were sports fans, rockers, heavy metallists, hippies, punks and brawlers. That total includes 12 200 juveniles. For a variety of illegal acts 1 100 juveniles from unofficial organisations were sentenced under the criminal code, and 4 400 were punished under the administrative code in 1988.

There has been an increase in the number of juveniles among persons who were guilty of offences under the anti-alcohol legislation. For consuming spirits and for being drunk in public places 187 200 juveniles were detained in 1987 and in 1988 the figure was 202 200, higher by 8.0%.

The number of juveniles who committed crimes under the influence of alcohol incresed from 20 600 to 25 600, or by 24.6%, over the period 1987-1988. About half of the juveniles sentenced under the criminal code for premeditated murder, inflicting grievous bodily harm and rape, together with 52.6% of those juveniles sentenced for hooliganism, committed their crimes under the influence of alcohol.

In 1988 the courts made compulsory medical treatment orders for 30 400 alcoholics under the age of 30 and for 1 000 drug addicts under the age of 30.

Source: **Stat. Press-Byull.** 1989, 9, s. 59-60.

**Persons aged 14-29 who committed crimes:
by Union Republic, 1986-1988** (thousands)

	1986	1987	1988
USSR	**817.2**	**738.3**	**709.6**
Russian SFSR	543.6	490.2	466.9
Ukrainian SSR	103.6	95.0	91.9
Belorussian SSR	22.1	19.5	20.3
Uzbek SSR	31.6	27.4	24.8
Kazakh SSR	43.3	41.5	41.4
Georgian SSR	6.4	5.5	5.7
Azerbaidzhan SSR	6.0	5.4	4.9
Lithuanian SSR	7.9	7.6	7.3
Moldavian SSR	11.2	9.3	10.2
Latvian SSR	9.1	8.9	8.5
Kirgiz SSR	7.4	7.1	7.7
Tadzhik SSR	5.4	4.6	5.1
Armenian SSR	3.3	2.9	2.2
Turkmen SSR	4.9	4.5	4.9
Estonian SSR	5.3	4.7	3.6

**Persons aged 14-29 who committed crimes as percentage of
relevant age group, 1986-1988**

Age group	1986	1987	1988
14-17	21.0	22.6	26.1
18-24	40.7	40.7	39.4
25-29	38.3	36.7	34.5

Source of both tables: **Stat. Press-Byull.** 1989, 9, s. 61.

Persons aged 14-29 convicted of crimes: by Union Republic, 1985-1988 (thousands)

	1985	1986	1987	1988
USSR	**661.6**	**601.3**	**473.0**	**389.7**
Russian SFSR	440.0	395.5	304.0	246.4
Ukrainian SSR	83.2	77.4	61.5	50.9
Belorussian SSR	20.7	15.9	12.8	13.2
Uzbek SSR	21.2	20.1	17.8	15.2
Kazakh SSR	39.0	38.6	32.9	26.5
Georgian SSR	6.3	6.0	4.6	4.0
Azerbaidzhan SSR	6.1	5.5	4.3	3.8
Lithuanian SSR	6.5	6.3	5.4	4.7
Moldavian SSR	9.0	8.5	6.6	5.8
Latvian SSR	7.0	6.3	5.4	5.0
Kirgiz SSR	6.2	5.9	4.8	4.0
Tadzhik SSR	4.7	4.4	3.9	3.1
Armenian SSR	3.2	2.9	2.4	1.7
Turkmen SSR	4.5	4.1	3.4	3.2
Estonian SSR	4.0	3.9	3.2	2.2

Source: **AiF** 1990, 4, s. 3.

Percentage of persons under age 30 in total of persons convicted for various crimes, 1987 and 1988

	1987	1988
All types of crime	**52.1**	**57.4**
Embezzlement of state or public property except pilfering	52.4	56.6
incl. theft	63.9	64.8
Pilfering of state and public property	34.9	33.4
Premeditated murder	41.5	41.2
Grievous bodily harm (premeditated)	41.8	41.0
Rape	86.0	86.7
Crimes against citizens' personal property	76.4	77.2
incl. theft	82.9	76.0
Speculation	31.9	33.6
Production, sale, storage of spirits on domestic premises	9.5	9.5
Hooliganism	74.2	77.0
Drug offences	70.7	68.2
Public transport and motoring offences	53.9	53.1

Source: **AiF** 1990, 4, s. 3.

171

**Persons convicted of leading a parasitic way of life*,
1980-1988** (thousands)

	Total	'Spongers' (unemployed)
1980	53.6	27.5
1981	58.1	37.8
1982	60.2	41.4
1983	69.2	49.4
1984	76.8	56.9
1985	63.9	47.6
1986	31.9	24.2
1987	9.7	7.1
1988	1.9	1.1

* Vagrancy, begging and 'sponging' (by unemployed persons).

During the first six months of 1989 the total of persons convicted under this heading was 500, of which 300 were 'spongers' (unemployed).

In the Russian SFSR the total number of persons sentenced during 1988 under Article 209 of the Republic's Criminal Code (Vagrancy, begging and 'sponging') was one million.

Up to 1989 the statistical data were kept a close secret. Today there is no reason to presume that the number of vagrants, beggars and 'spongers' has declined, but apparently, less attention is given to them.

Source: **AiF** 1990, 10, s. 8.

Persons aged 18-29 officially cautioned to discontinue a parasitic way of life: by Union Republic, 1980 and 1988

	1980 Number	As %*	1988 Number	As %*
USSR	**112 110**	**38.7**	**81 909**	**37.0**
Russian SFSR	66 170	39.3	46 672	37.7
Ukrainian SSR	21 380	35.8	8 542	36.4
Belorussian SSR	3 266	46.1	1 489	38.9
Uzbek SSR	2 725	36.6	6 367	25.3
Kazakh SSR	4 448	35.7	5 494	35.2
Georgian SSR	4 307	57.3	4 056	49.1
Azerbaidzhan SSR	2 082	50.6	2 206	58.3
Lithuanian SSR	1 669	31.3	1 127	41.4
Moldavian SSR	1 123	39.9	795	36.1
Latvian SSR	1 182	22.4	265	35.9
Kirgiz SSR	877	33.8	1 141	31.9
Tadzhik SSR	1 084	44.3	1 694	49.2
Armenian SSR	435	55.3	437	50.2
Turkmen SSR	638	40.6	977	41.0
Estonian SSR	427	33.4	516	31.3

* As percentage of all persons cautioned to discontinue a parasitic way of life.

Source: **Stat. Press-Byull.** 1990, 3, s. 40.

Sources of livelihood of the population, 1979 and 1989

	Thousands 1979	1989	% increase
Total	**262 085**	**285 743**	**9.0**
Employees	134 860	141 892	5.2
Students	6 633	6 772	2.1
Pensioners, recipients of social welfare*	40 126	50 503	5.9
Dependents and those only in private, part-time work	80 195	86 049	7.3
Other sources and no source reported	271	527	94.5

As percentages

Employees	51.5	49.7
Students	2.5	2.4
Pensioners, recipients of social welfare*	15.3	17.6
Dependents and those only in private, part-time work	30.6	30.1
Other sources and no source reported	0.1	0.2

* At the start of 1989 there were 58.6 million pensioners (compared to 47.6 million in 1979) and they accounted for 15% of the total population. In the censuses those persons for whom a pension is the main source of livelihood are classified as pensioners, while those pensioners who are in continuous employment are included among the employed.

The 1989 census took account of persons with two sources of livelihood (in 1979 only one was recognised) and they made up 15% of the population. This group consists mainly of working pensioners and persons supplementing their main employment with private, part-time work or receiving a stipend, pension, grant or help from relatives.

Source: **Ekonomika i zhizn** 1990, 10, s. 16.

174

State budget expenditure on grants to mothers, 1970–1988
(million roubles)

	1970	1980	1988
For expectant, nursing and single mothers, mothers of large and low income families	1 301	2 624	5 321

The grants to nursing and single mothers and mothers of large families are for the care of a child up to the age of one year.

Source: **Stat. Press-Byull.** 1990, 1, s. 52.

Number of mothers with large families receiving a monthly state grant, 1970–1988 (thousands)

	1970	1980	1988
Total	3 211	2 150	2 054
with 4 children	1 172	717	924
with 5 children	782	472	471
with 6 children	546	325	268
with 7 and more	711	636	391

Mothers of two children receive a one-time grant from the state on the birth of a third and subsequent child. Those with three children receive a monthly benefit on the birth of a fourth and subsequent child.

In the 11th Five year Plan period, with the object of improving state assistance to families, one-time grants were introduced for working mothers and those who have study-leave from their employment. The level of benefit was set at 50 roubles on the birth of a first child and 100 roubles on the birth of a second and third child, with the existing level of grant for a fourth and subsequent child being maintained.

Women who have given birth to five or more children and have reared them until age seven receive additional concessions in respect of their pensions.

Source: **Stat. Press-Byull.** 1990, 1, s. 52.

Average monthly pension in roubles, 1985 and 1988
(end of year)

	State pensions		Collective farm pensions and grants	
	1985	1988	1985	1988
All pensioners*	**78.7**	**86.3**	**47.0**	**54.3**
Pensions for:				
Old age	87.2	93.9	47.2	54.5
Occupational injury and illness				
Group I	96.2	100.3	65.9	78.9
Group II	83.0	88.0	50.9	58.1
Group III	43.6	44.2	31.8	34.7
Other illness				
Group I	89.5	93.2	62.2	76.1
Group II	74.4	80.5	46.0	53.7
Group III	33.5	34.5	–	–
Loss of breadwinner				
with 1 dependent	37.8	39.6	26.8	29.1
with 2 dependents	77.9	82.1	49.4	54.1
with 3 or more dependents	90.8	92.9	76.9	82.9

* On the records of the social security organs.

In 1988 state expenditure on pensions amounted to 55 billion roubles. That was 22% above the level for 1985 and 6% above the level for 1987.

Source: **Stat. Press-Byull.** 1989, 9, s. 128-9.

Old age pensioners receiving pensions 5-10 years early, 1975-1987 (end of year) millions

	1975	1980	1985	1987
Total	2.2	3.8	5.6	6.8
Those still working	0.7	1.4	2.2	2.5

Source: **Sotsialnoe razvitie SSSR**, s. 90.

Persons receiving pensions, 1988 (end of year)

	Total	State pensions	Collective farm pensions*
	in millions		
All pensioners	**58.6**	**48.2**	**10.4**
Old age	43.2	33.8	9.4
Loss of breadwinner	5.7	5.3	0.4
blue- and white-collar	4.5	4.5	-
military	0.8	0.8	-
collective farmer	0.4	-	0.4
Invalidity	6.5	5.9	0.6
occupational injury			
and illness	0.5	0.5	0.04
other illness	5.2	4.6	0.6
military	0.8	0.8	-
Personal pensions	0.5	0.5	-
Long service pensions	0.1	0.1	-
	in percentages		
Old age	73.6	70.1	90.0
Loss of breadwinner	9.8	11.0	4.0
blue- and white-collar	7.7	9.4	-
military	1.4	1.6	-
collective farmer	0.7	-	4.0
Invalidity	11.1	12.2	6.0
occupational injury			
and illness	0.9	1.0	0.4
general illness	8.9	9.6	5.6
military	1.3	1.6	-
Personal pensions	0.9	1.1	-
Long service pensions	0.2	0.3	-

* And grants.

Source of this and the following table: **Vestnik Statistiki** 1989, 11, s. 27-8.

Persons receiving pensions: by Union Republic, 1985-1988 (end of year) in millions

	1985	1987	1988 Total	Collective farm members
USSR all	**55.7**	**57.5**	**58.6**	**10.4**
for old age	**39.3**	**41.8**	**43.2**	**9.4**
Russian SFSR all	31.2	32.2	32.6	3.8
for old age	22.5	23.8	24.5	3.5
Ukrainian SSR all	12.0	12.4	12.6	3.4
for old age	8.5	9.2	9.5	3.1
Belorussian SSR all	2.2	2.2	2.3	0.6
for old age	1.5	1.6	1.7	0.6
Uzbek SSR all	2.0	2.1	2.2	0.7
for old age	1.3	1.3	1.4	0.6
Kazakh SSR all	2.2	2.3	2.3	0.2
for old age	1.4	1.5	1.6	0.2
Georgian SSR all	1.0	1.0	1.1	0.3
for old age	0.6	0.7	0.7	0.2
Azerbaidzhan SSR all	0.9	1.0	1.0	0.2
for old age	0.6	0.6	0.6	0.2
Lithuanian SSR all	0.8	0.8	0.8	0.2
for old age	0.5	0.6	0.6	0.2
Moldavian SSR all	0.7	0.8	0.8	0.3
for old age	0.5	0.5	0.6	0.2
Latvian SSR all	0.6	0.6	0.6	0.1
for old age	0.4	0.5	0.5	0.1
Kirgiz SSR all	0.5	0.6	0.6	0.2
for old age	0.4	0.4	0.4	0.1
Tadzhik SSR all	0.5	0.5	0.5	0.2
for old age	0.3	0.3	0.3	0.16
Armenian SSR all	0.4	0.5	0.4	0.1
for old age	0.3	0.3	0.3	0.1
Turkmen SSR all	0.3	0.3	0.4	0.1
for old age	0.2	0.2	0.2	0.1
Estonian SSR all	0.4	0.4	0.4	0.04
for old age	0.3	0.3	0.3	0.03

Age distribution of pensioners, 1987
(from sample surveys) in percentages

	Total	Old age	Loss of breadwinner	Invalidity
All pensioners	100	100	100	100
Under 16	4.4	-	34.9	-
16-19	1.7	-	13.3	0.2
20-29	0.6	-	0.5	4.7
30-39	1.3	-	0.7	9.9
40-49	2.4	0.4	1.3	15.9
50-54	4.5	3.5	0.7	14.1
55-59	17.8	20.6	1.1	17.5
60-64	22.8	27.7	2.3	14.0
65-69	13.7	16.4	3.9	7.3
70 and over	30.8	31.4	41.3	16.4

Among blue- and white-collar workers in 1988 there were 10 million persons in receipt of old age pensions. This category accounted for 4%-6% of employees in industry, agriculture, construction and transport. Every tenth employee was a pensioner in trade, community catering and in the majority of the non-productive sectors. Over 400 000 pensioners are working a shortened day in blue- and white-collar jobs.

The age breakdown of working pensioners was as follows:

Men		Women	
Under 60	25%	Under 55	10%
60-64	46%	55-59	42%
65-69	16%	60-64	29%
Over 70	19%	Over 65	19%

The highest proportion of pensioners who work is found among those whose pensions are granted on concessionary terms (35%). The total number of persons in that category rose from 3.8 million in 1980 to 7.2 million in 1988.

Source: **Vestnik Statistiki** 1989, 11, s. 26, 29.

Old age pensioners receiving a minimum pension, 1985 and 1988 (end of year)

	Millions		% of all old age pensioners	
	1985	1988	1985	1988
Blue- and white-collar workers	2.7	1.8	8.9	5.4
Collective farm workers	5.2	5.7	58.4	61.2

The minimum level of old age pension for blue- and white-collar workers has not risen since 1981, and is 50 roubles per month. For collective farm workers it was increased in 1985 from 28 to 40 roubles. In respect of pensions which were determined ten and more years ago, the mimimum level is slighly higher. For blue- and white- collar workers it is 55 roubles (since 1985), and for collective farm workers it is 50 roubles (since 1988). Out of the 41 million persons with an income below the subsistence minimum one fifth are pensioners.

Source: **Stat. Press-Byull.** 1989, 9, s. 129.

Persons first declared invalids, 1970-1987

	1970	1980	1987
Thousands			
Total	569	583	567
Blue- and white-collar workers	475	521	511
Collective farm workers	94	62	56
Per 10 000 workers			
Total	53	46	43

Source: **Sotsialnoe razvitie SSSR**, s. 229.

Blue- and white-collar employees of pension and pre-pension age* as percentage of all blue- and white-collar employees: by Union Republic, 1 June 1987

	Pension age	Pre-pension age
USSR	**7.3**	**8.2**
Russian SFSR	7.7	8.5
Ukrainian SSR	7.3	8.5
Belorussian	7.4	8.9
Uzbek SSR	4.2	5.2
Kazakh SSR	4.5	6.7
Georgian SSR	12.3	9.0
Azerbaidzhan SSR	7.5	7.2
Lithuanian SSR	9.3	8.9
Moldavian SSR	4.5	6.9
Latvian SSR	11.9	9.5
Kirgiz SSR	4.9	6.1
Tadzhik SSR	4.6	5.8
Armenian SSR	8.4	8.0
Turkmen SSR	5.4	5.6
Estonian SSR	12.2	9.2

* For women the pre-pension age is 50-54 years; for men it is 55-59 years.

In 1977 the proportion of workers of pension age was 5.1% and of pre-pension age 7.1%. An increase in the proportion of workers in these age groups has occurred in all Union Republics.

Source: **Nar. khoz. SSSR 1988**, s. 45.

**Personal pensioners and their average monthly pension,
1985 and 1988**

	1985	1988
Pensioners and their families (thousands)		
Total	498.6	589.2
Local	281.4	350.0
Republican	167.0	182.7
Union	50.2	56.5
Average monthly pension (roubles)		
All	95.4	107.0
Local	83.9	99.2
Republican	107.4	114.8
Union	120.5	130.3

Personal pensions are determined for individuals who have
given special service to the state in the fields of
revolutionary, state, social and economic activity; and to
persons who have given outstanding service in the fields of
culture, science and technology. In the event of the death
of such individuals the pensions are paid to members of the
family. Union and Republican personal pensions are assigned
by a commission of the Union Republic's Council of
Ministers, and local personal pensions are assigned by the
executive committee of the Soviet of People's Deputies.

Source: **Stat. Press-Byull.** 1989, 10, s. 113.

Female population: by age group, 1989*
(thousands)

	Total	Urban	Rural
All ages	151 056	99 645	51 411
Under 5	13 077	7 789	5 288
5-9	11 983	7 347	4 636
10-14	11 137	6 860	4 277
15-19	10 384	7 115	3 269
20-24	10 133	6 812	3 321
25-29	12 127	8 373	3 754
30-34	11 756	8 466	3 290
35-39	10 522	7 835	2 687
40-44	7 066	5 317	1 749
45-49	7 836	5 403	2 433
50-54	9 317	6 277	3 040
55-59	8 255	5 218	3 037
60-64	8 978	5 707	3 271
65-69	5 719	3 540	2 179
70 and over	12 708	7 540	5 168
Ages 15-49	69 824	49 321	20 503

* Census data.

Source: **Vestnik Statistiki** 1990, 1, s. 47.

Women per 1 000 men of corresponding age group in
urban population, 1959–1987

	1959	1970	1979	1987
All ages	**1 211**	**1 159**	**1 151**	**1 127**
Under 5	959	962	968	956
5–9	966	959	968	963
10–14	977	963	970	972
15–19	1 025	994	1 007	1 032
20–24	1 057	993	1 019	1 007
25–29	1 025	1 003	1 022	965
30–34	1 184	1 033	1 023	1 026
35–39	1 567	1 042	1 060	1 039
40–44	1 485	1 142	1 078	1 060
45–49	1 470	1 588	1 111	1 119
50–54	1 542	1 553	1 297	1 159
55–59	1 867	1 672	1 809	1 242
60–64	1 880	1 815	1 832	1 770
65–69	1 976	2 239	1 991	2 079
70 and over	2 475	2 585	2 702	2 764

Source: **Naselenie SSSR 1987**, s. 96.

Women per 1 000 men of corresponding age group in
rural population, 1959-1987

	1959	1970	1979	1987
All ages	**1 229**	**1 188**	**1 150**	**1 137**
Under 5	963	969	977	965
5-9	966	965	976	971
10-14	954	963	974	978
15-19	966	903	853	888
20-24	985	955	908	912
25-29	1 057	1 057	930	968
30-34	1 233	1 030	973	974
35-39	1 551	1 034	1 058	980
40-44	1 751	1 215	1 044	1 078
45-49	1 762	1 583	1 086	1 122
50-54	1 668	1 799	1 366	1 124
55-59	2 106	2 024	1 844	1 232
60-64	1 832	1 880	2 093	1 782
65-69	1 816	2 117	2 172	2 215
70 and over	1 971	2 145	2 411	2 851

Source: **Naselenie SSSR 1987**, s. 96.

Women as percentage of urban and rural populations: by Union Republic, 1970-1989

	1970	1979	1989
Urban population			
USSR	**53.7**	**53.4**	**53.0**
Russian SFSR	54.1	53.8	53.3
Ukrainian SSR	53.7	53.6	53.3
Belorussian SSR	53.0	52.9	52.8
Uzbek SSR	51.7	51.0	51.1
Kazakh SSR	51.8	52.4	52.3
Georgian SSR	53.3	53.4	53.2
Azerbaidzhan SSR	51.1	50.6	50.8
Lithuanian SSR	52.8	52.9	52.8
Moldavian SSR	53.2	53.1	52.1
Latvian SSR	54.3	54.2	53.9
Kirgiz SSR	53.0	51.8	52.5
Tadzhik SSR	51.0	50.8	50.9
Armenian SSR	51.1	51.6	50.9
Turkmen SSR	50.4	50.7	50.8
Estonian SSR	54.4	54.1	53.7
Rural population			
USSR	**54.2**	**53.4**	**52.4**
Russian SFSR	54.8	54.0	52.8
Ukrainian SSR	56.0	55.4	54.6
Belorussian SSR	54.8	54.3	53.8
Uzbek SSR	51.1	50.8	50.4
Kazakh SSR	51.9	51.1	50.5
Georgian SSR	52.8	52.6	51.8
Azerbaidzhan SSR	51.9	52.0	51.7
Lithuanian SSR	53.3	52.6	52.2
Moldavian SSR	53.5	52.8	53.0
Latvian SSR	54.3	53.5	52.5
Kirgiz SSR	51.7	51.2	50.4
Tadzhik SSR	50.7	50.5	50.1
Armenian SSR	51.3	50.9	49.8
Turkmen SSR	51.1	50.9	50.7
Estonian SSR	54.1	53.2	52.1

Source: **Nar. khoz. SSSR 1988**, s. 20.

Average expectation of life at birth for women: urban and rural areas, 1958-1988 (in years)

	Total	Urban	Rural
1958-1959	71.7	71.4	71.8
1971-1972	73.6	73.6	73.4
1978-1979	72.6	73.1	71.8
1983-1984	72.8	73.3	71.7
1985	72.9	73.5	71.7
1986	73.6	74.2	72.6
1987	73.8	74.3	72.9
1988	73.6	73.9	72.8

This indicator is currently 4-7 years lower than in Great Britain, USA, Federal Republic of Germany, France and Japan.

Source: **Vestnik Statistiki** 1990, 1, s. 53.

Abortions, 1980-1988

	Thousands	Per 1 000 women aged 15-49
1980	7 003	102.3
1981	6 834	99.6
1982	6 912	100.3
1983	6 765	97.7
1984	6 780	97.2
1985	7 034	100.3
1986	7 116	101.2
1987	6 818	97.1
1988*	6 068	86.6

* A further 1 460 000 abortions were performed by the vacuum-aspiration mini-abortion method.

Source: **Vestnik Statistiki** 1990, 1, s. 55.

Abortions: by Union Republic, 1975–1985

	1975	1980	1985
Thousands			
USSR	**7 135**	**7 003**	**7 034**
Russian SFSR	4 670	4 506	4 552
Ukrainian SSR	1 146	1 197	1 179
Belorussian SSR	195	202	201
Uzbek SSR	160	161	199
Kazakh SSR	391	378	367
Georgian SSR	95	89	69
Azerbaidzhan SSR	59	62	54
Lithuanian SSR	46	45	42
Moldavian SSR	93	96	103
Latvian SSR	58	60	58
Kirgiz SSR	64	65	69
Tadzhik SSR	39	40	41
Armenian SSR	45	32	34
Turkmen SSR	34	34	31
Estonian SSR	40	36	35
Per 1 000 women aged 15–49			
USSR	**105.7**	**102.3**	**100.3**
Russian SFSR	126.3	122.8	123.6
Ukrainian SSR	88.3	94.1	92.2
Belorussian SSR	78.7	81.1	80.0
Uzbek SSR	51.9	43.8	46.9
Kazakh SSR	108.7	99.2	90.7
Georgian SSR	74.0	67.7	52.4
Azerbaidzhan SSR	43.1	39.0	30.8
Lithuanian SSR	53.0	50.9	46.3
Moldavian SSR	89.7	90.7	96.0
Latvian SSR	91.4	92.5	88.7
Kirgiz SSR	84.1	76.6	73.8
Tadzhik SSR	53.4	45.3	39.5
Armenian SSR	60.5	38.8	38.4
Turkmen SSR	60.8	51.1	40.9
Estonian SSR	107.1	96.7	91.4

Source: **Naselenie SSSR 1987**, s. 319.

Abortions: by Union Republic, 1987 and 1988*

	1987	1988
Thousands		
USSR	**6 496**	**5 767**
Russian SFSR	4 166	3 832
Ukrainian SSR	1 068	774
Belorussian SSR	158	135
Uzbek SSR	223	234
Kazakh SSR	330	295
Georgian SSR	76	74
Azerbaidzhan SSR	50	40
Lithuanian SSR	38	35
Moldavian SSR	112	95
Latvian SSR	55	50
Kirgiz SSR	74	68
Tadzhik SSR	42	43
Armenian SSR	33	27
Turkmen SSR	36	35
Estonian SSR	35	30
Per 1 000 women aged 15-49		
USSR	**92.5**	**82.3**
Russian SFSR	113.6	105.2
Ukrainian SSR	84.6	61.9
Belorussian SSR	63.2	54.1
Uzbek SSR	49.7	50.8
Kazakh SSR	80.9	72.2
Georgian SSR	57.8	56.5
Azerbaidzhan SSR	28.0	22.4
Lithuanian SSR	41.4	38.0
Moldavian SSR	104.8	88.3
Latvian SSR	84.3	76.8
Kirgiz SSR	75.7	67.7
Tadzhik SSR	38.6	38.6
Armenian SSR	36.7	30.2
Turkmen SSR	44.6	43.1
Estonian SSR	90.3	77.3

*Data from institutions controlled by the USSR Ministry of Health.

Source: **Naselenie SSSR 1988**, s. 413.

Women's sources of livelihood, 1959-1989*
(percentages)

	1959	1970	1979	1989
All women	100	100	100	100
Employees	41.5	44.0	47.8	45.0
Those only in private, part-time work	7.8	1.3	0.4	0.8
Students	0.7	1.4	2.4	2.2
Pensioners, recipients of social welfare	6.0	16.7	19.6	23.0
Dependents	43.9	36.5	29.7	28.9

* Census data.

Source: **Vestnik Statistiki** 1990, 1, s. 47.

Women as percentage of workers in various sectors of industry, 1974-1985*

	1974	1978	1981	1985
All sectors	48	48	46	46
Machine building and metal working	42	43	42	42
Cellulose and paper	49	49	47	46
Cement	36	36	36	36
Textiles	72	72	70	70
Garments	86	87	89	89
Leather, fur, shoe production	69	69	70	69
Food processing	58	57	57	56
includes:				
bakery	74	73	71	71
confectionery	74	73	72	72

* Annual average figures.

Source: **Nar. khoz. SSSR 1988**, s. 40.

Despite the system of measures intended to improve their working conditions, a large number of women are still engaged in hard physical labour. Thus, out of the industrial workers engaged in hard physical labour, one fifth are women; in construction the figure is over a quarter. The proportion of women so engaged is above the all-Union level in industry in the Russian SFSR, Belorussia, Uzbekistan, Kazakhstan, Georgia, Azerbaidzhan, Lithuania, Moldavia, Kirgizia, Turkmenistan and Estonia. In construction it is above the all-Union level in the Russian SFSR, the Ukraine, Belorussia and Kazakhstan.

Despite the implementation of measures for the improvement of working conditions, the number of workers employed in heavy and unhealthy - and particularly heavy and particularly unhealthy - conditions has remained vitually unchanged. At the present time more than a half of industrial workers enjoy privileges and compensations for these working conditions. Of that number one third are women. In such sectors as the chemical, petrochemical, woodworking, glass making, china and pottery, and food processing industries almost one half are women; in light industry the corresponding figure is two thirds.

Source: **Nar. khoz. SSSR 1988**, s. 40 (excerpt).

******

Of those who work in particularly heavy and particularly unhealthy conditions in industry, 44% are women. In construction the corresponding figure is 17%.

In 1988 a total of 2.7 million women were working in conditions which did not conform to the norms and regulations for health protection.

A night shift is worked by 38% of women blue-collar workers. In Moldavia the figure is about 50%.

Women make up 12% of all bricklayers, 34% of road building workers, 20% of rail track layers, 13% of navvies and 6% of workers with concrete. In industry a large number of women are engaged in subsiduary activities - as loaders and transport staff (8% of the total number of women blue-collar workers).

During her working day a woman spends 3 hours 13 minutes on household management. During a holiday she spends 6 hours 18 minutes on household management.

Source: **AiF** 1990, 9, s. 1 (excerpt).

Female blue- and white-collar employees: by Union Republic, 1970–1988*

	1970	1980	1985	1988
Thousands				
USSR	**45 800**	**57 569**	**60 011**	**59 273**
Russian SFSR	28 585	34 314	35 138	34 329
Ukrainian SSR	8 113	10 424	10 755	10 664
Belorussian SSR	1 611	2 139	2 265	2 271
Uzbek SSR	1 091	1 784	2 082	2 149
Kazakh SSR	2 200	2 942	3 167	3 187
Georgian SSR	634	902	1 003	1 022
Azerbaidzhan SSR	518	768	889	904
Lithuanian SSR	570	758	816	829
Moldavian SSR	477	768	825	818
Latvian SSR	550	652	674	660
Kirgiz SSR	367	534	598	606
Tadzhik SSR	223	361	419	450
Armenian SSR	346	552	636	649
Turkmen SSR	189	293	331	357
Estonian SSR	326	378	393	378
As percentage of all employees				
USSR	**51**	**51**	**51**	**51**
ussian SFSR	53	52	52	51
Ukrainian SSR	50	52	52	52
Belorussian SSR	52	53	53	53
Uzbek SSR	41	43	43	43
Kazakh SSR	47	49	49	49
Georgian SSR	43	46	46	46
Azerbaidzhan SSR	41	43	43	43
Lithuanian SSR	49	52	52	52
Moldavian SSR	51	51	51	52
Latvian SSR	53	54	55	54
Kirgiz SSR	47	48	48	49
Tadzhik SSR	38	39	38	39
Armenian SSR	41	46	47	48
Turkmen SSR	39	41	41	42
Estonian SSR	53	54	55	54

* Annual average figures.

Source: **Nar. khoz. SSSR 1988**, s. 42.

Women as percentage of collective farm workers: by Union Republic, 1970-1988*

	1970	1980	1985	1988
USSR	**50**	**47**	**44**	**45**
Russian SFSR	49	44	41	40
Ukrainian SSR	52	49	46	45
Belorussian SSR	52	48	44	43
Uzbek SSR	48	50	49	55
Kazakh SSR	40	39	37	38
Georgian SSR	48	51	51	47
Azerbaidzhan SSR	46	51	51	53
Lithuanian SSR	46	43	40	45
Moldavian SSR	51	52	50	47
Latvian SSR	47	44	41	42
Kirgiz SSR	43	44	44	44
Tadzhik SSR	43	46	47	52
Armenian SSR	44	46	45	48
Turkmen SSR	48	49	49	52
Estonian SSR	47	42	40	41

* Annual average figures for workers engaged in the common economy of collective farms, excluding workers in fishery collectives.

In 1988 the annual average number of women collective farmers was 5.3 million.

Source: **Nar. khoz. SSSR 1988**, s. 43.

193

Female blue- and white-collar employees, 1960-1989
(annual average figures)

Year	Thousands	% of all employees
1960	29 250	47.2
1970	45 800	50.8
1980	57 569	51.2
1988	59 273	50.6
1989	58 700	50.6

Source: **Vestnik Statistiki** 1990, 1, s. 48.

Women specialists* with higher and specialised secondary education employed in the national economy, 1970-1988 (thousands)

	Total	Higher	Specialised secondary	As %**
1970	9 900	3 568	6 332	59
1980	16 956	6 410	10 546	59
1985	20 166	7 840	12 326	60
1987	21 617	8 470	13 147	61
1988	22 400	8 800	13 600	61

* Russian: **spetsialisty**.

** As % of all specialists with such education.

Source: **Nar. khoz. SSSR 1988**, s. 48.

Percentage of women among top managers of enterprises and organisations* in various economic sectors: by Union Republic, 1 January 1989

Key: Column 1 Industry
                2 Agriculture
                3 Transport
                4 Communications
                5 Construction

| | | Sectors | | | |
	1	2	3	4	5
USSR	9.5	6.4	0.6	8.4	0.9
Russian SFSR	10.8	7.8	0.5	10.8	1.0
Ukrainian SSR	8.8	5.7	0.7	4.8	0.8
Belorussian SSR	9.1	7.0	0.8	11.4	0.4
Uzbek SSR	4.2	3.0	0.5	3.9	0.9
Kazakh SSR	9.4	5.5	0.6	4.3	0.8
Georgian SSR	3.6	1.8	0.8	0.0	0.3
Azerbaidzhan SSR	3.3	1.5	0.0	0.7	0.2
Lithuanian SSR	9.1	5.7	0.0	4.7	0.5
Moldavian SSR	7.4	4.6	0.5	5.6	1.9
Latvian SSR	8.6	4.4	0.8	5.4	6.3
Kirgiz SSR	10.1	4.3	0.6	10.3	1.0
Tadzhik SSR	6.2	2.8	0.6	4.3	0.5
Armenian SSR	1.2	1.3	0.5	0.0	0.0
Turkmen SSR	7.3	1.3	0.0	9.2	0.4
Estonian SSR	6.5	0.5	0.0	9.1	0.0

* The total number of enterprises and organisations surveyed was 173 000.

Source: **Vestnik Statistiki** 1989, 12, s. 46.

Women Deputies elected in 1989

	Number	% of all Deputies
Elected as People's Deputies of USSR	352	15.7
Elected to USSR Supreme Soviet	100	18.5
to Union Soviet	44	16.2
to Soviet of Nationalities	56	20.7

Source: **Vestnik Statistiki** 1990, 1, s. 47.

Women teachers in general education day schools, 1960/61-1988/89 (start of academic year)

Year	Thousands*	% of all teachers*
1960/61	1 312	70
1970/71	1 669	71
1980/81	1 653	71
1988/89	2 164	74

Sub-totals for 1988/89

Primary school heads	0.5	85
Heads of incomplete secondary schools	15	44
Heads of secondary schools	26	39
Deputy heads of incomplete secondary schools	12	69
Deputy heads of secondary schools	106	73
Teachers of classes 1-10/11 excl. heads	1 810	83
Teachers of music, singing, drawing, technical drawing, physical culture and work training	194	43

* Persons holding second, part-time, posts are counted only once. The figures include heads, who, as a rule, also undertake classroom teaching.

Source: **Vestnik Statistiki** 1990, 1, s. 51.

Women teachers in general education schools: by Union Republic, 1988/89 (start of academic year)

	Total	Urban	Rural
Thousands			
USSR	**2 135**	**1 166**	**969**
Russian SFSR	988	591	397
Ukrainian SSR	357	209	148
Belorussian SSR	84	48	36
Uzbek SSR	174	69	105
Kazakh SSR	167	67	100
Georgian SSR	64	30	34
Azerbaidzhan SSR	65	35	30
Lithuanian SSR	30	19	11
Moldavian SSR	34	13	21
Latvian SSR	21	14	7
Kirgiz SSR	44	13	31
Tadzhik SSR	32	14	18
Armenian SSR	36	23	13
Turkmen SSR	26	12	14
Estonian SSR	13	9	4
As percentage of all teachers			
USSR	**74.4**	**83.1**	**66.0**
Russian SFSR	82.3	86.0	77.4
Ukrainian SSR	78.1	82.7	72.3
Belorussian SSR	78.4	83.2	73.0
Uzbek SSR	55.4	74.7	47.2
Kazakh SSR	77.0	83.8	73.0
Georgian SSR	73.0	81.8	66.8
Azerbaidzhan SSR	57.3	76.1	44.3
Lithuanian SSR	81.8	85.3	76.2
Moldavian SSR	74.7	80.5	71.5
Latvian SSR	84.4	86.2	81.5
Kirgiz SSR	67.7	81.4	63.4
Tadzhik SSR	38.3	63.5	29.4
Armenian SSR	71.3	80.1	59.3
Turkmen SSR	50.0	65.5	41.4
Estonian SSR	85.2	86.3	82.8

Source: **Narodnoe obrazovanie**, s. 139.

Women doctors of all specialties*, 1970-1988
(end of year)

Year	Thousands	% of all doctors
1970	479.6	72
1980	683.1	69
1985	802.4	69
1986	828.3	69
1987	815.4	66
1988	820.5	65

* Includes two categories of dentist. [Ed.]

Source: **Nar. khoz. SSSR 1988**, s. 222.

Women as percentage of students in higher and specialised secondary education: by sectoral affiliation of their institutions, 1970/71-1988/89 (start of academic year)

	1970	1980	1985	1988
Higher education				
Total	49	52	55	54
Industry, construction transport, communications	38	42	44	40
Agriculture	30	34	36	35
Economics and law	60	67	71	70
Health care, physical culture and sport	56	58	60	63
Education, art, cinematography	66	69	74	71
Specialised secondary education				
Total	54	56	58	57
Industry, construction transport, communications	40	43	43	39
Agriculture	37	37	35	33
Economics and law	83	85	84	83
Health care, physical culture and sport	87	90	90	88
Education, art, cinematography	81	85	87	87

Source: **Narodnoe obrazovanie**, s. 175, 226.

Women students in higher and specialised secondary
education as percentage of all students:
by Union Republic, 1970/71-1988/89*

	1970	1980	1985	1988
Higher education				
USSR	**49**	**52**	**55**	**54**
Russian SFSR	51	53	56	55
Ukrainian SSR	47	52	57	54
Belorussian SSR	52	55	60	59
Uzbek SSR	40	43	45	46
Kazakh SSR	51	52	56	54
Georgian SSR	49	48	53	49
Azerbaidzhan SSR	37	40	47	43
Lithuanian SSR	53	55	62	60
Moldavian SSR	52	56	58	59
Latvian SSR	51	57	61	62
Kirgiz SSR	51	54	59	55
Tadzhik SSR	35	36	42	41
Armenian SSR	46	48	54	50
Turkmen SSR	34	37	43	44
Estonian SSR	51	54	59	55
Specialised secondary education				
USSR	**54**	**56**	**58**	**57**
Russian SFSR	56	58	59	58
Ukrainian SSR	52	56	58	57
Belorussian SSR	55	59	62	60
Uzbek SSR	42	49	51	52
Kazakh SSR	53	56	58	57
Georgian SSR	45	46	52	52
Azerbaidzhan SSR	38	45	47	44
Lithuanian SSR	50	52	52	51
Moldavian SSR	56	63	63	63
Latvian SSR	50	51	55	52
Kirgiz SSR	55	58	59	60
Tadzhik SSR	38	42	42	47
Armenian SSR	43	51	53	54
Turkmen SSR	39	43	49	51
Estonian SSR	48	50	51	51

* At start of academic year.

Source: **Narodnoe obrazovanie**, s. 176, 227.

Percentage of women students pursuing higher and specialised secondary education while still working: by Union Republic, 1988/89*

	Higher	Specialised secondary
USSR	**52**	**56**
Russian SFSR	53	57
Ukrainian SSR	54	61
Belorussian SSR	59	59
Uzbek SSR	44	47
Kazakh SSR	48	53
Georgian SSR	49	43
Azerbaidzhan SSR	33	34
Lithuanian SSR	62	58
Moldavian SSR	59	65
Latvian SSR	64	53
Kirgiz SSR	46	51
Tadzhik SSR	43	35
Armenian SSR	39	37
Turkmen SSR	36	48
Estonian SSR	56	55

* At start of academic year.

Source: **Narodnoe obrazovanie**, s. 176, 227.

Permanent pre-school units, 1970-1988 (end of year)

	1970	1980	1985	1988
Total (thousands)	102.7	127.7	140.1	147.4
in urban areas	61.5	69.1	73.5	75.6
in rural areas	41.2	58.6	66.6	71.8
Children (thousands)	9 281	14 337	16 140	17 354
in urban areas	7 380	10 887	12 075	12 832
in rural areas	1 901	3 450	4 065	4 522
Provision per 100 children of corresponding age	37	54	58	58
in urban areas	61	69	70	66
in rural areas	15	32	38	40

Source: **Nar. khoz. SSSR 1988**, s. 194.

Provision in permanent pre-school units per 100 children of corresponding age: by Union Republic, 1970-1988

	1970	1980	1985	1988
USSR	**37**	**54**	**58**	**58**
Russian SFSR	49	65	70	71
Ukrainian SSR	38	57	60	61
Belorussian SSR	30	57	67	71
Uzbek SSR	15	34	36	36
Kazakh SSR	30	46	52	53
Georgian SSR	22	37	41	44
Azerbaidzhan SSR	12	19	20	20
Lithuanian SSR	25	50	61	61
Moldavian SSR	22	61	67	70
Latvian SSR	37	55	61	63
Kirgiz SSR	18	28	30	30
Tadzhik SSR	11	16	17	16
Armenian SSR	25	36	37	39
Turkmen SSR	19	28	30	31
Estonian SSR	50	63	69	68

Overcrowding persists in many pre-school units, especially in urban areas. There are more than one million children in conditions where the established norms are exceeded. Furthermore, over 1.9 million children need places in kindergarten or nurseries.

Source: **Nar. khoz. SSSR 1988**, s. 194.

Life expectancy

The most rapid increases in the average expectation of life in the USSR occurred at the end of the 1940s and during the first half of the 1950s. An average annual improvement of two years resulted from the introduction by health service organs of sulphonamide preparations and antibiotics, and from their very wide availability to the population. A decline in mortality rates occurred up until the mid 1960s when life expectancy in the USSR was only two years less for men and six months less for women than the average in the world's advanced capitalist countries.

Average expectation of life at birth: by country, 1965-1987 (in years)

| | Men | | Women | |
	USSR	Others*	USSR	Others*
1965-66	65.8	67.9	73.8	74.3
1979-80	62.2	70.7	72.5	77.7
1983-85	-	72.2	-	79.1
1986-87	65.0	-	73.8	-

* USA, Federal Republic of Germany, France, Great Britain and Japan.

In the postwar period life expectancy was at its lowest level during the years 1978-1981. That is explained largely by the rise in mortality which occurred among people in the working age groups.

An extensive programme of administrative-organisational and educational measures to combat drunkenness and alcoholism contributed to a significant reduction of mortality, particularly from accidents, poisoning and traumas. As a consequence, life expectancy rose to 65.0 years for men and to 73.8 for women in 1986-1987. The impact on life expectancy of changes in mortality rates for the main causes of death are shown in the next table.

Effect of changes in mortality on expectation of life, 1967-1987 (in years)

| | 1967-84 | | 1985-87 | |
	Men	Women	Men	Women
All causes of death	-3.5	-1.4	2.7	1.2
Diseases of circulatory system	-2.2	-1.7	0.6	0.6
Accidents, poisoning and traumas	-1.0	-0.3	1.4	0.3
Diseases of respiratory organs	-0.3	-0.1	0.5	0.3
Infectious and parasitic diseases	0.3	0.1	0.1	0.1
Neoplasms	-0.2	0.2	-0.1	0.03

Despite the reduction in mortality during 1985-1987, the average expectation of life in the USSR remains at a level lower than in advanced capitalist countries. This is due mainly to the higher level of infant mortality (2.4-5 times higher than in the USA, the Federal Republic of Germany, Great Britain, France and Japan), and from higher death rates among the working population. That applies particularly in the case of male deaths due to diseases of the circulatory system, accidents, poisoning and traumas, and diseases of the respiratory organs.

Source: **Stat. Press-Byull.** 1989, 5, s. 108-9.

Average expectation of life at birth, 1971–1988 (in years)

From	All	Men	Women
1971–72	69.5	64.5	73.6
1978–79	67.9	62.5	72.6
1983–84	67.9	62.6	72.8
1984	67.7	62.4	72.6
1984–85	68.1	62.9	72.7
1985	68.4	63.3	72.9
1985–86	69.0	64.2	73.3
1986	69.6	65.0	73.6
1986–87	69.8	65.0	73.8
1987	69.8	65.1	73.8
1988	69.5	64.8	73.6

Source: **Nar. khoz. SSSR 1988**, s. 30.

Average expectation of life at birth: by Union Republic, 1979–1980 (in years)

	All	Men	Women
USSR	**67.7**	**62.2**	**72.5**
Russian SFSR	67.5	61.5	73.0
Ukrainian SSR	69.7	64.6	74.0
Belorussian SSR	71.1	65.9	75.6
Uzbek SSR	67.6	64.0	70.7
Kazakh SSR	67.0	61.6	71.9
Georgian SSR	71.2	67.1	74.8
Azerbaidzhan SSR	68.1	64.2	71.8
Lithuanian SSR	70.5	65.5	75.4
Moldavian SSR	65.6	62.4	68.8
Latvian SSR	68.9	63.6	73.9
Kirgiz SSR	66.0	61.1	70.1
Tadzhik SSR	66.3	63.7	68.6
Armenian SSR	72.8	69.5	75.7
Turkmen SSR	64.6	61.1	67.8
Estonian SSR	69.4	64.2	74.2

Source: **Nar. khoz. SSSR 1988**, s. 31.

Average expectation of life at birth:
by Union Republic, 1984-1985 (in years)

	All	Men	Women
USSR	**68.1**	**62.9**	**72.3**
Russian SFSR	68.1	62.3	73.3
Ukrainian SSR	69.7	64.8	74.0
Belorussian SSR	72.6	67.4	77.2
Uzbek SSR	67.7	64.3	70.8
Kazakh SSR	67.7	62.6	72.5
Georgian SSR	71.6	67.3	75.2
Azerbaidzhan SSR	69.5	65.3	73.1
Lithuanian SSR	70.5	65.5	75.4
Moldavian SSR	65.4	62.0	68.6
Latvian SSR	69.5	64.4	74.2
Kirgiz SSR	66.6	62.5	70.2
Tadzhik SSR	68.7	66.3	70.8
Armenian SSR	73.0	69.8	75.7
Turkmen SSR	64.7	61.1	68.1
Estonian SSR	69.7	64.6	74.4

Source: **AiF** 1989, 9, s. 3.

Average expectation of life at birth:
by Union Republic, 1985-1986 (in years)

	All	Men	Women
USSR	**69.0**	**64.2**	**73.3**
Russian SFSR	69.3	63.8	74.0
Ukrainian SSR	70.5	65.9	74.5
Belorussian SSR	71.4	66.7	75.5
Uzbek SSR	68.2	65.1	71.0
Kazakh SSR	68.9	64.0	73.3
Georgian SSR	71.6	67.4	75.1
Azerbaidzhan SSR	69.9	65.7	73.4
Lithuanian SSR	71.5	66.8	75.9
Moldavian SSR	66.4	63.1	69.5
Latvian SSR	70.2	65.5	74.5
Kirgiz SSR	67.9	64.1	71.1
Tadzhik SSR	69.7	67.2	71.8
Armenian SSR	73.3	70.5	75.7
Turkmen SSR	64.8	61.4	67.8
Estonian SSR	70.4	65.5	74.9

Source: **Nar. khoz. SSSR 1988**, s. 31.

Average expectation of life at birth: by Union Republic, 1986-1987 (in years)

	All	Men	Women
USSR	**69.8**	**65.0**	**73.8**
Russian SFSR	70.1	64.9	74.6
Ukrainian SSR	71.1	66.5	74.9
Belorussian SSR	72.0	67.3	76.0
Uzbek SSR	68.6	65.6	71.2
Kazakh SSR	69.7	64.9	73.9
Georgian SSR	72.1	67.9	75.7
Azerbaidzhan SSR	70.2	66.0	73.7
Lithuanian SSR	72.5	67.9	76.6
Moldavian SSR	67.8	64.5	70.7
Latvian SSR	70.9	66.3	75.0
Kirgiz SSR	68.6	64.9	71.7
Tadzhik SSR	70.1	67.6	72.1
Armenian SSR	73.9	71.0	76.2
Turkmen SSR	65.2	61.8	68.2
Estonian SSR	71.0	66.4	75.1

Source: **AiF** 1989, 9, s. 3.

Average expectation of life at birth: by Union Republic, 1988 (in years)

	All	Men	Women
USSR	**69.5**	**64.8**	**73.6**
Russian SFSR	69.9	64.8	74.4
Ukrainian SSR	70.9	66.4	74.8
Belorussian SSR	71.7	67.0	75.9
Uzbek SSR	68.7	65.6	71.4
Kazakh SSR	69.8	64.8	74.1
Georgian SSR	72.2	68.0	75.8
Azerbaidzhan SSR	69.9	65.7	73.5
Lithuanian SSR	72.4	67.7	76.6
Moldavian SSR	68.1	64.3	71.3
Latvian SSR	71.0	66.3	75.1
Kirgiz SSR	68.2	64.2	71.8
Tadzhik SSR	69.7	66.8	72.1
Armenian SSR	62.3	61.6	62.4
Turkmen SSR	65.9	62.4	69.2
Estonian SSR	71.0	66.6	75.0

Source: **Nar. khoz. SSSR 1988**, s. 31.

Cases of selected diseases in USSR and USA, per 100 000 population

	USSR 1987	USA 1984	USSR / USA
Typhoid fever	3.2	0.16	+20.0
Bacterial dysentery	179.4	73.5	+2.7
Viral hepatitis	304.6	133.2	+2.3
incl. serum hepatitis	41.8	11.0	+3.8
Measles	67.4	1.1	+61.3
Whooping cough	7.2	0.96	+7.5
Meningococcal infection	5.4	1.16	+4.7
Malaria	0.56	0.42	+1.2
Tuberculosis	44.0	9.4	+4.7
Gonorrhea	59.8	372.0	-6.2
Syphilis	5.6	12.2	-2.2

Source: **AiF** 1990, 4, s. 7.

Cases of temporary loss of work capacity from various causes, 1980-1988 per 100 workers*

	1980	1986	1987	1988
All cases	**111.3**	**103.0**	**94.5**	**106.3**
Illness	82.1	72.7	66.3	73.0
includes:				
'Flu and colds	42.7	35.8	28.9	35.7
Accidents	4.9	4.0	4.1	4.2
Diseases of:				
circulatory system	5.3	5.2	5.3	5.1
musculo-skeletal system	5.3	5.6	5.9	6.1
gastrointestinal tract	3.1	3.1	3.1	3.1
Complications of pregnancy and the postnatal period	2.0	2.3	2.3	2.3
Caring for sick persons	28.2	28.2	26.1	31.4
Sanitorium-health resort treatment, quarantine	0.8	0.5	0.5	0.6

* From a sample of enterprises.

Source: **Nar. khoz. SSSR 1988**, s. 232.

Calendar days of temporary loss of work capacity from various causes, 1980-1988 per 100 workers*

	1980	1986	1987	1988
All cases	**1 155**	**1 054**	**1 011**	**1 141**
Illness	980	878	839	877
Includes:				
'Flu and colds	320	259	219	266
Accidents	113	92	94	96
Diseases of:				
circulatory system	88	88	88	84
musculo-skeletal system	71	77	79	81
gastrointestinal tract	55	56	55	54
Complications of pregnancy				
and the postnatal period	31	36	37	37
Care of sick persons	166	166	162	255
Sanitorium-health resort				
treatment, quarantine	7	3	4	4

* From a sample of enterprises.

The total loss of working time due to temporary loss of work capacity was 1.13 billion man-days in 1988. Of those, 243 million days were accounted for by care of sick persons, and on average 900 000 persons are not at work for that reason each day. The increase in the number of days of temporary loss of work capacity arises from the epidemic of influenza in January-February 1989, and also from the extension of the period for caring for sick persons during which pay is received.

Source: **Nar. khoz. SSSR 1988**, s. 232.

Temporary loss of work capacity: by Union Republic, 1987 per 100 workers*

	Cases All	Illness	Work days lost All	Illness
USSR	**94.47**	**66.32**	**1 011.4**	**839.2**
Russian SFSR	103.29	70.65	1 095.0	894.3
Ukrainian SSR	83.20	61.58	866.5	739.1
Belorussian SSR	87.66	59.74	863.2	703.0
Uzbek SSR	69.82	53.91	827.0	723.7
Kazakh SSR	91.58	64.57	1 061.5	890.8
Georgian SSR	49.14	43.00	599.7	565.5
Azerbaidzhan SSR	71.92	60.05	805.7	729.6
Lithuanian SSR	67.18	50.82	897.4	796.9
Moldavian SSR	91.97	61.23	1 006.3	813.5
Latvian SSR	90.81	70.70	1 043.7	924.3
Kirgiz SSR	81.64	60.18	836.3	708.2
Tadzhik SSR	75.50	56.09	787.4	674.8
Armenian SSR	70.17	56.46	657.1	577.0
Turkmen SSR	67.03	53.47	818.2	724.1
Estonian SSR	91.38	65.86	1 072.4	917.0

* From a sample of enterprises.

Source: **Sotsialnoe razvitie SSSR**, s. 227-8.

Persons first declared invalids:
by type of illness, 1987

Key: Column 1 Blue- and white-collar workers
               2 Collective farmers
               3 Blue- and white-collar workers
               4 Collective farmers

Columns	1	2	3	4
	Thousands		Per 10 000 workers	
All	**511.3**	**56.0**	**43.1**	**45.2**
Circulatory system	161.2	14.6	13.6	11.8
Neoplasms	105.3	12.2	8.9	9.9
Traumas	56.4	6.5	4.8	5.2
Nervous system	35.4	4.3	3.0	3.5
Musculo-skeletal system	32.4	3.6	3.0	3.5
Respiratory organs	29.2	4.7	2.5	3.8
Psychiatric	22.6	1.8	1.9	1.5
Digestive organs	16.4	2.0	1.4	1.6
Tuberculosis	15.9	2.8	1.3	2.3
Occupational diseases and poisoning	2.5	0.2	0.2	0.2

Of the total number of persons who were first declared
invalids in 1987 over 400 000 (71%) had complete loss of
work capacity; 169 000 (30%) were under the age of 45. The
main causes of invalidity (63%) were diseases of the
circulatory system, neoplasms and traumas.

The total number of invality pensioners on the records of
the social security organs is practically stable and stood
at over 6 million at the start of 1988.

Source: **Sotsialnoe razvitie SSSR, s. 229.**

Cases of selected infectious diseases, 1980–1988

	1980	1985	1988
Thousands			
Severe intestinal infections	1 324	1 601	1 815
Typhoid and Paratyphoid A, B, and C	16.9	17.6	11.5
Scarlatina	230	278	215
Diphtheria	0.35	1.51	0.87
Whooping cough	13.9	53.9	45.4
Mumps	0.30	0.28	0.20
Severe poliomyeltis	0.17	0.14	0.16
Measles	356	273	165
Influenza etc*	60 359	71 869	79 906
Viral hepatitis incl. serum hepatitis	802	934	716
Per 100 000 population			
Severe intestinal infections	499	578	636
Typhoid and Paratyphoid A, B, and C	6	6	4
Scarlatina	87	100	75
Diphtheria	0.13	0.55	0.30
Whooping cough	5	19	16
Mumps	0.11	0.10	0.07
Severe poliomyeltis	0.06	0.05	0.06
Measles	134	98	58
Influenza etc*	22 761	25 928	27 999
Viral hepatitis incl. serum hepatitis	302	337	251

* Acute infections of the upper respiratory tract.

Source: **Nar. khoz. SSSR 1988**, s. 233.

Cases of severe intestinal infections: by Union Republic, 1988 per 10 000 population

	All cases	As % of 1987 figs	Bacterial dysentery Cases	As % of 1987 figs.
USSR	**64**	**106**	**21**	**107**
Russian SFSR	83	107	31	108
Ukrainian SSR	31	104	10	124
Belorussian SSR	24	141	14	177
Uzbek SSR	71	99	8	89
Kazakh SSR	51	96	16	86
Georgian SSR	33	101	5	98
Azerbaidzhan SSR	22	91	3	80
Lithuanian SSR	21	135	10	154
Moldavian SSR	57	95	15	80
Latvian SSR	25	166	12	152
Kirgiz SSR	62	96	10	88
Tadzhik SSR	113	105	17	90
Armenian SSR	21	87	5	84
Turkmen SSR	63	102	7	75
Estonian SSR	45	140	19	216

In 1988 a total of 1.8 million cases of severe intestinal infection were notified. That figure is 8% above the average for the years 1985-1987. These illnesses are caused in the main by the unsatisfactory sanitary conditions of population centres, reservoirs and products of the food industry. This type of morbidity has not declined in 1989.

Source: **Stat. Press-Byull.** 1989, 9, s. 54.

**Cases of viral hepatitis and influenza etc.*:
by Union Republic, 1988 per 10 000 population**

	Viral hepatitis		Influenza etc.*	
	Cases	As % of 1987 figs.	Cases	As % of 1987 figs.
USSR	**25**	**82**	**2 805**	**133**
Russian SFSR	15	96	3 341	134
Ukrainian SSR	17	98	3 163	136
Belorussian SSR	23	127	2 920	138
Uzbek SSR	94	65	1 028	119
Kazakh SSR	40	112	1 954	130
Georgian SSR	20	65	1 605	134
Azerbaidzhan SSR	21	81	1 369	108
Lithuanian SSR	21	101	1 704	193
Moldavian SSR	29	97	1 926	141
Latvian SSR	24	151	2 425	141
Kirgiz SSR	82	76	1 333	122
Tadzhik SSR	53	47	1 264	124
Armenian SSR	14	73	1 727	120
Turkmen SSR	47	61	1 143	121
Estonian SSR	10	101	2 678	154

* Severe infections of the upper respiratory tract.

The absence of disposable syringes, other disposable items and sterile apparatus is the basic reason for the spread of serum hepatitis, the proportion of which amongst all cases of hepatitis has risen from 10% in 1985 to 16% in 1988. Morbidity from viral hepatitis has risen in the majority of Union Republics during 1989.

Source: **Stat. Press-Byull.** 1989, 9, s. 55.

Patients suffering from alcoholism and alcoholic psychosis: by Union Republic, 1984-1988 per 100 000 population

	First diagnosed	Recorded cases
USSR		
1984	206	1 560
1986	196	1 618
1987	181	1 628
1988	154	1 598
Russian SFSR		
1984	243	1 875
1986	242	1 980
1987	223	2 009
1988	198	2 000
Ukrainian SSR		
1984	228	1 709
1986	192	1 690
1987	180	1 678
1988	148	1 619
Belorussian SSR		
1984	257	1 757
1986	219	1 851
1987	196	1 879
1988	143	1 758
Uzbek SSR		
1984	69	472
1986	46	465
1987	40	452
1988	33	436
Kazakh SSR		
1984	172	1 222
1986	183	1 308
1987	187	1 324
1988	126	1 278
Georgian SSR		
1984	39	327
1986	29	284
1987	29	279
1988	29	282
Azerbaidzhan SSR		
1984	23	278
1986	13	253
1987	15	260
1988	16	241
Lithuanian SSR		
1984	158	1 575
1986	202	1 612
1987	184	1 613
1988	133	1 602

Table continues

	First diagnosed	Recorded cases
Moldavian SSR		
1984	274	1 679
1986	293	1 888
1987	255	1 948
1988	206	1 838
Latvian SSR		
1984	275	1 777
1986	302	1 945
1987	229	1 997
1988	213	2 013
Kirgiz SSR		
1984	105	868
1986	92	838
1987	69	789
1988	62	742
Tadzhik SSR		
1984	71	478
1986	54	481
1987	41	466
1988	28	425
Armenian SSR		
1984	20	262
1986	16	219
1987	13	194
1988	11	175
Turkmen SSR		
1984	39	496
1986	50	511
1987	39	442
1988	47	433
Estonian SSR		
1984	185	1 316
1986	159	1 478
1987	143	1 489
1988	114	1 490

Source: **Vestnik Statistiki** 1989, 6, s. 61-2.

******

In 1987, 17% of the country's population thought that it was impossible to achieve success in the battle against drunkenness, alcoholism and drug addiction. In 1988 the number of pessimists doubled. This year [1989] as many as 58% of the population do not believe that victory can be won over this social evil.

Text continues

Such were the results of sociological enquiries presented
by the Vice-Chairman of the Russian SFSR's Council of
Ministers, N. Trubilin, at a meeting of the USSR Supreme
Soviet's Committee on health protection.

The scale of drunkenness and drug addiction is growing.
Today just the recorded number of alcoholics is 5 million.
Every year, 20 thousand people die from alcohol-related
causes. The growth in "drunk" crime continues.

The threat to the next generation is also increasing. The
number of children with mental impairment rose from 900
thousand in 1984 to 1.1 million in 1988. Today 260
thousand mentally retarded children are pupils in special
schools of the Russian SFSR alone. In the first eight
months of this year 133 thousand juveniles were punished
for drunkenness under the administrative code. In a word,
the brief drop noticed shortly after the well-known Decree
of 1985 has now changed into a strong and swift upward
surge.

Addressing the Deputies, the Chief of a Directorate at the
USSR Ministry of Health, A. Demenkov, stated that the
number of institutions for the treatment of alcohol and
drug addiction had increased by three and a half times
since 1981....More than half of these institutions are
urgently in need of repairs and it is necessary simply to
close down many simply because of their ruinous condition.
The point is that local managers, when reporting the
opening of new dispensaries, did not indicate that they had
allocated the poorest buildings - apparently thinking that
alcoholics and drug addicts, as social outcasts, did not
deserve better.

At the time a great deal of enthousiasm was expressed for
the opening of addiction treatment rooms at industrial
enterprises. Today, as the representative of the Ministry
of Health reported, they are being closed on a mass scale
in connection with the transfer to economic accounting.

It has become unprofitable for enterprises to take on
persons who have undergone a course of treatment for
alcoholism and drug addiction. Indeed, why mention them
when, according to data from the State Committee on
Education, one out of three young people leaving school,
occupation-technical school or technikum could not find
work last year? This year some graduates from higher
educational establishments also encountered this problem.
Is it any wonder that those with nowhere to study or to
work account for the main increase in juveniles found
guilty of drunkenness?

Source: **Izvestiya**, 1989, 30 oktyabrya, s. 1 (excerpts).

Patients suffering from drug addiction and toxicomania: by Union Republic, 1984-1988 per 100 000 population

	First diagnosed	Recorded cases
USSR		
1984	2.5	13.7
1986	5.8	17.1
1987	8.6	21.5
1988	6.0	24.3
Russian SFSR		
1984	1.7	11.2
1986	4.5	13.4
1987	8.0	17.9
1988	5.6	20.6
Ukrainian SSR		
1984	6.0	14.9
1986	13.0	24.9
1987	13.9	32.4
1988	8.9	37.4
Belorussian SSR		
1984	0.2	1.4
1986	1.9	3.2
1987	2.4	4.8
1988	2.4	5.9
Uzbek SSR		
1984	1.7	12.3
1986	5.0	15.5
1987	6.2	20.8
1988	5.1	24.2
Kazakh SSR		
1984	2.1	17.7
1986	5.0	19.5
1987	9.7	26.5
1988	6.6	30.9
Georgian SSR		
1984	2.4	17.9
1986	2.2	17.2
1987	3.0	17.7
1988	2.9	19.2
Azerbaidzhan SSR		
1984	1.6	8.3
1986	1.8	7.8
1987	4.5	11.1
1988	6.7	14.1
Lithuanian SSR		
1984	0.4	5.9
1986	2.8	7.2
1987	6.1	10.1
1988	2.9	11.2

Table continues

	First diagnosed	Recorded cases
Moldavian SSR		
1984	0.5	1.8
1986	3.4	5.7
1987	4.7	8.0
1988	2.4	8.3
Latvian SSR		
1984	1.8	6.0
1986	5.4	12.3
1987	7.8	19.0
1988	5.8	22.5
Kirgiz SSR		
1984	3.3	33.4
1986	4.8	32.7
1987	9.2	29.0
1988	7.0	26.7
Tadzhik SSR		
1984	0.3	4.8
1986	2.0	6.2
1987	3.7	9.1
1988	2.8	10.5
Armenian SSR		
1984	1.1	12.3
1986	1.2	7.9
1987	1.5	6.3
1988	1.0	6.5
Turkmen SSR		
1984	6.8	162.7
1986	13.3	152.3
1987	21.4	129.9
1988	13.7	109.8
Estonian SSR		
1984	1.6	5.2
1986	1.4	5.9
1987	4.6	10.3
1988	4.0	14.0

Source: **Vestnik Statistiki** 1989, 6, s. 61-2.

Cases of plague, 1927–1988

Years	Absolute numbers
1927–1936	1 037
1937–1946	415
1947–1956	235
1957–1966	53
1967–1976	33
1988	2

In August 1989 a small girl from a livestock-farming family died of plague in Makhambet district of Kazakhstan. A quarantine was imposed; 63 persons who had been in direct contact with her were hospitalised for observation but no one else proved to be infected. This was the second case of plague to be notified in the USSR in 1989.

In the country as a whole there are 14 plague foci, including the Central Asian desert area, where the above case was notified. The total area involved exceeds 20 million hectares.

Measures are taken to prevent outbreaks of plague among the population and these include the work of 29 anti-plague stations and 6 anti-plague research institutes. Complete eradication of the disease is out of the question while it is still carried by numbers of small scavenging rodents.

Source: **AiF** 1989, 36, s. 8.

AIDS

By early 1990, according to the USSR Ministry of Health, 28 patients had contracted AIDS and 19 of them had died. The number of HIV carriers was 457, of whom more than 200 were children.

It is estimated that by the end of 1990 there will be 1 625 persons who are infected, and that by 1992 the number of HIV carriers may be 24 000.

Source: **Med. gaz.** 1990, 30, s. 1 (extracts).

Cases of leprosy, 1970–1988

Years	Absolute numbers
1970	7 042
1971	6 953
1972	6 793
1973	6 635
1974	6 454
1975	6 303
1976	6 148
1977	5 984
1978	5 822
1979	5 682
1980	5 497
1981	5 316
1982	5 158
1983	4 975
1984	4 808
1985	4 648
1986	4 504
1987	4 373
1988	4 214

During the past ten years 12-15 patients have been registered as suffering from leprosy each year. Taking into account the rate of decline of this disease, the number of patients may amount to around 2 251 (plus or minus 46) by the year 2 000.

The average age of patients is 40 years and above. In its early stages the disease is curable, but cured patients remain under medical observation for the rest of their lives. At present, out of 4 000 patients, 3 000 have succesfully undergone a full course of treatment. About a thousand patients are in hospitals.

The largest number of cases of the disease are notified in Karakalpak ASSR, Kzyl-Orda oblast (Kazakh SSR) and also along the estuaries of large rivers - the Volga, Don, Amudari and Syrdari. There are 16 anti-leprosy institutions in the USSR; not all have ward blocks. The largest of them are the Astrakhan (Scientific Research Institute for the Study of Leprosy), Tersa, Abinsk, and Kazakh institutes. Each of them has 80-150 beds. World-wide the number of registered leprosy patients is 15 million: they live mainly in India, the countries of South-East Asia and Africa.

Source: **AiF** 1990, 5, s. 8.

Patients suffering from cancer, 1980–1988

	1980	1985	1988
First diagnosed:			
thousands	544	616	677
per 100 000 population			
non-standardised	205	222	237
standardised	173	186	192.4
Recorded cases:			
thousands	2 226	2 635	2 937
per 100 000 population	836	946	1 025

Source: **Nar. khoz. SSSR 1988**, s. 234.

Patients first diagnosed as suffering from cancer: by selected localisations, 1988

	Thousands		Per 100 000 popn.*	
	Men	Women	Men	Women
All neoplasms	**338.6**	**338.4**	**254.1**	**160.2**
Localisation:				
lip, oral cavity,				
pharynx	21.8	5.9	16.1	2.7
oesophagus	12.2	6.5	9.2	2.7
stomach	54.4	40.8	40.8	17.9
rectum	13.3	16.5	10.1	7.3
larynx	13.0	0.9	9.5	0.5
trachea, bronchi,				
lungs	91.0	19.1	67.8	8.2
skin	31.6	46.4	24.0	20.8
mammary gland	0.4	53.5	0.3	27.9
uterus	–	44.1	–	21.6
lymphatic and				
haemopoietic tissue	16.7	14.8	12.5	8.0
other organs	82.4	89.9	63.8	42.6

* Standardised.

Source: **Nar. khoz. SSSR 1988**, s. 234.

Tuberculosis, 1985-1988

	1988	1988 as % of 1985 figs.
Cases first diagnosed:		
thousands	119.8	94.5
per 100 000 population	42.0	91.9
incl. respiratory cases:		
thousands	107.5	94.5
per 100 000 population	37.7	92.0
Deaths:		
thousands	21.8	83.9
per 100 000 population	7.6	80.9
incl. respiratory cases:		
thousands	20.1	83.5
per 100 000 population	7.0	80.5

At the beginning of 1990 curative institutions had 603 000 patients on record as suffering from active tuberculosis. Among the rural population the incidence of this disease was 1.4 times higher than among the urban population. Of the total number of patients first diagnosed as suffering from active tuberculosis, two thirds were men and almost a half were persons aged between 20 and 40 years. In this age group among those with tuberculosis of the respiratory organs more than 40% were bacteria carriers; these were mainly alcoholics and persons of no fixed abode. Due to the low effectiveness of preventive examinations the disease manifests itself in an advanced form in more than a third of patients.

In Kazakhstan the incidence of the disease has remained at a high level for many years. In 1988 there were 74 cases per 100 000 population, which is 1.8 times higher than the average for the country as a whole. In Azerbaidzhan, Moldavia and the Republics of Central Asia this indicator exceeds the all-Union level by 10-26%.

In 1988 a total of 17 600 blue- and white-collar workers and collective farmers suffering from tuberculosis were given the status of invalids. The level of invalidity is 1.3 per 10 000 blue- and white-collar workers, and 2.1 per 10 000 collective farmers. It is high among blue- and white-collar workers in Kazakhstan, Uzbekistan and Turkmenistan, being 1.5-2 times above the all-Union level. It is high among collective farmers in Uzbekistan, Tadzhikstan and the Russian SFSR, being 10%-14% above the all-Union level. Of the persons whose invalidity is due to tuberculosis, half are under 45 years.

Text continues

Notwithstanding the continuing reduction in death from tuberculosis, the rate is 2-10 times above that for Japan, France, the Federal Republic of Germany, Great Britain and the USA. Mortality from this cause is 1.3 times higher among the rural population than among the urban population, and this excess is still more significant in persons over the age of 50.

Men die from tuberculosis 4.5 times more frequently than women. This difference increases with age: among persons aged 30-39 male mortality is 6 times higher than female, and among persons aged 40-59 it is 8 times higher. In Azerbaidzhan, the Ukraine, Turkmenistan and Kazakhstan the death rate exceeds the all-Union level by 11%-42%.

At the same time, over the period 1981-1988 hospital beds for patients with tuberculosis fell by 16% and the number of doctors specialising in this field decreased by 11%. In Lithuania, Tadzhikistan, Uzbekistan, Moldavia and Estonia hospital beds decreased by 24%-36%. In Belorussia, Moldavia, Estonia and Georgia the number of specialists declined by 20%-22%.

At the present time the supply of hospital beds in the Ukraine, Estonia, Georgia and Belorussia is one third lower than the norm; in Armenia it is half the norm. The anti-tuberculosis dispensaries are poorly equipped; about half have no fluorography room and 7% have no X-ray room.

The material-technical basis of the anti-tuberculosis institutions is in an unsatisfactory state. Thus, for example, in Kazakhstan out of 180 dispensaries and hospitals only 46 are in purpose-designed buildings. There has been a failure to fulfill a range of measures for the construction of a tuberculosis hospital in Alma-Ata, an oblast dispensary in Shevchenko, and tuberculosis sanatoria in Gurev and Semipalatinsk oblasti.

Source: **Vestnik Statistiki,** 1990, 2, s. 63-4.

Cases of venereal diseases first diagnosed:
by Union Republic, 1980-1987 per 100 000 population

	1980	1985	1986	1987
All forms of syphilis				
USSR	**19.7**	**9.7**	**7.6**	**5.6**
Russian SFSR	23.0	9.7	7.2	5.1
Ukrainian SSR	15.0	7.8	7.3	5.7
Belorussian SSR	8.4	3.5	2.8	1.6
Uzbek SSR	10.9	12.5	7.6	6.1
Kazakh SSR	18.1	10.3	8.2	4.7
Georgian SSR	23.7	17.1	21.5	25.5
Azerbaidzhan SSR	13.4	5.0	5.0	4.7
Lithuanian SSR	9.8	3.2	2.4	2.9
Moldavian SSR	49.0	17.7	9.7	7.4
Latvian SSR	11.1	8.9	8.8	6.1
Kirgiz SSR	39.1	18.6	9.6	6.1
Tadzhik SSR	8.5	16.3	10.6	7.9
Armenian SSR	16.3	10.2	8.5	5.9
Turkmen SSR	17.0	10.2	14.2	12.1
Estonian SSR	29.1	6.8	5.4	3.3
Acute and chronic gonorrhoea				
USSR	**148.0**	**113.0**	**94.6**	**86.3**
Russian SFSR	196.4	147.6	117.9	105.7
Ukrainian SSR	99.5	82.7	77.7	73.5
Belorussian SSR	117.5	96.2	85.9	87.0
Uzbek SSR	37.4	29.8	27.2	23.4
Kazakh SSR	143.3	111.8	96.8	89.3
Georgian SSR	47.0	76.4	112.3	95.9
Azerbaidzhan SSR	23.0	16.8	18.7	15.2
Lithuanian SSR	155.1	123.3	96.3	87.2
Moldavian SSR	154.7	119.8	110.7	115.2
Latvian SSR	161.9	111.3	92.6	79.9
Kirgiz SSR	89.4	68.7	58.1	55.9
Tadzhik SSR	51.1	30.2	24.4	24.5
Armenian SSR	66.7	45.0	44.3	54.8
Turkmen SSR	63.5	37.2	31.5	35.0
Estonian SSR	236.6	154.8	117.2	102.5

At the end of 1987 the total nuumber of patients suffering
from syphilis who were on the records of curative
institutions stood at 152 000, a rate of 54 per 100 000
population.

Source: **Sotsialnoe razvitie SSSR**, s. 235.

Accidents, 1988

	1988	Figures for 1988 as % of		
		1985	1986	1987
Poisoning and traumas thousands	19 046	99	104	103
per 1 000 popn.	67	96	102	102
incl. children thousands	3 980	111	106	103
per 1 000 popn. under 14	54	106	103	101

Each year nearly 19 million persons suffer traumas or poisoning at their place of work or during the course of their domestic lives. In 1988 about 13 million accidents (67% of the total) occurred during domestic life, at school or on the streets (excluding road traffic incidents). The number of such accidents was 6% higher than in 1987. and represented a rate of 45 per 1 000 population. More than 3 million persons (17%) had accidents at work, on the way to or from work, or when fulfilling their civic duty.

The level of traumas due to road traffic incidents remains high. In 1988 a total of 345 000 persons - including 46 000 children (13%) - suffered injuries from this cause. The figure was 12% higher than in 1987 and the number of cases with a fatal outcome rose by 19%. Drivers who were under the influence of alcohol gave rise to injuries to 62 000 persons and pedestrians in the same condition gave rise to 12 000 cases of injury. There were fatal outcomes for 9 000 and 1 600 persons in the two categories. Consumption of alcohol is a contributory factor in every fifth case of injury or death which arises from road traffic incidents.

The level of injuries rises especially in icy conditions, a fact which is frequently linked to the unsatisfactory state of road maintenance. According to the findings of a survey undertaken by Goskomstat SSSR in 25 cities, the number of traumas was 37% higher in January 1989 than in September 1988. The figure was two to three times higher in: Gorki, Bryansk, Kalinin, Dnepropetrovosk, Kuibyshev, Tual, Kirov, Orlov, Donetsk, Novgorod, and Petrozavodsk. More than a quarter of people who were injured sustained fractures; their average duration of absence from work was one and a half months. In Moscow, according to a sample survey, during a 26 day period in January over a thousand people suffered injuries each day.

225

Injuries at work, 1975-1987

	1975	1980	1985	1987
Fatalities and cases entailing loss of work capacity				
Thousands	1 067	878	706	690
Per 10 000 worker	94	72	56	55
Fatalities				
Thousands	19.6	20.5	16.7	14.6
Per 10 000 worker	1.73	1.69	1.33	1.15
Work days lost				
Thousands	21 166	18 111	16 098	16 112
Per 10 000 worker	1 870	1 491	1 280	1 275

Source: **Sotsialnoe razvitie SSSR, s. 70.**

******

In 1988 the number of persons involved in accidents at work was 668 000 of whom 14 400 died. By comparison with 1980 injuries with a fatal outcome in the economy as a whole declined by 32%. The level of injuries was 1.9 times higher than the all-Union level at enterprises and organisations of the fuel and energy complex, 1.6 times higher in the machinery construction complex and 1.4 times higher in the agro-industrial and the wood-chemical complexes.

In 1988 the loss of working time due to accidents at work amounted to 15.8 million man-days.

Source: **Nar. khoz. SSSR 1988, s. 229.**

Injuries at work: by Union republic, 1987
per 10 000 workers

Key: Column 1 Fatalities and cases involving loss of
                  work capacity
                2 Fatalties
                3 Work days lost

| | Columns | | |
	1	2	3
USSR	**55**	**1.15**	**1 275**
Russian SFSR	65	1.21	1 463
Ukrainian SSR	52	1.13	1 184
Belorussian SSR	44	0.89	1 059
Uzbek SSR	18	0.78	516
Kazakh SSR	67	1.17	1 705
Georgian SSR	10	0.71	364
Azerbaidzhan SSR	10	0.92	378
Lithuanian SSR	43	0.80	1 123
Moldavian SSR	43	1.07	1 083
Latvian SSR	53	0.83	1 212
Kirgiz SSR	31	1.28	845
Tadzhik SSR	25	1.00	685
Armenian SSR	17	0.82	646
Turkmen SSR	19	1.12	606
Estonian SSR	54	0.95	1 297

Source: **Sotsialnoe razvitie SSSR, s. 70.**

227

Traumas constitute one of the main causes of complete loss of ability to work. The number of persons from the workforce who were first categorized as invalids on account of traumas has hardly declined. In 1988 the number was 64 600, which is a rate of 5 per 10 000 workers. In Lithuania and Latvia the invalidity rate exceeds the Union average by 14% and 16% respectively, while in Kirgizia and Uzbekistan the corresponding figures are 20% and 24%.

In 1988 a total of 287 000 persons died as a consequence of accidents, poisoning and injuries at work, in their domestic lives and in road traffic incidents. The figure was 14% higher than that for 1987.

Source: **Stat. Press-Byull.** 1989, 9, s. 142-3.

******

Road traffic accidents, 1989

	1989	As % of 1988 figs.
Total accidents	318 805	116.7
Dead	58 460	123.9
Injured	346 484	116.4

Source: **Ekonomika i zhizn** 1990, 8, s. 11.

Fires and deaths from fires: by Union Republic, first nine months of 1989

	Fires	As % of 1988 figs.*	Deaths	Increase on 1988 figs.*
USSR	**109 482**	**113.9**	**5 922**	**359**
Russian SFSR	69 098	110.7	3 992	219
Ukrainian SSR	13 457	112.4	721	14
Belorussian SSR	4 537	114.3	280	88
Uzbek SSR	6 968	145.0	182	12
Kazakh SSR	4 554	117.7	297	20
Georgian SSR	1 596	113.9	54	7
Azerbaidzhan SSR	566	114.3	40	11
Lithuanian SSR	1 719	117.7	56	−17
Moldavian SSR	1 605	125.0	82	1
Latvian SSR	1 369	106.0	70	10
Kirgiz SSR	1 070	116.3	39	10
Tadzhik SSR	693	116.9	13	3
Armenian SSR	895	152.7	19	0
Turkmen SSR	614	143.5	37	3
Estonian SSR	741	109.0	40	−22

* Relates to first nine months of 1988.

Source: **Ekonomika i zhizn** 1990, 3, s. 17.

Deaths from drowning: by Union Republic, 1985-1988
(absolute numbers)

	1985	1986	1987	1988
USSR	**24 238**	**19 947**	**19 634**	**22 706**
Russian SFSR	13 786	10 638	10 562	12 547
Ukrainian SSR	3 794	3 280	3 163	3 548
Belorussian SSR	853	707	562	777
Uzbek SSR	1 845	1 559	1 630	1 727
Kazakh SSR	1 294	1 154	1 274	1 219
Georgian SSR	173	207	166	216
Azerbaidzhan SSR	207	269	264	275
Lithuanian SSR	399	375	259	368
Moldavian SSR	394	353	277	322
Latvian SSR	287	291	214	295
Kirgiz SSR	290	246	327	442
Tadzhik SSR	327	330	383	372
Armenian SSR	60	69	85	100
Turkmen SSR	410	353	355	352
Estonian SSR	119	116	113	146

Source: **Stat. Press-Byull.** 1989, 10, s. 107.

Deaths from drowning: by Union Republic, 1985-1988
per 100 000 population

	1985	1986	1987	1988
USSR	**8.7**	**7.1**	**6.9**	**8.0**
Russian SFSR	9.6	7.4	7.2	8.5
Ukrainian SSR	7.5	6.4	6.2	6.9
Belorussian SSR	8.6	7.0	5.6	7.6
Uzbek SSR	10.1	8.3	8.4	8.7
Kazakh SSR	8.1	7.2	7.8	7.4
Georgian SSR	3.3	3.9	3.1	4.1
Azerbaidzhan SSR	3.1	4.0	3.8	4.0
Lithuanian SSR	11.1	10.4	7.1	10.0
Moldavian SSR	9.5	8.5	6.6	7.6
Latvian SSR	11.0	11.0	8.0	11.0
Kirgiz SSR	7.2	6.0	7.8	10.3
Tadzhik SSR	7.1	7.0	7.8	7.4
Armenian SSR	1.8	2.0	2.5	2.9
Turkmen SSR	12.7	10.6	10.4	10.1
Estonian SSR	7.7	7.5	7.2	9.3

Source: **Stat. Press-Byull.** 1989, 10, s. 107.

Deaths of men per 10 000 population
of specified age group, 1988

	Total	Urban	Rural
All ages	1 019.9	934.5	1 188.6
Under 1	2 802.1	2 378.4	3 418.2
1-4	264.8	147.5	445.7
5-9	76.1	67.9	89.4
10-14	65.4	61.6	71.2
15-19	124.3	121.0	130.0
20-24	202.4	179.9	246.0
25-29	252.6	206.0	390.8
30-34	325.0	284.6	435.8
35-39	428.0	389.1	539.0
40-44	580.5	538.5	706.1
45-49	965.4	905.6	1 102.2
50-54	1 326.1	1 277.5	1 421.6
55-59	2 075.5	2 084.5	2 060.4
60-64	3 010.3	3 052.0	2 935.9
65-69	4 262.6	4 372.0	4 088.1
70-74	6 555.4	6 728.3	6 261.2
75-79	9 399.4	9 778.6	8 870.9
80-84	13 472.4	14 338.9	12 491.2
85 and over	20 894.9	23 117.4	19 001.7

Source: **Naselenie SSSR 1988**, s. 583.

Deaths of women per 10 000 population of specified age group, 1988

	Total	Urban	Rural
All ages	1 005.4	913.5	1 185.4
Under 1	2 151.8	1 749.5	2 733.8
1-4	229.5	124.6	390.2
5-9	50.8	45.1	60.0
10-14	40.3	37.7	44.3
15-19	65.8	59.6	77.8
20-24	77.7	68.1	97.6
25-29	88.6	74.1	131.8
30-34	109.8	97.8	143.9
35-39	156.2	142.8	196.7
40-44	217.7	199.6	272.1
45-49	350.5	330.7	394.8
50-54	511.5	492.5	550.1
55-59	851.2	846.3	859.7
60-64	1 356.8	1 388.9	1 300.3
65-69	2 146.5	2 250.8	1 982.7
70-74	3 747.1	3 962.8	3 418.6
75-79	6 064.6	6 548.2	5 432.5
80-84	9 861.1	10 684.2	8 852.9
85 and over	17 615.0	18 732.8	16 420.0

Source: **Naselenie SSSR 1988**, s. 583.

Main causes of death, 1985-1988
(thousands)

	1985	1987	1988
All causes of death	2 947	2 805	2 889
Diseases of circulatory system	1 630	1 574	1 606
Neoplasms	423	453	465
Accidents, poisoning and traumas	313	249	287
Diseases of respiratory organs	267	223	226
Diseases of digestive organs	87	81	81
Infectious diseases	65	60	58

Source: **Stat. Press-Byull.** 1989, 10, s. 106

Main causes of death, 1985-1988 per 100 000 age-standardised population

	1985	1987	1988
All causes of death	1 222	1 117	1 125
Diseases of circulatory system	705	647	647
Neoplasms	176	183	185
Accidents, poisoning and traumas	120	92	105
Diseases of respiratory organs	104	84	85
Diseases of digestive organs	36	32	32
Infectious diseases	23	21	20

Source: **Stat. Press-Byull.** 1989, 10, s. 106.

Main causes of death: by country and sex, per 100 000 population of corresponding sex and working age group

	Men		Women	
	USSR	Others*	USSR	Others*
All causes of death	659	363	254	178
Diseases of circulatory system	217	109	82	38
Neoplasms	151	103	81	78
Accidents, poisoning and traumas	178	79	38	25
Diseases of respiratory organs	34	12	10	6

* USA, Federal Republic of Germany, France, Great Britain and Japan.

Amongst men of working age the major source for increasing the duration of life is a reduction in the number of premature deaths from diseases of the circulatory system, and from accidents, poisoning and traumas. Amongst women the main source is to be found in diseases of the circulatory system. The pace at which mortality from these causes declines is largely determined by the effectiveness of measures introduced to improve the population's health.

Source: **Stat. Press-Byull.** 1989, 5, s. 108-9. The years in question are not specified. [Ed.]

Main causes of death amongst population of working age, 1980-1988 per 100 000 age-standardised population

	1980	1985	1987	1988
All causes of death	553	522	445	450
Diseases of circulatory system	161	162	145	143
Accidents, poisoning and traumas	175	144	106	118
Neoplasms	107	112	111	111
Diseases of respiratory organs	35	31	21	21

Source: **Nar. khoz. SSSR 1988**, s. 27.

Main causes of death among men, 1980–1988 per 100 000 age-standardised population

	1980	1987	1988
Total population			
All causes of death	**1 729.1**	**1 527.4**	**1 539.9**
Diseases of circulatory system	879.6	816.3	808.8
Neoplasms	250 2	276.8	280.5
Diseases of respiratory organs	192.9	134.8	134.7
Accidents, poisoning and traumas	243.0	150.6	168.4
Urban population			
All causes of death	**1 742.6**	**1 546.8**	**1 554.2**
Diseases of circulatory system	899.8	846.0	833.6
Neoplasms	292.7	310.2	310.7
Diseases of respiratory organs	152.0	101.8	102.1
Accidents, poisoning and traumas	232.9	140.5	161.2
Rural population			
All causes of death	**1 739.2**	**1 534.4**	**1 556.6**
Diseases of circulatory system	858.9	784.9	784.3
Neoplasms	199.4	231.9	239.6
Diseases of respiratory organs	245.9	183.3	183.7
Accidents, poisoning and traumas	269.4	178.5	193.9

Source: **Naselenie SSSR 1988**, s. 663.

Main causes of death among women, 1980–1988 per 100 000 age-standardised population

	1980	1987	1988
Total population			
All causes of death	**950.8**	**874.4**	**879.2**
Diseases of circulatory system	594.4	556.5	552.4
Neoplasms	126.7	131.7	131.9
Diseases of respiratory organs	89.4	58.5	58.1
Accidents, poisoning and traumas	58.4	43.1	51.3
Urban population			
All causes of death	**962.3**	**892.9**	**898.6**
Diseases of circulatory system	611.7	578.9	573.3
Neoplasms	153.0	153.3	152.3
Diseases of respiratory organs	59.7	36.7	37.6
Accidents, poisoning and traumas	54.7	41.8	52.7
Rural population			
All causes of death	**949.7**	**864.5**	**866.4**
Diseases of circulatory system	578.7	534.0	532.1
Neoplasms	93.7	101.0	102.4
Diseases of respiratory organs	127.8	89.6	87.9
Accidents, poisoning and traumas	62.4	47.3	50.6

Source: **Naselenie SSSR 1988**, s. 663.

Main causes of death among men: by Union Republic, 1980-1988 per 100 000 age-standardised population

	1980	1987	1988
RUSSIAN SFSR			
All causes of death	**1 868.2**	**1 587.0**	**1 589.5**
Diseases of circulatory system	943.3	852.9	837.1
Neoplasms	283.9	305.3	307.9
Diseases of respiratory organs	183.6	116.6	117.4
Accidents, poisoning and traumas	294.9	170.4	188.6
UKRAINIAN SSR			
All causes of death	**1 636.1**	**1 520.3**	**1 524.4**
Diseases of circulatory system	913.0	848.3	834.3
Neoplasms	222.8	268.1	276.2
Diseases of respiratory organs	168.5	132.7	132.2
Accidents, poisoning and traumas	196.0	142.8	150.6
BELORUSSIAN SSR			
All causes of death	**1 476.3**	**1 436.2**	**1 466.9**
Diseases of circulatory system	746.8	796.4	793.3
Neoplasms	204.9	253.1	267.3
Diseases of respiratory organs	230.6	154.6	148.6
Accidents, poisoning and traumas	178.9	130.8	143.6
UZBEK SSR			
All causes of death	**1 390.1**	**1 274.8**	**1 300.3**
Diseases of circulatory system	705.6	651.1	694.8
Neoplasms	156.7	172.8	161.1
Diseases of respiratory organs	193.8	162.0	156.1
Accidents, poisoning and traumas	133.3	90.6	97.4

	1980	1987	1988
KAZAKH SSR			
All causes of death	1 673.0	1 431.4	1 435.3
Diseases of circulatory system	706.5	664.0	660.7
Neoplasms	291.1	290.4	290.5
Diseases of respiratory organs	233.7	159.8	158.1
Accidents, poisoning and traumas	225.5	145.8	152.9
GEORGIAN SSR			
All causes of death	1 361.2	1 311.4	1 304.6
Diseases of circulatory system	855.1	836.8	826.0
Neoplasms	143.2	155.5	148.8
Diseases of respiratory organs	105.2	80.3	81.3
Accidents, poisoning and traumas	104.6	86.0	94.7
AZERBAIDZHAN SSR			
All causes of death	1 439.3	1 420.7	1 448.3
Diseases of circulatory system	746.2	835.3	866.9
Neoplasms	205.7	218.3	214.9
Diseases of respiratory organs	176.1	118.0	124.1
Accidents, poisoning and traumas	94.5	75.4	78.2
LITHUANIAN SSR			
All causes of death	1 453.3	1 352.7	1 355.7
Diseases of circulatory system	689.6	720.4	705.7
Neoplasms	233.3	261.9	268.2
Diseases of respiratory organs	147.6	91.7	92.4
Accidents, poisoning and traumas	250.8	164.0	180.0

	1980	1987	1988
MOLDAVIAN SSR			
All causes of death	1 711.6	1 725.9	1 811.6
Diseases of circulatory system	925.6	983.9	1 022.9
Neoplasms	167.8	216.3	226.3
Diseases of respiratory organs	180.5	147.8	157.4
Accidents, poisoning and traumas	202.0	153.4	177.9
LATVIAN SSR			
All causes of death	1 669.5	1 541.2	1 548.7
Diseases of circulatory system	941.2	896.5	891.9
Neoplasms	247.9	294.3	290.6
Diseases of respiratory organs	95.7	68.4	68.2
Accidents, poisoning and traumas	249.4	158.4	170.0
KIRGIZ SSR			
All causes of death	1 589.3	1 405.3	1 463.7
Diseases of circulatory system	665.4	671.1	687.2
Neoplasms	187.5	200.2	192.5
Diseases of respiratory organs	342.9	240.0	263.2
Accidents, poisoning and traumas	196.9	124.3	136.5
TADZHIK SSR			
All causes of death	1 303.3	1 087.4	1 136.6
Diseases of circulatory system	560.3	478.2	521.8
Neoplasms	152.2	145.8	151.6
Diseases of respiratory organs	250.5	174.1	166.3
Accidents, poisoning and traumas	112.7	69.6	82.5

Table continues

	1980	1987	1988
ARMENIAN SSR			
All causes of death	**1 113.3**	**1 056.8**	**1 468.2**
Diseases of circulatory system	536.7	552.6	583.4
Neoplasms	171.7	180.6	185.1
Diseases of respiratory organs	166.5	110.4	117.7
Accidents, poisoning and traumas	83.1	65.5	437.8
TURKMEN SSR			
All causes of death	**1 664.2**	**1 491.8**	**1 520.9**
Diseases of circulatory system	848.3	796.2	799.2
Neoplasms	221.8	191.4	205.6
Diseases of respiratory organs	252.2	193.5	187.1
Accidents, poisoning and traumas	121.1	98.2	103.6
ESTONIAN SSR			
All causes of death	**1 688.6**	**1 529.0**	**1 521.1**
Diseases of circulatory system	968.6	912.2	897.5
Neoplasms	262.5	278.4	291.9
Diseases of respiratory organs	87.0	50.8	45.8
Accidents, poisoning and traumas	233.0	164.3	160.7

Source: **Naselenie SSSR 1988,** s. 664-8.

Main causes of death among women: by Union Republic, 1980-1988 per 100 000 age-standardised population

	1980	1987	1988
RUSSIAN SFSR			
All causes of death	**955.4**	**859.8**	**854.6**
Diseases of circulatory system	607.6	560.7	551.8
Neoplasms	135.3	137.7	137.7
Diseases of respiratory organs	70.3	40.3	41.0
Accidents, poisoning and traumas	67.8	46.0	48.8
UKRAINIAN SSR			
All causes of death	**923.6**	**882.1**	**891.3**
Diseases of circulatory system	628.7	598.5	601.5
Neoplasms	117.1	128.4	130.7
Diseases of respiratory organs	72.1	51.0	49.3
Accidents, poisoning and traumas	43.8	38.1	39.3
BELORUSSIAN SSR			
All causes of death	**819.5**	**811.5**	**815.5**
Diseases of circulatory system	507.6	535.5	533.2
Neoplasms	105.8	119.8	121.3
Diseases of respiratory organs	112.3	63.5	62.0
Accidents, poisoning and traumas	36.8	34.0	36.6
UZBEK SSR			
All causes of death	**934.2**	**896.8**	**895.4**
Diseases of circulatory system	524.7	497.8	510.2
Neoplasms	94.3	105.7	102.4
Diseases of respiratory organs	141.3	116.8	107.9
Accidents, poisoning and traumas	40.6	34.1	35.0

	1980	1987	1988
KAZAKH SSR			
All causes of death	**904.4**	**789.9**	**792.0**
Diseases of circulatory system	467.1	426.5	428.1
Neoplasms	142.8	142.5	141.3
Diseases of respiratory organs	118.5	74.8	74.2
Accidents, poisoning and traumas	62.3	44.1	43.9
GEORGIAN SSR			
All causes of death	**812.1**	**773.6**	**773.4**
Diseases of circulatory system	560.5	540.4	535.0
Neoplasms	92.0	91.1	94.3
Diseases of respiratory organs	64.6	45.5	47.2
Accidents, poisoning and traumas	26.7	24.7	25.4
AZERBAIDZHAN SSR			
All causes of death	**870.8**	**811.3**	**825.5**
Diseases of circulatory system	491.6	501.7	520.8
Neoplasms	112.8	106.3	100.5
Diseases of respiratory organs	112.2	75.5	80.4
Accidents, poisoning and traumas	34.9	28.3	27.3
LITHUANIAN SSR			
All causes of death	**824.0**	**762.3**	**755.2**
Diseases of circulatory system	505.6	492.9	479.6
Neoplasms	134.6	129.1	132.1
Diseases of respiratory organs	59.4	28.6	29.8
Accidents, poisoning and traumas	53.5	45.2	47.1

Table continues

	1980	1987	1988
MOLDAVIAN SSR			
All causes of death	1 201.7	1 164.9	1 179.9
Diseases of circulatory system	744.1	747.3	761.1
Neoplasms	108.8	121.8	122.2
Diseases of respiratory organs	96.0	64.7	68.0
Accidents, poisoning and traumas	74.7	61.9	65.1
LATVIAN SSR			
All causes of death	911.9	878.1	863.3
Diseases of circulatory system	609.0	587.2	575.7
Neoplasms	135.7	144.2	137.8
Diseases of respiratory organs	33.8	23.4	21.0
Accidents, poisoning and traumas	63.7	48.6	54.9
KIRGIZ SSR			
All causes of death	934.5	853.6	891.3
Diseases of circulatory system	463.4	449.6	466.9
Neoplasms	100.9	104.2	112.1
Diseases of respiratory organs	203.0	137.2	149.5
Accidents, poisoning and traumas	49.3	44.0	45.9
TADZHIK SSR			
All causes of death	953.7	801.5	810.3
Diseases of circulatory system	440.3	366.8	389.4
Neoplasms	84.7	90.1	84.2
Diseases of respiratory organs	198.8	140.5	132.9
Accidents, poisoning and traumas	36.7	29.1	31.0

Table continues

	1980	1987	1988
ARMENIAN SSR			
All causes of death	720.5	692.4	1 214.7
Diseases of circulatory system	412.6	402.7	383.3
Neoplasms	93.3	103.2	99.5
Diseases of respiratory organs	98.5	63.1	56.7
Accidents, poisoning and traumas	24.3	29.6	577.7
TURKMEN SSR			
All causes of death	1 112.6	1 023.7	1 018.2
Diseases of circulatory system	597.2	558.2	563.0
Neoplasms	143.1	130.4	122.1
Diseases of respiratory organs	193.2	142.5	130.9
Accidents, poisoning and traumas	36.1	35.9	36.4
ESTONIAN SSR			
All causes of death	916.2	878.1	882.5
Diseases of circulatory system	619.8	599.0	596.2
Neoplasms	137.8	141.9	141.7
Diseases of respiratory organs	23.6	18.3	15.8
Accidents, poisoning and traumas	64.0	46.7	51.8

Source: **Naselenie SSSR 1988**, s. 664-8.

Maternal mortality*: by Union Republic, 1980-1988

	1980	1985	1988
Absolute numbers			
USSR	**2 737**	**2 561**	**2 312**
Russian SFSR	1 498	1 282	1 175
Ukrainian SSR	333	308	284
Belorussian SSR	45	28	40
Uzbek SSR	250	330	270
Kazakh SSR	198	190	198
Georgian SSR	23	22	21
Azerbaidzhan SSR	60	73	40
Lithuanian SSR	14	13	11
Moldavian SSR	51	45	31
Latvian SSR	9	12	12
Kirgiz SSR	53	55	72
Tadzhik SSR	138	108	88
Armenian SSR	19	18	22
Turkmen SSR	40	66	42
Estonian SSR	6	11	6
Per 100 000 births			
USSR	**56.4**	**47.7**	**43.0**
Russian SFSR	68.0	54.0	50.0
Ukrainian SSR	44.8	40.4	38.2
Belorussian SSR	29.1	17.0	24.5
Uzbek SSR	46.3	48.6	38.9
Kazakh SSR	55.6	47.9	48.6
Georgian SSR	25.7	22.5	22.8
Azerbaidzhan SSR	38.7	41.1	21.7
Lithuanian SSR	27.0	22.2	19.4
Moldavian SSR	64.1	49.8	35.0
Latvian SSR	25.3	30.2	29.1
Kirgiz SSR	49.4	42.8	53.8
Tadzhik SSR	94.2	59.1	43.6
Armenian SSR	27.0	22.4	29.4
Turkmen SSR	40.8	56.8	33.4
Estonian SSR	27.0	46.6	23.9

* Due to complications of pregnancy, birth and the postnatal period.

The level of maternal mortality is still significantly higher in the USSR than in a number of socialist and capitalist countries of Europe.

Source: **Stat. Press-Byull.** 1989, 9, s. 116.

Infant mortality, 1975-1988
(Deaths of infants under the age of one year)

| | Thousands | | | Per 1 000 live births | | |
	Total	Urban	Rural	Total	Urban	Rural
1975	141	68	73	30.6	25.8	37.0
1980	132	67	65	27.3	23.5	32.5
1985	140	69	71	26.0	21.7	32.0
1986	141	69	72	25.4	21.1	31.4
1987	142	70	72	25.4	21.1	31.5
1988	134	66	68	24.7	20.7	30.4

The infant mortality rate in the USSR is 2.4-5 times higher than in the USA, France, Great Britain, the Federal Republic of Germany and Japan. The lowest rates in the world - less than 6 infant deaths per 1 000 live births - are reported from Japan, Sweden and Finland. The level of infant mortality varies significantly among the territories of the USSR. The highest rates (37-53 per 1 000) are reported from the Republics of Central Asia, where a high birth rate is also recorded. The lowest rates occur in Lithuania and Latvia, where 11-11.5 children per 1 000 live births die in their first year.

The infant mortality rate serves as one of the most important indicators for evaluating the work of the health service. With the object of improving on the actual state of affairs several medical establishments follow the practice of concealing infant deaths by classifying them as miscarriages etc. There is also failure by parents to report infant deaths at the Register Office. According to the findings of an investigation carried out by organs of the state statistical service, the under-recording of infant deaths was up to 86% in various areas of the Republics of Central Asia; up to 60% in the Transcaucasian Republics; up to 60% in Moldavia; up to 50% in the Russian SFSR; and up to 19% in the Ukraine.

Notwithstanding systematic efforts in this matter, the situation regarding the recording of infant deaths is not improving. Analysis shows that the level of infant mortality in rural areas of the Republics of Central Asia, Azerbaidzhan and Kazakhstan is 1.5-2 times higher than the figure reported on the basis of registered facts of death.

Source: **AiF** 1989, 45, s. 3.

Infant mortality rate*: by major territorial-administrative divisions, 1975-1988

Abbreviations: AO = Autonomous oblast   AOk = Autonomous okrug

	1975	1980	1985	1987	1988
USSR	**30.6**	**27.3**	**26.0**	**25.4**	**24.7**
Russian SFSR	23.7	22.1	20.7	19.4	18.9
Nenets AOk	45.6	39.2	17.1	14.8	16.8
Karelian ASSR	25.9	21.0	19.2	16.5	16.3
Komi ASSR	27.7	22.3	21.9	20.2	20.1
Mari ASSR	22.6	17.6	18.6	16.7	16.2
Mordvin ASSR	18.9	17.4	18.1	17.4	14.5
Chuvash ASSR	24.4	18.4	15.5	17.1	16.1
Kalmyk ASSR	33.5	28.5	20.6	21.1	28.7
Tatar ASSR	20.2	17.1	15.4	15.8	16.0
Adyge AO	19.2	18.7	15.7	21.5	15.2
Karachai-Cherkes AO	15.2	15.7	24.2	22.7	19.6
Dagestan ASSR	45.3	32.7	31.8	27.8	26.2
Kabardino-Balkar ASSR	26.9	22.5	21.2	21.3	19.4
North Osetin ASSR	18.9	19.4	19.3	15.4	16.2
Chechen-Ingush ASSR	23.3	30.4	35.7	37.1	39.4
Komi-Permyak AOk	32.5	34.3	26.9	19.1	19.6
Bashkir ASSR	22.4	20.3	18.8	19.5	18.7
Udmurt ASSR	22.3	19.0	20,2	17.4	17.4
Gorno-Altai AO	33.9	36.5	22.6	21.3	20.6
Khanty-Mansi AOk	22.3	25.7	21.0	17.7	18.4
Yamalo-Nenets AOk	26.9	23.7	24.4	20.9	19.3
Khakass AO	28.8	20.6	18.8	17.0	17.6
Taimyr (Dolgano-Nenets) AOk	38.2	19.8	39.2	25.5	18.7
Evenki AOk	65.3	29.4	60.8	27.5	29.0
Ust-Ordinski Buryat AOk	35.6	28.4	29.0	19.7	20.1
Aginski-Buryat AOk	39.1	34.9	26.6	15.1	16.1
Buryat ASSR	27.4	27.4	26.8	21.7	20.3
Tuva ASSR	34.8	53.4	44.4	36.7	34.6
Jewish AO	34.0	31.2	39.3	32.9	33.9
Koryak AOk	29.3	20.7	20.2	18.8	11.4
Chukot AOk	32.6	27.7	23.8	14.3	15.7
Yakut ASSR	28.4	30.3	24.3	22.5	19.5

247

Table continues

	1975	1980	1985	1987	1988
Ukrainian SSR	19.7	16.6	15.7	14.5	14.2
Lithuanian SSR	19.6	14.5	14.2	12.3	11.5
Latvian SSR	20.3	15.4	13.0	11.3	11.0
Estonian SSR	18.2	17.1	14.0	16.1	12.4
Georgian SSR	32.7	25.4	24.0	24.3	21.9
Abkhazian ASSR	19.2	27.3	27.2	22.6	18.6
Adzhar ASSR	56.5	36.9	29.5	34.4	27.2
South Osetin AO	32.6	22.5	16.6	14.5	15.0
Azerbaidzhan SSR	37.5	30.4	29.4	28.6	26.5
Nakhichevan ASSR	43.6	33.1	28.6	23.6	21.9
Nagorno-Karabakh AO	40.5	32.5	28.9	24.0	27.4
Armenian SSR	30.6	26.2	24.8	22.6	25.3
Uzbek SSR	53.8	47.0	45.3	45.9	43.3
Karakalpak ASSR	50.4	46.5	59.2	69.6	60.1
Kirgiz SSR	42.5	43.3	41.9	37.8	36.8
Tadzhik SSR	80.8	58.1	46.8	48.9	48.9
Gorno-Badakhshan AO	74.5	59.4	44.1	32.9	36.0
Turkmen SSR	56.5	53.6	52.4	56.4	53.3
Kazakh SSR	38.8	32.7	30.1	29.4	29.2
Belorussian SSR	18.7	16.3	14.5	13.4	13.1
Moldavian SSR	43.4	35.0	39.0	25.9	23.0

* Deaths of infants under the age of one year, per 1 000
live births.

Source: **Stat. Press-Byull.** 1989, 7, s. 147-9.

Infant deaths*: by Union Republic capitals and cities with over one million inhabitants, 1988

	Absolute numbers	Per 1 000 live births
Alma-Ata	429	21.3
Ashkhabad	551	53.1
Baku**	1 027	28.4
Vilnius	94	11.5
Gorki	320	16.5
Dnepropetrovsk	248	15.2
Donetsk	239	17.2
Dushanbe	564	38.4
Erevan	561	25.6
Kazan	314	18.0
Kiev	593	16.0
Kishinev	268	20.7
Kuibyshev	391	22.6
Leningrad**	1 323	19.0
Minsk	380	14.1
Moscow**	2 334	19.7
Novosibirsk	468	22.1
Odessa	209	15.3
Omsk	338	17.8
Perm	275	16.2
Riga	139	11.2
Rostov-na-Donu	345	25.1
Sverdlovsk	317	15.3
Tallin	113	15.3
Tashkent	1 258	28.3
Tbilisi	480	26.8
Ufa	396	22.0
Frunze	340	28.9
Kharkov	359	16.1
Chelyabinsk	285	15.8

* Infants under the age of one year.

** The figure includes outlying settlements which are subordinated to the city.

Source: **Vestnik Statistiki** 1989, 11, s. 69-70.

Perinatal mortality*: by Union Republic, 1988

	Perinatal deaths	Still-births	Died in first week
Absolute numbers			
USSR	**94 267**	**52 846**	**41 421**
Russian SFSR	42 462	21 984	20 478
Ukrainian SSR	10 717	6 710	4 007
Belorussian SSR	2 106	1 156	950
Uzbek SSR	13 183	7 778	5 405
Kazakh SSR	7 617	4 137	3 480
Georgian SSR	1 457	798	659
Azerbaidzhan SSR	2 545	1 706	839
Lithuanian SSR	542	311	231
Moldavian SSR	1 549	822	727
Latvian SSR	417	230	187
Kirgiz SSR	1 974	1 153	821
Tadzhik SSR	4 758	3 086	1 672
Armenian SSR	1 542	983	559
Turkmen SSR	3 023	1 787	1 236
Estonian SSR	375	205	170
Per 1 000 live and still births			
USSR	**17.35**	**9.73**	**7.62**
Russian SFSR	17.91	9.27	8.64
Ukrainian SSR	14.28	8.94	5.34
Belorussian SSR	12.81	7.03	5.78
Uzbek SSR	18.78	11.08	7.70
Kazakh SSR	18.52	10.06	8.46
Georgian SSR	15.72	8.61	7.11
Azerbaidzhan SSR	13.68	9.17	4.51
Lithuanian SSR	9.50	5.45	4.05
Moldavian SSR	17.33	9.20	8.13
Latvian SSR	10.05	5.54	4.51
Kirgiz SSR	14.64	8.55	6.09
Tadzhik SSR	23.22	15.06	8.16
Armenian SSR	20.37	12.99	7.38
Turkmen SSR	23.68	14.00	9.68
Estonian SSR	14.84	8.11	6.73

* Deaths of infants during the interval between the 28th week of pregnancy and the end of the first seven days of life.

Source: **Naselenie SSSR 1988**, s. 485-8.

Main causes of infant* deaths, 1985 and 1988

	Absolute numbers 1985	1988	Per 10 000 live births 1985	1988
All causes	**139 793**	**133 977**	**259.7**	**246.6**
Infectious and parasitic diseases	22 252	20 413	41.3	37.6
Diseases of: Nervous system and sense organs	2 306	2 533	4.3	4.7
Respiratory organs	49 672	43 083	92.3	79.3
Digestive organs	1 724	2 078	3.2	3.8
Congenital abnormalities	17 846	17 826	33.2	32.8
Conditions arising in perinatal period	36 778	37 926	68.3	69.8
Accidents, poisoning and trauma	5 174	4 944	9.6	9.1

* Infants under the age of one year.

Source of this and the following table: **Stat. Press-Byull.** 1989, 10, s. 104-5.

Four main causes of infant deaths: by Union Republic, 1988 per 10 000 live births

Key: Column 1 Infectious and parasitic diseases
                2 Diseases of the respiratory organs
                3 Congenital abnormalities
                4 Conditions arising in perinatal period

Columns	1	2	3	4
USSR	**37.6**	**79.3**	**32.8**	**69.8**
Russian SFSR	17.2	34.9	38.6	77.7
Ukrainian SSR	12.1	21.1	40.5	46.8
Belorussian SSR	10.9	23.4	41.2	42.0
Uzbek SSR	91.0	208.5	18.2	82.9
Kazakh SSR	44.6	106.7	33.3	77.5
Georgian SSR	31.3	98.4	8.7	66.5
Azerbaidzhan SSR	41.3	149.1	16.2	37.7
Lithuanian SSR	6.3	9.3	46.2	33.0
Moldavian SSR	23.0	66.4	44.6	71.0
Latvian SSR	9.9	7.5	34.0	43.0
Kirgiz SSR	79.2	178.8	20.1	61.8
Tadzhik SSR	126.7	178.1	12.8	73.8
Armenian SSR	31.0	64.0	29.0	65.0
Turkmen SSR	142.7	234.2	24.8	79.8
Estonian SSR	4.4	11.6	29.5	60.3

The indicators show greatest variation in respect of those causes from which death could have been avoided by proper care and a timely visit to the doctor. Thus, mortality from infectious and parasitic diseases in the Central Asian Republics is 14 times higher and mortality from diseases of the respiratory organs is 22 times higher than in the Baltic Republics. Out of the total number of deaths from acute intestinal infections, 80% occur in the Republics of Central Asia and the Kazakh SSR, where mortality from these causes increases by 10-20 times in the summer months.

Deaths from alcoholism-related causes*: by Union Republic, per 100 000 population

	1984	1986	1987
USSR	**17.2**	**8.3**	**7.4**
Russian SFSR	23.0	10.6	9.1
Ukrainian SSR	17.3	9.2	9.2
Belorussian SSR	15.3	8.2	8.5
Uzbek SSR	1.5	1.0	0.6
Kazakh SSR	6.1	3.8	3.1
Georgian SSR	3.1	2.5	1.8
Azerbaidzhan SSR	1.1	0.7	0.5
Lithuanian SSR	25.3	12.2	11.2
Moldavian SSR	19.5	9.7	7.8
Latvian SSR	11.5	7.4	5.1
Kirgiz SSR	6.4	2.1	2.4
Tadzhik SSR	1.6	1.0	1.1
Armenian SSR	0.5	0.2	0.2
Turkmen SSR	1.7	1.2	0.6
Estonian SSR	21.5	11.4	10.4

* Alcohol poisoning, chronic alcoholism, alcoholic psychosis and cirrhosis of the liver due to alcohol.

Source: **Vestnik Statistiki** 1989, 6, s. 62.

Suicide, 1975-1987

	Thousands	Per 100 000 population
1975	66	26
1980	71	27
1984	81	30
1985	68	25
1986	53	19
1987	54	19

The rate for deaths from suicide varies among the Union Republics from 2-8 per 100 000 population in the Transcaucasian republics and Central Asia (excepting the Kirgiz SSR) to 23-29 per 100 000 in the Russian SFSR and the Baltic republics. A high suicide rate is closely linked to the prevalence of alcoholism; the sharp reduction in suicide after 1984 coincides with the introduction of measures aimed at combating drunkenness and alcoholism.

Source: **Sots. Is.** 1989, 2, s. 97.

Suicide: by sex and age group, 1985 and 1987
per 100 000 relevant group

	1985 Men	Women	1987 Men	Women
All ages	**50.5**	**11.3**	**30.3**	**9.3**
Under 20	4.6	1.3	3.5	1.1
20-24	38.5	6.5	22.2	5.5
25-29	61.9	7.6	34.5	5.5
30-39	72.9	11.0	42.3	7.1
40-49	98.9	17.1	53.8	12.2
50-59	98.5	19.4	56.1	15.4
60-69	66.7	20.8	47.8	17.5
70 and over	82.7	26.3	72.3	27.5

The rate of death by suicide is over three times higher among men than among women of all ages; it is over six times higher among men than among women in the age group 25-39.

Source: **Sots. Is.** 1989, 2, s. 97.

254

Suicide, 1988

Number of suicides in USSR	56 000

Rate per 100 000 population

USSR	19
Great Britain*	9
USA*	12
Federal Republic of Germany*	21
France*	22

* Year not specified. [Ed.]

Source: **Nar. khoz. SSSR 1988**, s. 28.

Suicide: by sex and age group, 1988
per 100 000 persons of relevant sex and age

	Men	Women
All ages	**30.8**	**9.3**
Under 20	4.1	1.5
20-24	22.5	5.6
25-29	34.4	5.6
30-39	43.8	7.2
40-49	54.8	11.5
50-59	54.9	14.8
60-69	48.2	17.6
70 and over	75.5	27.7

Source: **Nar. khoz. SSSR 1988**, s. 28.

255

Public opinion

In the autumn of 1989 the journal **Ogonek**, which was strongly dedicated to the principle of glasnost, started to publish series of articles which report the results of Soviet public opinion surveys. Most appear under the rubric **For and Against**. As a rule, no methodological information accompanies the articles, but it appears that they all derive from interviews carried out by the All-Union Centre for the Study of Public Opinion through its 25 regional offices. In some cases answers to fairly disparate questions are published in the same issue of the journal. There is also a small amount of repetition of questions in different issues. The numbering of the reports is mine and for some I composed the title. [Ed.]

Report No. 1: Economic and political issues

Question: **We are in the fifth year of perestroika. Do you consider that the changes which have taken place during this time will lead to a significant improvement of the position in the country in the near future?**

Yes, the changes will lead to a noticeable improvement of the position	12.1%
Yes, but the changes will be insignificant	34.9%
No, the changes will not give rise to improvements; everything will stay as it is	16.4%
No, the position will only get worse	18.5%
Don't know	18.1%

******

Question: **How do you rate the material position of your family by comparison with 2-3 years ago?**

Rather improved	23.8%
Remains unchanged	52.7%
Rather worse	23.5%

******

Question: **Should cooperatives be further developed or did they ought to be abolished?**

Cooperatives should be developed	45.1%
Cooperatives should be removed	29.8%
It is all the same to me	10.0%
Don't know	15.1%

Opinion survey continues

Agreement with statements presented*: **Those who want the good of their people should above all**

(1) be concerned about the unity and solidarity of the USSR

Armenia	10.6%
Baltic SSRs	10.2%
Russian SFSR	63.4%
Ukraine	30.9%

(2) strive for a "strong centre and strong Republics"

Armenia	4.8%
Baltic SSRs	9.6%
Russian SFSR	19.5%
Ukraine	17.2%

(3) concentrate all efforts on the preservation of the national language and culture

Armenia	52.9%
Baltic SSRs	25.6%
Russian SFSR	8.8%
Ukraine	20.6%

(4) strive for the Republic's economic independence

Armenia	26.0%
Baltic SSRs	43.5%
Russian SFSR	14.8%
Ukraine	32.4%

(5) strive for the Republic's full political self-determination, not excluding separation from the USSR

Armenia	17.3%
Baltic SSRs	47.0%
Russian SFSR	9.9%
Ukraine	20.6%

(6) Don't know

Armenia	1.9%
Baltic SSRs	2.9%
Russian SFSR	7.5%
Ukraine	4.9%

---

* The totals can exceed 100% because respondents could choose more than one answer.

Source: **Ogonek** 1989, 43, s. 5. (Survey date: August-September 1989.)

Question: **In your opinion, how may the economic position of the country change in the near future?**

It will improve	23.7%
It will get worse	10.0%
It will remain unchanged	28.1%
It will improve at first and then will get worse	3.2%
It will get worse at first and then will improve	35.0%

****

Question*: **Which of the following opinions comes closest to your attitude towards the work which you do?**

For me work is the most important thing in life	14.9%
For me work is very important, but there are other things no less important	54.5%
I work in order to get paid	25.6%
Work is an unpleasant necessity; if it was possible, I would not work	6.4%

* The total of responses exceeds 100% because some respondents gave two answers. [The same table was published in a later number of **Ogonek** with a figure of 53.1% against the second statement.]

******

Question*: **Have you had to make payments in any form for services in state medical institutions?**

Yes, I have made payment in money	12.2%
Yes, I have made payment with gifts or services	18.0%
No, I have never had to make payments for treatment in state medical institutions	71.3%

* The total exceeds 100% because some respondents gave two answers.

******

Question: **Do you think that you take sufficient care of your health?**

I take less care than is needed	49.1%
I take far too little care	23.6%
My state of health does not require particular care	8.3%
I take as much care as is needed	16.6%
Don't know	2.8%

Opinion survey continues

Question: **How worried are you about the state of the environment in your town, settlement or immediate surroundings?**

Extremely worried	51.4%
Fairly worried	32.1%
Not much worried	6.7%
Not worried	4.9%
Don't know	4.9%

******

Question: **Do you agree with the view that perestroika and glasnost in the USSR will be wrecked by the bureaucratic apparatus?**

I agree	16.0%
I disagree	45.3%
Don't know	38.7%

Source: **Ogonek** 1989, 44, s. 5.

Report No. 3: Foreign policy

Question: **What do you consider is most positive in the foreign policy of the USSR during the last 2-3 years?**

Conclusion of the agreement on the abolition of medium- and short-range rockets	25.8%
Decision to withdraw Soviet troops from Afghanistan	29.0%
Decision on the unilateral reductions of the army and armaments	8.5%
Decision to withdraw part of the Soviet troops from Hungary, the GDR, Czechoslovakia and Mongolia	6.4%
Improvement of the USSR's political, economic and cultural relations with countries of the West	15.9%
Increased authority of M. S. Gorbachev in the international arena	12.5%
Don't know; I don't follow these things	1.1%
I don't think our actions in the international arena in recent years have been positive	0.8%

Opinion survey continues

Question: **How do you rate the relations between East and West?**

Good	12.9%
Average	72.7%
Poor	3.0%
Don't know	11.4%

******

Question: **How do you personally rate the foreign policy of the USA?**

Rather positively	30.0%
Rather negatively	19.5%
Don't know	50.5%

******

Question: **What are the future possiblities for the preservation of peace in Europe?**

Favourable	70.0%
Unfavourable	5.5%
Don't know	24.5%

******

Question: **Which country, in your opinion, interferes in the internal affairs of other states?**

Only the USA	43.6%
Only the USSR	1.3%
Both the USA and the USSR	37.6%
Neither the USA nor the USSR	1.8%
Don't know	15.7%

******

Question: **Which country, in your opinion, is intensifying the arms race?**

Only the USA	54.8%
Only the USSR	0.9%
Both the USA and the USSR	8.5%
Neither the USA nor the USSR	9.7%
Don't know	26.1%

Opinion survey continues

Question: **Which side is stronger in military terms – the USSR and countries of the Warsaw Pact or the USA with the countries of NATO?**

USSR and Warsaw Pact countries	11.1%
USA and NATO countries	7.3%
Both sides are roughly as strong; there is a military parity between them	58.4%
Don't know	23.2%

******

Question: **Is it possible to secure the defence of the country adequately without nuclear weapons?**

Yes	52.9%
No	21.3%
Don't know	25.8%

******

Question: **What would be your attitude to the USA and the USSR withdrawing their troops from the territories of their European allies?**

I would support it	90.3%
I would not support it	2.0%
Don't know	7.7%

Source: **Ogonek** 1989, 45, s. 5.

Report No. 4: Family and marital issues

Question: **Do you agree that everyone ought to get married and raise a family sooner or later?**

Yes	84.5%
No, not everyone is obliged to	12.3%
Don't know	3.2%

261

Opinion survey continues

Question: **For what reason above all, in your opinion, do people get married and raise a family? (More than one answer can be given.)**

So as not to be alone	23.6%
To have a comfortable home, and a domestic life with amenities	23.9%
To have children and continue the family line	56.1%
To remain with the person you love	19.0%
To feel needed by someone and to have someone to care about	36.8%
To have a permanent sexual partner	7.1%
To have someone with you who will understand and support you in any situation in life	44.8%
It is customary to get married - everyone does - though not everyone creates a happy family	6.7%
It is a person's moral duty to have a family and children	26.3%
Don't know	2.3%

******

Question: **What do you see as the negative sides of family life? (More than one answer can be given.)**

Family life hinders career development	7.8%
In family life too much importance is devoted to domestic matters (the saucepans, nappies, the shops etc.)	39.6%
A family limits personal freedom	20.7%
In family life there is too much monotony; the same people and the same obligations day after day	17.9%
Family life imposes an excessive obligation for the welfare of others	16.2%
You have to work too hard in order to secure the material welfare of the family	44.0%
In a family children bring much anxiety and distress	16.4%
In a family deceit, betrayal and conflicts are unavoidable	14.6%
Living in a family it is impossible to preserve love	3.6%
Don't know	20.0%

******

Question: **What is your attitude towards a man and woman who live together as husband and wife but do not register their relationship?**

I think it is unacceptable	22.5%
There are cases when it is acceptable	33.6%
It is completely acceptable	34.2%
Don't know	9.7%

Opinion survey continues

Question: **What is your attitude towards a woman who gives birth to a child out of wedlock?**

I approve of such women	8.5%
Various situations occur in life and each specific case must be judged separately	72.4%
I do not approve of such women	19.1%

******

Question: **What would you say about couples who are able to have children but do not want to?**

They should not be criticised	13.1%
Various situations occur in life and each specific case must be judged separately	51.4%
They deserve to be criticised	35.5%

******

Question: **What would you say about a man who is unfaithful to his wife?**

He should not be criticised	6.8%
Various situations occur in life and each specific case must be judged separately	51.4%
He deserves to be criticised	35.5%

******

Question: **What would you say about a woman who is unfaithful to her husband?**

She should not be criticised	4.5%
Various situations occur in life and each specific case must be judged separately	48.7%
She deserves to be criticised	46.9%

Source: **Ogonek** 1989, 47, s. 3.

Report No. 5: Economic questions

Question: **What influence, in your opinion, do the processes of democratisation in the political sphere have on the country's economic position?**

A positive influence	18.9%
More positive than negative	27.2%
More negative than positive	19.5%
Undoubtedly negative	5.0%
Don't know	29.5%

******

Question: **Do you consider that in the next year or two the sharp rise in prices will be successfully halted?**

I think so	15.0%
I think not	57.2%
I consider that in effect prices will not rise	1.0%
Don't know	26.9%

******

Question: **What would you say about your family income?**

We live below the poverty line	2.6%
We scarcely make ends meet	31.1%
We economise and live more or less in decency	52.7%
We live without any particular material worries	10.1%
Don't know	3.5%

******

Question: **What, above all, should be done to raise people's interest in the results of their work?**

Transfer enterprises to the collective ownership of those who work in them	23.6%
Adjust income distribution fairly; abolish unjustified privileges in the acquisition of goods	34.6%
Sharply increase the difference in pay between those who work well and those who work badly	30.6%
Strengthen discipline at work and control over order	31.7%
Don't know	6.8%

(The total exceeds 100% because some respondents gave two answers.)

Source: **Ogonek** 1989, 48, s. 3.

Report No. 6: Attitudes towards work

Question: **Are you satisfied with your work on the whole?**

Fully satisfied	38.8%
More satisfied than dissatisfied	29.8%
More dissatisfied than satisfied	13.8%
Rather dissatisfied	7.5%
Don't know	10.1%

******

Question: **What attracts you about your current work?**

It corresponds to my skills and abilities	31.2%
I am used to this place of work	20.4%
It is important and useful for society	19.3%
It is close to home	14.8%
There are good relationships in the collective	14.7%
It is interesting and provides opportunities for cultural and professional development	13.8%
Guaranteed pay	9.7%
The work is well paid	6.7%
It allows one to occupy a respected place in society	6.0%
It gives an opportunity to prove oneself and work wholeheartedly	5.8%
It is light, clean, safe and in a good building	5.6%
The pay there corresponds to the work I put in	5.5%
It does not attract me in any way	5.3%
It is a means of obtaining living accommodation	5.2%
There is good, qualified management	2.3%
There is good organisation of the work	2.2%
There is good organisation of production and sales orders etc.	2.0%
There is a good canteen, prophylactorium, rest home etc.	1.9%
There is a good kindergarten (nursery)	1.9%
Other reasons	1.3%

******

Question: **What do you dislike about your present work?**

Inadequate pay	27.4%
I like [sic] everything about my work	17.9%
Poor organisation of the work	17.7%
Poor organisation, or lack of organisation, of production and sales orders etc.	15.2%
No opportunity to obtain living accommodation	13.1%
The work is far from home	11.0%
Lack of differentiation in pay	9.2%
Dirty, heavy work in poor conditions	8.1%
There is poor, unqualified mangement	7.3%
Absence of a canteen, prophylactorium etc.	6.8%

265

Opinion survey continues

Irregular earnings, absence of guaranteed pay	6.2%
The work is hazardous to life	5.3%
The work does not correspond to my skills and abilities	4.5%
It is uninteresting and does not give opportunities for cultural and professional development	4.2%
It gives no opportunity to prove oneself and work wholeheartedly	3.9%
There is no kindergarten or nursery	2.9%
There are poor relations with the management and in the collective	2.4%
The work does not allow one to occupy a respected place in society	2.2%
The work is not useful for society	1.7%
Other reasons	1.9%

******

Question: **What is your attitude to the fact that the state has virtually removed all limitations on supplementary jobs?**

I approve	83.8%
I am indifferent	9.6%
I do not approve	6.6%

******

Question: **Do you have a supplementary job at present (including work in a cooperative etc.)?**

Yes	13.5%
No	86.5%

******

Question: **Do you intend to start up in a supplementary job in the near future?**

Yes	14.9%
No	69.7%
Don't know	15.4%

Opinion survey continues

Question: **What are the personal aspirations and needs which induce you to take on a supplementary job?**

A desire to use my working time actively	6.8%
An aspiration to use all my professional skills and abilities	10.6%
A need to occupy myself in types of activity which differ from my main work	5.3%
Necessity to increase family income	56.7%
Opportunity to benefit people and society	12.2%
Aspiration to determine my work myself and to run my own affairs	7.4%
Other reasons	1.0%

Source: **Ogonek** 1989, 49, front inside cover and s. 1.

Report No. 7: The environment

The first set of data in this report has been omitted on the ground that it had already appeared in an earlier number of **Ogonek** and is given in Report No. 2. The question asked was: **How worried are you about the state of the environment in your town, settlement or immediate surroundings?** [Ed.]

******

Question: **If you are worried about the state of the environment where you live, what causes your worry?**

Beautiful places are disappearing	11.0%
The country's natural riches are being squandered	7.8%
People's health is getting worse	52.4%
The natural order in the vegetable and animal world is being destroyed	13.9%
Opportunities for relaxation in nature are being reduced	11.9%
Other	3.0%

267

Opinion survey continues

Question: **How has the state of the environment in your town or settlement changed during the last decade?**

It has got significantly worse	43.6%
It has got a little worse	25.5%
It has not changed	8.9%
It has improved a little	5.6%
It has improved significantly	1.7%
Difficult to say	14.7%

****

Question: **What in particular dissatisfies you in your town and its immediate surroundings?**

Pollution of the air by gases	14.0%
Pollution of the river, lake, sea	9.3%
Increased level of radiation	3.3%
Insanitary state of the terrain – refuse, waste tips	9.9%
Change in the climate	3.1%
Bad, polluted drinking water	5.3%
Harmful chemical substances in vegetables and fruit	8.7%
Acid rain	2.2%
Shrinking of reservoirs, emergence of deserts or bogs, other changes in the countryside	1.7%
Disappearance of various types of bird, fish, animal and vegetation	3.0%
Unsuitability of water for polyps	0.6%
Increased level of noise	5.3%
Absence of parks and squares and green spaces	3.8%
Disappearance of woods, their unsatisfactory state	3.1%
Dirty streets, decrepit buildings	10.9%
Ruin of old monuments, neglect of old estates and parks	4.0%
Presence of large numbers of harmful insects and other pests	2.7%
Trampling down, damaging, littering of parks and places for relaxation	6.2%
Deterioration of the soil, reduction of its natural fertility	2.6%
Others	0.5%

******

Question: **Is anything being done to improve the environment in your town or settlement?**

Yes	22.9%
No	28.1%
Don't know	49.0%

268

Opinion survey continues

Question: **Who is the initiator of improvements in the state of the environment in your town?**

Regional committee, town committee of the Party	6.2%
Unofficial groups, associations	5.8%
Soviet of people's deputies, executive committee of the Soviet	7.8%
Several active citizens	10.8%
Newspapers, radio, television	13.8%
Environmental health doctors, environmental health stations	6.4%
Others	1.9%
Don't know	47.3%

Source: **Ogonek** 1989, 50, s. 3. The interviewing was carried out amongst the urban population.

Report No. 8: Sexual behaviour of young people

Question: **What is your attitude towards the possibility of sexual relationships between young people before marriage?**

For young men

Premarital sexual relations are not admissible	30.3%
Admissible only with a future wife	29.3%
Admissible with any woman	10.4%
Not only admissible but useful and necessary	12.1%
Don't know	18.6%

For young women

Premarital sexual relations are not admissible	39.6%
Admissible only with a future husband	34.4%
Admissible with any partner	5.7%
Not only admissible but useful and necessary	5.0%
Don't know	16.0%

Opinion survey continues

Question: **If you think that premarital sexual relations amongst young people are admissible, at what age do you think they are acceptable?**

13 years	0.5%
14-15	0.7%
16-17	8.6%
18-19	40.7%
20 and older	34.4%
Don't know	15.6%

******

Question: **How would you define the extent of premarital sexual relations amongst young people?**

Very rare	3.0%
Fairly frequent but not on a mass scale	33.3%
On a mass scale	41.7%
Don't know	22.2%

******

Question: **What do you think has led to the spread in recent years of premarital sexual relations amongst young people in our country?**

Moral decline in society as a whole, absence of moral upbringing	41.0%
Absence of religious upbringing	13.4%
Inadequate sex education of youth, no idea of the consequences of early sexual relations	36.3%
Changing ideas about love; love is associated mainly with sex	17.7%
Earlier physical maturity among boys and girls	15.5%
Becoming familiar with alcohol earlier	10.4%
Imitation of Western life-style	14.9%
Striving of young people for self-determination, self-expression and to prove their maturity	11.5%
A freer attitude towards sex, an idea of sex as a part of relations between friends	12.6%
Others	2.0%
Don't know	8.2%

******

Question: **Which do you think are the most serious amongst the possible consequences of premarital sexual relations?**

Worsening of relationships between youth and the older generation	13.9%
Difficulties in obtaining education and a career due to early pregnancy	11.1%

Opinion survey continues

Onset of impotence among men at an earlier age	7.3%
Spread of venereal diseases, AIDS	50.0%
Appearance of a large number of deserted children	42.9%
Increase of infertility among women as a result of abortions	21.5%
Appearance of a large number of unstable families formed "of necessity"	30.0%
Other	1.1%
Don't know	11.4%
I think that premarital sexual relations do not have serious consequences	3.4%

******

Question: **What channels of information about sex life do you think most acceptable and effective?**

Discussion of problems of sex life with peers	5.3%
Talks with parents	21.4%
A special course in schools and educational institutions	45.6%
Consultations with specialist doctors	22.2%
Specialised popular-scientific literature	42.5%
Specialised popular-scientific films, specialised television programmes	28.7%
Personal experience	5.9%
Other means	0.7%
Don't know	6.2%
The education of young people in questions about sex life is not necessary at all	3.0%

******

Question: **What, in your opinion, should be the central issue in the sex education of young people?**

Moral aspect of early sexual relations, instilling a sense of responsibility for one's actions	59.5%
Means and methods for the prevention of pregnancy	17.2%
Means and methods for the prevention of venereal diseases	19.3%
Influence of premarital sexual relations on the creation of a family, on long-term family life	16.1%
Influence of early sexual relations on one's own health and the health of future children	16.2%
Influence of early sexual relations on receiving education and acquiring a career	4.4%
Other	0.4%
Don't know	12.5%
Sex education is not necessary at all	2.1%

Source: **Ogonek** 1990, 3, s. 32-3.

271

Report No. 9: Food supply problems

Question: **What makes it most difficult for you to obtain food-stuffs?**

A lot of time is spent looking for food and queuing	61.0%
Having to travel to another town, district, oblast	16.1%
Having to buy in the collective farm market at dearer prices	34.4%
Having to produce food-stuffs oneself on a subsiduary smallholding	14.8%
Other	1.9%
I do not encounter difficulties	5.1%

******

Question: **What share of your income goes on the purchase of food-stuffs?**

Almost all	22.1%
More than half	38.2%
About half	24.6%
Don't know	5.7%

******

Question: **How often do you experience a shortage of food-stuffs which are essential to you?**

I do not experience shortages	6.9%
Quite rarely	16.1%
Quite often	43.4%
Constantly	29.7%
Don't know	4.1%

******

Question: **What dissatisfies you most about your food?**

Monotony of diet	25.9%
Poor quality of food-stuffs	41.5%
Presence of harmful substances in food-stuffs	23.6%
Absence of cheap food	43.2%
No delicacies, food for special occasions	21.3%
Other	2.8%
It is all satisfactory	4.6%

Opinion survey continues

Question: **Do you get sufficient bread, macaroni, cereals?**

Not sufficient   6.2%
Sufficient   82.8%
Too much   7.3%
Don't know   4.2%

******

Question: **Do you get sufficient vegetable oil, butter, lard?**

Not sufficient   23.5%
Sufficient   67.0%
Too much   1.9%
Don't know   7.8%

******

Question: **Do you get sufficient meat, fish, poultry?**

Not sufficient   76.8%
Sufficient   19.0%
Too much   0.3%
Don't know   4.2%

******

Question: **Do you get sufficient vegetables, fruit, berries?**

Not sufficient   63.6%
Sufficient   30.5%
Too much   1.3%
Don't know   4.7%

******

Question: **What is your attitude towards the increasing use of coupons and ration cards when food-stuffs are in short supply?**

Positive   50.7%
Indifferent   5.9%
Negative   34.4%
Don't know   9.2%

273

Opinion survey continues

Question: **What forms of food-stuffs distribution do you use?**

Orders placed at work	7.4%
Snack-bars and shops at the workplace	15.9%
Special departments, shops for war veterans, invalids, etc. at place of residence	9.0%
Once-only coupons for food at the workplace	6.1%
Food ration cards at the place of residence	18.2%
Any other	11.4%
I use none of the listed forms	40.7%

******

Question: **What form of food-stuffs distribution seems most convenient to you?**

Once-only coupons for food at the workplace	9.5%
Food ration cards at the place of residence	24.0%
Orders placed at work	20.5%
Buffets and shops at the workplace	17.5%
Special departments, shops for war veterans, invalids, etc. at place of residence	8.3%
Another form	9.7%
Don't know	17.9%

******

Question: **How do you rate your diet in general?**

Sufficient in quantity and good in quality	18.1%
Sufficient in quantity but poor in quality	26.7%
Inadequate in quantity but good in quality	9.0%
Inadequate in quantity and poor in quality	30.9%
Don't know	15.9%

Source: **Ogonek** 1990, 5, front inside cover and s. 1.

Report No. 10: Looking foward to 1990

Question: **Do you think that 1990 will be a better year for you than the last one, 1989?**

Yes, certainly	4%
I hope so very much	40%
I think it will not be worse	13%
Probably unchanged	22%
I think it will be worse	14%
Don't know	9%

******

Question: **Do you think that the following will increase or decline in 1990?**

The movement for protection of the environment

Will increase	73%
Will decline	1.7%
Difficult to say	19%
I know nothing about it	7%

The activity of the National Fronts

Will increase	39%
Will decline	7%
Difficult to say	31%
I know nothing about it	24%

Strikes

Will increase	29%
Will decline	19%
Difficult to say	43%
I know nothing about it	9%

The fight to preserve monuments of national culture

Will increase	59%
Will decline	3%
Difficult to say	26%
I know nothing about it	11%

Conflicts within the country

Will increase	37%
Will decline	17%
Difficult to say	38%
I know nothing about it	8%

Emigration from the USSR

Will increase	48%
Will decline	9%
Difficult to say	30%
I know nothing about it	12%

Opinion survey continues

Organised crime

Will increase	44%
Will decline	15%
Difficult to say	34%
I know nothing about it	7%

Members leaving the Communist Party

Will increase	40%
Will decline	10%
Difficult to say	35%
I know nothing about it	15%

Refusals to serve in the army

Will increase	35%
Will decline	12%
Difficult to say	37%
I know nothing about it	17%

Rationing of food-stuffs and goods

Will increase	51%
Will decline	16%
Difficult to say	29%
I know nothing about it	4%

Public expressions of opinion* in defence of your native people

Will increase	50%
Will decline	3%
Difficult to say	33%
I know nothing about it	14%

The movement to commemorate the victims of stalinism

Will increase	50%
Will decline	9%
Difficult to say	29%
I know nothing about it	11%

The Church's participation in the life of society

Will develop	72%
Will decline	1.5%
Difficult to say	18%
I know nothing about it	8%

* Russian: **vystupleniya**

276

Opinion survey continues

Question: **Do you support the actions of M. S. Gorbachev as Head of State?**

Fully support	43%
Partly support	35%
Do not support	12%
Don't know	11%

Question: **Do you support the political line of the Communist Party of the Soviet Union**

Fully support	26%
Partly support	29%
Do not support	20%

Question: **Do you support the economic policy of the country's government?**

Fully support	24%
Partly support	42%
Do not support	18%

Question: **Do you support the further extension of criticism in the press?**

Fully support	64.5%
Partly support	17.1%
Do not support	3.5%

Source: **Ogonek,** 1990, 15, front inside cover to s. 3 (excerpts).

Abbreviated titles of sources

Journals and newspapers

AiF	Argumenty i Fakty
Med. gaz.	Meditsinskaya gazeta
Sots. Is.	Sotsiologicheskie issledovaniya
Stat. Press-Byull.	Statisticheski Press-Byulleten

Books

Narodnoe khozyaistvo SSSR 1988

Goskomstat SSSR, **Narodnoe khozyaistvo SSSR v 1988 g.:
statisticheski ezhegodnik,** Moskva, Finansy i Statistika,
1989.

Narodnoe obrazovanie

Goskomstat SSSR, **Narodnoe obrazovanie i kultura v SSSR:
statisticheski sbornik,** Moskva, Finansy i Statistika, 1989.

Naselenie SSSR 1987

Goskomstat SSSR, **Naselenie SSSR 1987: statisticheski
sbornik,** Moskva, Finansy i Statistika, 1988.

Naselenie SSSR 1988

Goskomstat SSSR, **Naselenie SSSR 1988: statisticheski
sbornik,** Moskva, Finansy i Statistika, 1989.

Sotsialnoe razvitie SSSR

Goskomstat SSSR, **Sotsialnoe razvitie i uroven zhizni
naseleniya SSSR: statisticheski sbornik,** Moskva, Finansy i
Statistika, 1989.

Index

deaths
    alcoholism-related   202, 253
    by age groups   48, 231-2
    by sex and age groups   231-2
    by SSR   49-50, 56-9, 237-44
    from accidents, poisoning and traumas   202-3, 233-44
    from AIDS   219
    from diseases of circulatory system   203, 233-44
    from diseases of digestive organs   233-44
    from diseases of respiratory organs   203, 233-44
    from drowning   230
    from fires   229
    from injuries at work   226-7
    from plague   219
    from tuberculosis   222
    in large towns   64-5
    infant   203, 246-52
    international comparisons of   234
    main causes of   233-44
    maternal   245
    perinatal   250
Deputies **see** women Deputies
diet   147
    views on   272-4
diseases
    causing invalidity   209-10
    causing loss of work capacity   207-8
    comparison with USA   207
    infectious   211
    venereal   224
divorces
    by age of wife   80
    by duration of marriage   81-2
    by size of family   78, 80
    by SSR   77, 83-6
    children involved in   79-80
    in large towns   64-5
doctors **see** women doctors
drug addiction   217-8

economic issues, views on   256, 258, 264
economic policy of government, views on   277
economic regions, population of   4-7, 10-13, 17
educational attainment
    by SSR   137
    of employed persons   135-6
    of persons over ten   135-6
    of working youth   138
effluent, discharge of   146, 149-51
emigration from USSR   23
    views on   275
environment
    reports on   146-8
    views on   259, 267-9, 275

nationalist issues, views on   257, 275-6
natural increase   16, 51-2, 60-5
noxious substances, emissions of   146-8, 151-4

payment for medical care by patients   258
pension
    average monthly   176
    minimum for old age   180
pensioners
    age distribution of   179
    as % of population   174
    by SSR   178
    categories of   177
    invalidity   176-7, 180
    old age   176-7, 180-1
    personal   177, 182
perestroika, views on   256, 259
period fertility rates   40-2
plague   219
pollution
    atmospheric   148, 151-4
    by discharge of effluent   149-51
population
    age composition of   90
    decrease of in Russian SFSR   18
    emigration of   23
    female, by age group   92, 183
    male, by age group   91
    intercensal change in   16-7
    migration of   16, 20-22
    natural increase of   16, 51-2, 60-5
    of economic regions and
      major administrative divisions   4-15
    of towns   25-34
    of SSRs   2-3, 18
    of USSR   1
    sex composition of   89
    sex and age composition of USSR   93
    sex and age composition of SSRs   94-108
    urban and rural   19-22
pre-school units   126-7, 201
price rises, views on   264

rationing, views on   273, 276
refusals to serve in army, views on   276
remarriages
    of men   75
    of women   76
road traffic accidents   225, 228

sex composition of population   89
sexual behaviour of young people, views on   269-71
specialists   139-40, 194
stalinism, views on commemorating victims of   276
strikes, views on   275